EMERGING ISSUES
IN
RELIGIOUS EDUCATION

EMERGING ISSUES IN RELIGIOUS EDUCATION

edited by
Gloria Durka
and
Joanmarie Smith

PAULIST PRESS
New York/Ramsey, N.J./Toronto

Library of Congress
Catalog Card Number: 76-18052

ISBN: 0-8091-1971-4

Published by Paulist Press
Editorial Office: 1865 Broadway, N.Y., N.Y. 10023
Business Office: 545 Island Road, Ramsey, N.J. 07446

Printed and bound in the
United States of America

Contents

REFINING MODELS

DEEPENING MODELS

EVALUATING MODELS

TO
OUR
MOTHERS
ESTELLE AND GERTRUDE

"Many women have done excellently,
but you surpass them all."
Proverbs 31:29

Preface

The articles in this collection have not been previously published; they have been prepared especially for publication here. We solicited articles from persons who are working on the edge of their disciplines, that is, who are exploring in their thinking and research issues that the religious educator must confront tomorrow. The theories developed in these pages, however, benefited from exposure to and the critique of the authors' friends, colleagues and students.

The need for the study of foundational questions in religious education has become axiomatic. There is, as Robert O'Gorman has written in his introduction to Harold W. Burgess's *An Invitation to Religious Education*, "a widely recognized critical need to deal with the matter of theory in the field of religious education." Berard Marthaler underscored the point in his presidential address at the 1975 annual meeting of the Association of Professors and Researchers in Religious Education. But we think it is not enough to know the present state of the foundational or theoretical questions in the area. One must anticipate the new questions that will arise and the new theories that will develop from these questions. So quickly does change overtake us that answers, knowledge, methods and skills become obsolete almost at the moment of their achievement. It has been suggested that in the coming world the capacity to face the new appropriately will be more important than the ability to know and repeat the old. It is to this particular need that the collection is addressed.

The situation we have described is sometimes expressed as a call for new models. While this call certainly moves in the proper direction, it is perhaps even more appropriate than those who issue the call realize. We think that a critical analysis of the term "model" renders it more fruitful than its use today has been construed to be. We make the case that a model of reality is implicit not only in the procedures and programs in which religious educators engage, but also in every common and proper noun they use. We are saying, in effect, that experience is not the primary "given" but it is the model through which one experiences that is fundamental. Models are the condition and content of experience.

With this in mind we have grouped the articles in terms of the emphasis that we detect as sometimes confronting, extending, refin-

1

ing, deepening or evaluating models. Each of the authors is obviously working from a well-thought-out model which he or she modifies according to the classifications we have outlined. This classification is not exhaustive, however. A careful reader will also note that in almost every case an article could have been in more than one category and, in fact, each author could be said to confront, extend, refine, deepen and evaluate the model with which he or she is working. The editors must take responsibility therefore for their inclusion of a particular article under a particular heading. The choice, while not arbitrary, is obviously debatable.

Joanmarie Smith
Gloria Durka

CONFRONTING MODELS

Gloria Durka
Joanmarie Smith
Anthony Padovano
Gregory Baum
Reginald H. Fuller

1.
Challenging the Framework

Joanmarie Smith and Gloria Durka

Confronting some fundamental terms which attempt to ground theories of education, the authors are particularly concerned to demonstrate that the term "model" can be more appropriately used to describe the condition and content of our entire experience of reality.

Theories of knowledge and experience constitute the foundation of any framework in education. Words like "knowing" and "experiencing" are sprinkled liberally throughout religious education literature. Yet confronted with the questions: "What do you actually mean by knowledge?" or "What is experience?" one may be at a loss to describe these basic concepts, may realize that one's grasp of them is tenuous and ambiguous.

In this essay we will deal with the assumptions that have traditionally been attached to the notions of knowing and experiencing and critique and revise them in the light of recent studies. We will locate the role of modeling in this context and explore the implication of modeling as it has been described for religious education.

KNOWLEDGE

The description of knowledge most commonly offered is the grasp of reality as it is. This is the realist position. In general a realist claims that we can, and in fact do, experience reality as it is. We will attempt to demonstrate that this description of knowledge is no longer tenable and further suggest that the term "knowledge" should be replaced by the term "belief." We think that analysis of the technical definition of knowledge as justified true belief must dispense with the "true," leaving only models or interpretive schemes in which one believes more or less justifiably.

Any purported grasp of reality must depend upon our senses. We have been aware for some time that reality is both accessible to us through our senses and that on occasion these senses can deceive us.

Implicit in this recognition seems to be the assumption that when our senses are not deceiving us they are delivering the goods intact, that is, they are delivering reality just as it is.

Realization that our senses play a reconstructing role is more recent. Students in introductory philosophy and psychology courses still seem perplexed to learn that there is no noise in the forest if there is no ear to hear it. The idea that both a stimulus and a sensor is required in order for sensation to occur is sometimes clarified for these students by calling attention to the myriad radio and television programs that are present in the room. We do not have access to these programs, however, without an instrument which will tune into the electronic waves and convert them for our personal sensory equipment. Having to come to grips with this apparent fact, students seem to have less difficulty with the probability that we never have a pure sensation; we have only perceptions which are interpreted sensations. Yet it is precisely this point that undermines most realist theories of knowledge.

The attempt to strip our thinking or experience of bias the way we can strip our speech of metaphor apparently can never be completely successful. Psychologists tell us our experience is filtered through interpretations which are products of our entire personal history.[1] "We read nature as a Rorschach."[2] Sociologists claim that our reality is constructed and maintained by society.[3] Even the physical scientists have abandoned the position that their work is value-free, totally objective, uncontaminated by personal expectations and desires or the biases of society or culture.

Norwood Hanson, a philosopher and historian of science, has carefully examined the nature of perception in microphysics. He demonstrates to some effect that even in this seemingly most objective of fields the so-called "pure" data is actually "theory-laden."[4] In the light of such considerations, the "hardness" and "coldness" of facts dissolves. Hanson remarks:

> Given the *same* world, it might have been construed differently. We might have spoken of it, thought of it, perceived it differently. Perhaps facts are somehow moulded by the logical forms of the fact-stating language. Perhaps these provide a "mould" in terms of which the world coagulates for us in different ways.[5]

Hanson's studies, as well as the work of other philosophers and historians of science, indicate that we never have an *immediate* grasp of reality but only a *mediated* grasp. We suggest that the "moulds" in terms of which we experience reality are appropriately called "models."

MODELS

We choose to refer to these interpretive schemes as models for three reasons. First, we wish to avoid the purely cognitive or linguistic significance that appears attached to "theory" or even "interpretive schemes."

Secondly, "model" connotes some degree or at least effort toward explanation or understanding. We do not wish to be confined to the notion of predictability or control sometimes associated with the scientific endeavor.

Finally, we wish to suggest in our use of models some kind of holistic interpretive schemes of reality. Individual perceptions or propositions are not usually treated as some isolable data but rather fitted into some overall, quite complex, and rarely explicated stance toward reality.

However, some may find the use of "model" to describe our interaction with reality objectionable because the term is so widespread that its use can be considered faddish. Moreover, "model" has so many referents that to give it yet another one is at best confusing.

To say a word has become fashionable is practically pejorative these days. However, word fads usually occur when a term seems exceptionally appropriate. To discard a word simply because it is in vogue seems unreasonable. We also maintain that it is precisely the many referents and all the connotations the term "model" bears as a result of its uses, etymology and cognates that make it peculiarly appropriate to describe the interpretive schemes that mediate reality.

Uses

When used in conversation "model" has a number of meanings which are only somewhat related to each other. Model can mean a replica of something made to scale; for example, a model plane. It can also mean a design according to which something is constructed, as in homes built according to the colonial model. It can also refer to persons who model clothes and persons who model for artists.

What these various usages share, however tenuously, is their reference to visible, tangible entities. They also allude to the existence of something else, whether it is a larger plane, a figure yet to be painted or some abstract notion of an ideal marriage of which the model claims to be an embodied analogue. It is this last sense that has generated a recent extension of the term model. Scientists have been building scale models of their work where it was possible for some time. Then, however, they began to conceive of models that did not purport to be representations of their work but were rather picturable ideals of analogous systems. The billiard ball model of gas from which the Kinetic Theory of Gases can be developed is a classic example of this type of model. Mathematicians use what has been called a logical model to illustrate their abstract systems and give a possible interpretation of them. A set of points and lines in geometry is a logical model for Euclid's formal axioms.[6] Physical as well as social scientists and mathematicians use what are called mathematical models, which are symbolic representations of variables in physical or social systems. A mathematical model is to be distinguished from a logical model because a mathematical model resembles the primary system only in formal structure; there are no material or physical similarities.[7]

Another use of the term, however, has popularized it outside of mathematics and the sciences. Here the term "model" is used where the word "type" might formerly have been forced to serve.[8] Theologians like Avery Dulles, speaking of models of the church,[9] and David Tracy, exploring five models of theology,[10] employ the term in this last sense. The nuances of construction and imagination that accompany model appear to make the switch from "types" to "models" appropriate. A ring of imaging as well as imagining is suggested here. In fact, some models of this type are images; for example, the temple, the vine, and the flock in scripture.[11] Most often they are not "picture" models, but what Ian Ramsey calls "disclosure" models —models which, while not literal representations of reality, are "self authenticating models in which the universe discloses itself to us."[12]

Etymology

The derivation of model from the Latin *modus* for measure and manner surfaces two suggestions intrinsic to the notion: first, our capacity to experience is *measured* to the boundaries of the model we use; and second, the *manner* of our experience will reflect the contents of the model through which we experience.

Cognates

Finally, the cognates of "model" account for the nuances that accrue to the term. Mode, for example, can mean the arrangement of a musical scale as well as the style of expression in grammar. More generically, mode is simply a manifestation, form or arrangement of being. We have already alluded to the intimate connection between "moulds" and "models."

In summary, we think the character of "model" results from what Lewis Thomas calls the "internal marks of long use" and "inner conversation"[13] which make it especially valuable as a label for that imprecise, imaginative dealing we have with reality.

EXPERIENCE

A definition of model which is comprehensive enough to include almost every example cited is that of Ian Barbour who describes a model simply as an imaginative tool for ordering experience.[14] We would like to include in this description two additional elements: models both are the condition of and provide the content for our experience.

Experience is sometimes defined as the sum total of one's interaction with reality. We submit that this description more properly designates existence. To *exist* is to interact with reality. Perhaps experience —at least human experience—is more distinctively described as awareness of one's interaction with reality. We are constantly existing or totally interacting with reality. A simple exercise will demonstrate the point. At this moment every inch of our bodies is subjected to the pressure of the atmosphere and the material of our own clothing but how rarely do we "experience" this. As we read these words, however, we undoubtedly begin to attend to this ongoing aspect of our existence and experience it. Even while doing so, however, we realize our inability to experience the totality even of that limited interaction with reality.

Our experience of reality is not only piecemeal, and partial; it is also interpreted, or, as previously suggested, modeled. As John Hick says, all experience is "experiencing as."[15] The aforementioned experience of pressure is filtered by one's model, however crude and unexplicated, of "pressure," "atmosphere" and "material."

The report of persons born blind who begin to see illustrates the issue. Unlike the persons born blind, we with our eyes open cannot *not* see *things;* whereas the person born blind seeing for the first time does not see things or objects, but sees only patches of color.

It might be argued that one does sometimes have an experience that one cannot interpret. "Something is happening, but I don't know what it is!" On the face of it such a statement means one has no models available which could plausibly interpret the situation. Reflecting on instances where one might be said to have had an "unknown" experience one will discover that "unknown" is quite a complexly content-filled model. In the first place it will probably be remembered that one immediately filed the interpretation under "eventually knowable" and was even aware of what steps might be taken to get an interpretation. If, on the other hand, the experiences were filed under "unknowable," there undoubtedly were reasons for doing that, too. To summarize, an uninterpreted experience is simply not experienced.

IMPLICATIONS

A number of conclusions can be drawn from the premises explored above but perhaps the most significant of these is that faith, "the substance of things hoped for, the conviction of things not seen," (Hebrews 11:1) is the fundamental category of human existence.

Knowledge cannot be the essential structure of human existence because for all practical purposes it does not exist. Knowledge is defined as justified true belief. We have demonstrated that we do not grasp reality as it is; therefore, we can have no basis for determining the truth of any model or belief in any traditional sense of the term "truth."

Experience cannot be the fundamental category of existence either. Experience exists but it is conditioned and determined by the existence and content of our models.

Finally, believing or modeling is not the fundamental category of human existence since there is some still more basic activity which recognizes the inadequacy of any model to that which is being modeled. It seems obvious to us that the distinction between believing and faithing is legitimate and fruitful because faith is the dynamic which not only enables us to critique our believing but demands that we do so. It is faith that requires the construction and application of criteria to our believing. It is also faith which compels us to abandon a "good" model or belief for a "better" one.

In the light of these considerations, one might ask, what does education look like? Since in this framework one cannot claim to know, information can only be proposed. Teaching styles must reflect the realization that one does not have the truth. The attitude of proposing distinguishes teaching from preaching and indoctrination. Educators would do well to critique their programs in this light.

The term experience must be critiqued also. It is easy enough for educators to call attention to their learners' myriad interactions with the environment. It is almost impossible to determine what experiences anyone will have as a result of this attention. The model one brings to the experience will be the determining factor. The days of children reciting "Lead us not into Penn Station" are possibly being repeated in a much more subtle way. Our students may be having experiences quite other than we suspect. A model different from the one presented may be operating in their experience. This is much more difficult to discern than it was to hear the wrong words being used.

A framework treating models as human constructs which only reflect "the substance of things hoped for" less and less inappropriately might be viewed as follows:

Education is the process which promotes attentiveness to criteria. Models are only as credible as the reasons for believing them are cogent.

Education is the process which allows for tentativeness in belief. Our models are but "dim reflections in a mirror" (1 Cor.13:12).

The essence of our education is the process of fostering faith, that fundamental mode of human engagement to reality. Such would be the effect if education were regarded as commitment to better and better models.

Notes

1. George Kelly, *The Psychology of Personal Constructs.* New York: Norton, 1956.
2. George B. Leonard, *The Transformation.* New York: Delta Publishing Company, 1972, p. 82.
3. Peter Berger and Thomas Luckman, *The Social Construction of Reality.* New York: Doubleday & Co., 1966.
4. Norwood R. Hanson, *Patterns of Discovery.* Cambridge: Cambridge University Press, 1961, p. 19.
5. *Ibid.,* p. 36.
6. Ian G. Barbour, *Myths, Models and Paradigms.* New York: Harper and Row, 1974, p. 29.
7. *Ibid.,* p. 30.
8. David Tracy, *Blessed Rage for Order.* New York: Seabury Press, 1975, p. 34.
9. Avery Dulles, *Models of the Church.* New York: Doubleday and Co., Inc., 1974.
10. Tracy, *op. cit.* pp. 22-42.
11. Dulles, *op. cit.* p. 6.
12. Ian Ramsey, *Models and Mystery.* Oxford: Oxford University Press, 1964, p. 20.
13. Lewis Thomas, *The Lives of A Cell.* New York: Viking Press, 1974, p. 132.
14. Barbour, *op. cit.,* p. 6.
15. John Hick, *Faith and Knowledge.* Second Edition. New York: Macmillan, 1969, p. 142f.

2.
Theological and Ascetical Reflections
Anthony T. Padovano

Religious education is profoundly influenced by the theological and ascetical models it chooses. Anthony Padovano confronts the models which are operating in much of today's theologizing and ascetical writing and offers an imaginative alternative.

The nature of theology and the character of contemporary spirituality are two of the most vital issues emerging in the field of religious education. Religious education is an apt place for their emergence because it readily exposes the functional deficiencies of theoretical work. As we shall see, theology and asceticism have surprising practical consequences.

Before we consider each of the main issues in this article in turn, it will be helpful to remind ourselves of the meaningfulness of theoretical endeavors. Religious educators may be as liable to ignore the theoretical basis for their work as professional theologians are likely to disdain questions concerning the relevance and pastoral necessity of their speculations. The pastoral is the touchstone of validity for all theological, ascetical, and educational theory in the church. The church is people and the people are an assembly of pastoral gifts and needs. The church is not an academy, not a school of ideas, not a think-tank, not an atheneum where scenarios may conveniently be conjectured without reference to the impact they have on lives. The end result of the ignorance of theory and practice is the religious educator who becomes a religious technician and the professional theologian whose thinking is idle when it is not fanciful, useless for the ministry of the church when it is not obstructive.

We must make no mistake about the practical import of the philosophical or theoretical assumptions we make. This is evident even in the field of economics, perhaps the most practical of human endeavors. The world economic order functions as inequitably as it does not because practical structures are badly organized or unable to be effective, but because certain presuppositions have been made about the quality of life and the nature of justice. Capitalism requires a philosophy which rewards the productive and penalizes the unfortunate. Socialism begins with the theory that limited wealth rather than unrestrained riches, communal ownership rather than private enterprise in certain sectors of the economy are more humane for society in the long run. One cannot devise these systems without deciding beforehand questions concerning the nature of what is good for people and of what makes people more or less human. Communism is premised on a philosophy of economic equality and on a theory defining a priori the purpose of human labor. To be more domestic, the Social Security system in the United States, to cite one of many possible American projects, is in crisis not because it is badly managed on the operational level but because ethical and philosophical judgments led to the limitation of the birth rate on the one hand and the planned obsolescence of the elderly on the other. There are now too few young people and too many enforced retirees to make the system work. To be more ecclesiastical, the Second Vatican Council has failed to reach certain people not because theologians or religious educators were lacking in suggestions for practical reform but because reactionaries adopted a theory of the church which preferred power to people or rectitude with past formulations to attentiveness to the present and the future.

The Nature of Theology

Theology has failed to develop its resources properly because it tends, in its recent form, to favor unimaginative work. This is not due to the fact that the unimaginative become theologians; it derives from a misconception concerning the imaginative possibilities of the craft. This deficiency is attributable, I believe, to the adoption of a particular model for theological effort which is not easily theologically productive.

Theology becomes dull when it is conceived of as a service performed for church administrators. For many years, this has been the task assigned theology. Theology has not fully recovered from this role and often vacillates between a desire to please church officials and a need to excoriate them, both indications of excessive concern. It is not fair to presuppose that church administrators are tedious; the character of administration, however, precludes an enthusiasm for innovation, especially in ecclesiastical circles. Administration stabilizes rather than explores. It is true that sometimes there are exceptions to this rule but they remain exceptions.

Theology is further incapacitated by its fascination with the borrowing of university procedures or the adoption of graduate research principles as its norm for acceptability. Theology thrives no more in a strict university environment than it does in a rigidly magisterial system. Scholarship is intrinsic to the theological enterprise but scholarship should not be confused with documentation. Scholars are thinkers rather than readers. They are those who have absorbed the reading and research of apprenticeship and have now become masters in their fields precisely because they master it with their thinking. The vast majority of theological work done in the United States remains apprenticeship work. The tireless and tiresome bibliographers are hacks, not experts. They compile as a substitute for thought. It would be shortsighted, obviously, to exclude research from theology. The model we shall propose as an alternative to the present model will take account of the need for a comprehension of the past. Research, however, is something a genuine scholar has obviously done without being obvious about it. True scholars do not do their research in the course of their writing. Augustine, Aquinas, and Karl Rahner have no need of bibliography or footnotes. Bibliography and footnotes are often a way of supplying for a deficiency of innovative thinking.

The place of oral tradition in community awareness serves, I believe, as a more apt model for theological work than the exemplar of the graduate research student. The oral singer was not a reciter. He was a poet who was remarkable in his capacity to grasp the tradition of the community and yet sing the community song in a new way. He sang for the audience the song it needed to hear in the manner it required. A few observations and applications to the theological scene are in order.

In the ancient world, the oral singer or poet was the most vital contact a community had with its own identity. He was a man of the word, someone who knew how to verbalize people into life. He inspired not only by the tale he told but by the creativity of the telling and the persuasiveness of his own presence. The singer did not impart knowledge; he sharpened awareness. And he did this in an intensely personal manner.

The oral singer was the reliable bearer of the community's tradition. He was designated and accepted as the one on whom one could depend to know the tradition so well that its retelling was never the same. He was not the tired repeater of the same song whose tale was as worn as the description given by contemporary tour guides who mindlessly and prosaically reiterate a story they no longer care to relate. There is no reason why there could not be a certified, even an ordained ministry in the church, of those who have absorbed the community's tradition and who bring the community to life in terms of it.

The church should have ordained priests, certified singers at the core of its theological ministry. If ordination could be used for sacramental administration, it can also be used exclusively for preaching, solely for teaching, only for counselling, restrictively for executive leadership, or singularly for the designation of those who embody the tradition and captivate the community with the music of their love for tradition and the life they make from it.

The ancient world regarded originality differently from the way we do. Originators were not those who, perhaps self-consciously, developed something utterly new, surprisingly novel, unexpectedly unusual. Actually, this may be a less creative manner of proceeding. Originators may be the ones who recreate the familiar and allow it to take new forms. Originators are also the ones who sing the old song so that it continues to enchant and illumine, the ones who remind their hearers of those things they know already without having sufficiently attended to their meaning. Jesus is just such a singer, a religious thinker who fulfills the venerable Torah by dotting every letter and yet convincing people that no one ever spoke before like this man.

Theologians are at their best when they utilize the received wisdom of the community as a new insight. Everything about competent theologians resonates with ancient learning and contemporary relevance. When theologians are more consistent with their craft, they are poets, creators of fresh music from the traditional melodies of Christianity. Augustine writes compelling literature; Aquinas writes poetry and hymns; Chardin is a lyricist; and Karl Rahner writes essays on symbols and creative thinking, even on poetry and the Christian. When talented theologians use the past they are neither tedious nor forgettable. They vitalize the past in the power of their present charism. They avoid the superfluity of the sterile repeater of the historical record who chronicles where people may have been with no judgment as to whether they should have been there at all and no care as to where they are now.

Such repeaters of ancient songs are dispensable because mechanical reproduction, rote memory, or mere copying accomplish as much, with no need for the presence of the singer. They are tiresome and send people from the church not in anger but for relief. A competent theologian also avoids the excess of the frenetic, rejecting the temptation to lead people in new directions when a return to origins proves more productive. Such harbingers of novelty are disposable because the changing temper of the times dates them and ages their contributions overnight. They are wearisome and worrisome; they send people from the church not to explore new tasks for it but because there is no need to abide with a community which changes its locus every day. The genius of theology is the ingenuity of harmonizing the recognizable past with a new rendition.

Religious educators may make their finest contribution to the life of the community when they are tempered by the approach we are suggesting. They will captivate more easily when they are neither dated nor naive. They will unify when they weave new cloth from the former threads others have sewn less freely. They will bring forth things old and new in such a manner that people prefer neither because they are inseparable and because possessing both alone allows wholeness.

The oral poet was not expected to be precise. Precision is not the stuff of life. He remembered the old songs with the freshness of reminiscence. Reminiscence requires a personal relationship to the past. He did not transmit a venerable song making, at most, inconsequential changes and unnecessary additions. He breathed life into the song so that it was completely new and yet not unheard of nor unthinkable. He astonished as he recalled, created suspense from the predictable, always came home with his song but by roads so diverse that the journey and the arrival were worthy experiences.

The theoretical, we have said, is not without its concrete consequences. Because we have had an inadequate model for theological work, we have had more dull theologians than necessary and an abundance of theology no one needed. Because theologians were expected to be archaic or sensational, servile to the magisterium or in rebellion against it, they were either conservatives or liberals with no encouragement to be both. They offered old things when a new song was yearned for to help us feel at home in the alien land of the present; or they offered a new thing when the spirit of the age required the grace of a familiar name or recognizable theme. Because theologians tried to be either old or new, they limited themselves to one response in a world too complicated for single-mindedness.

The Character of Contemporary Spirituality

Intellectual energy is wasted when theology lives from its own resources rather than from the resources of life. The same holds true for asceticism. A great deal of ascetical activity has its own accomplishment as its goal rather than a further and fuller reference to life. Just as an inadequate theology becomes its own closed idea system and suffocates from the limited breath of life it bears, so a deficient asceticism becomes its own closed idea system and is crippled by its incapacity to function in the real world. Concreteness forces oxygen into theological work as human contact brings flexibility into spirituality.

There are valid reasons for the renewal of interest in ascetical theology today. Periods of crisis lead to self-reflection. The present crisis has been aggravated by bad theology, by a theology which squandered the ministry of theologians on trivia. The stone of rigid orthodoxy or unyielding liberalism was offered when bread was needed in the wilderness.

A crisis becomes especially acute when one senses in it the nearness of death. Such an awareness causes us to reduce life to its simplest terms, a reduction which is always required as a prelude to contemplation. We know something is dying in the church today. Whether we view this in one way or another, the proximity of death induces reflection. A dying church appears less reliable than God. The effort to encounter God directly becomes imperative and ascetical theology becomes preeminent.

Contemporary spirituality suffers from the problems we explored in our consideration of theology. Theology restricted to a research model generates an asceticism meant for a ghetto group. The religious educator who inherits these flaws becomes a dull teacher and an unreal spiritual guide. A theology, on the other hand, which labors to be different gives rise to an asceticism which is trendy and faddish. The religious educator who moves in this direction becomes academically superficial and ascetically simplistic.

Theology can adopt a servile attitude toward the magisterium, as we have noted. Correlatively, groups in the church, if not the official church, foster at times a spirituality which serves institutional purposes. There are a number of myths which accompany what one might call bureaucratic spirituality.

One of these myths is premised on the notion that it is always worthwhile to recommend prayer or speak piously. This is a misconception which cheapens invitations to prayer by making them clichés. Prayer becomes a means of defusing a situation of its life content so that something innocuous may occur. Obviously, I am not talking here of genuine prayer but of prayer employed as a manipulative exercise. The identical attitude is extended to pious speaking. Piety becomes a useless addendum to a conversation which was not going in that direction anyway. This confuses piety with devotion. Piety, as I am using the term, is simple-minded and escapist; devotion is deeper and faithful to life. Few things are more irrelevant and unwelcome than a pious face. Jesus reminded us of this when he asked us to wash our faces now and then.

Contemporary spirituality may also be vitiated by the myth that good asceticism must abstract from the life normal people live. Such false asceticism is fascinated with the notion that one is sanctified in direct proportion to his or her unconnectedness with the world, lack of interest in church reform, or distance from the possibility of doing or saying something memorable. One adopts this myth because one assumes the world is evil. Sometimes, however, the world is assumed to be not bad but stupid. This creates a spiritual theology tailored for an obtuse world, a theology of gibberish and slogans. Such a spiritual theology encourages one to use language in a way no one in his or her right senses would employ, a language so artificial and contrived that no one outside one's own group would ever care to use it.

The common problem in the theological and ascetical approaches we are criticizing lies in the substitution of ideology for life. Doctrines are declared to preserve the integrity of the system rather than to fill the emptiness in someone else's life. Spiritual procedures are recommended to keep ideals alive even if they happen to cause the death of hope in others.

Sound spiritual writing possesses significant characteristics. It is symbolic, suggesting more than it says. Its language is charged with meaning rather than cluttered with verbiage. Good spiritual writing is biblical: not mechanistically biblical—indeed, the better spiritual writing is, the less it quotes the Bible. Yet one is aware that such a writer has assimilated the biblical message and can therefore be oblique and creative with it. Quotations allow little flexibility. They are the stock trade of fundamentalists and propagandists. In much the same manner, the competent theologian gives evidence of having done his or her theological homework without giving evidence of the process in every manuscript he or she writes. Effective spiritual writers evoke human reactions from people. They make people feel human in much the same way as the gifted theologian makes people reflect on the worth of being alive. This is why effective theological work is essentially contemplative.

Religious education is profoundly influenced by the theological and ascetical models it chooses. Religious education is always theological in its content, value-influenced in its orientation. If the religious educator views theology as a conservative or liberal ideological commitment or envisions spirituality as esoteric or ephemeral, then he or she will inherit all the plagues of the past which have been visited not only on the sons and daughters of Egypt but on all the children of the ghetto.

3.
Prayer and Society

Gregory Baum

Gregory Baum helps us to surface the models implicit in our prayers. Our words betray a political stance, a particular understanding of human life, a total approach to the world and an imagination of the divine. In sum, Baum explores the social impact of our prayer.

In sociology the power of symbols is taken very seriously. Symbols, whether they be religious or not, have an effect on social life. Symbols form the patterns of the imagination which affect the way in which we perceive the world and respond to it. We do not encounter the world in a neutral way, we do not see things in some sort of objective immediacy; our encounter with the world is mediated by the symbols operative in our imagination. Symbols, then, are not only in the mind; they translate themselves into action and thus affect the world to which we belong and which we are. Symbols have weight and power in history, and to understand their meaning correctly it is not sufficient to look at them in their representation; we also have to study them in their social consequences.

In this article I wish to take this fundamental thesis from the sociology of religion without discussing it any further and apply it to a better understanding of the social reality of prayer. What I shall be concerned with is the impact of prayer on society, an impact of which the praying community remains largely unconscious. (My purpose is not to advocate a particular social or political viewpoint but to make the readers more aware of the hidden power of public prayer and hence to enable them to assume a more conscious Christian responsibility for these effects.)

The topic is indeed a large one. What I wish to do in this brief article is to present an outline; a more thorough study might follow and present concrete examples to make the investigation vivid and useful to the readers. I shall look at symbols in prayer and liturgy on four different levels, though no claim is made that these four levels cover all the significant aspects. Prayer affects society I) by specific refer-

ences to the political order, II) by advocating a particular understanding of human life, III) by projecting a total approach to the
world, and finally, IV) by fostering a particular imagination of the
divine.

I

Prayer has influence on society by its conscious and public reference to the political order. "God save the Queen" is an anthem conceived as a hymn; it is sung in church; it asks God's blessing on the
monarch. It is a hymn that defends and legitimates a particular form
of government, namely monarchy. Wherever the hymn is sung, it
promotes an outlook that takes monarchical government for granted.
When the anthem is sung in Canada it has no nationalistic overtones.
On the contrary it creates an international bond between members of
the Commonwealth. Only indirectly, by defining the Canadian reality
over against the American republic, does it have a specifically Canadian reference. In the United States we often find a flag in the sanctu-
ary: here religion and prayer are linked to national feeling. The combination of flag and altar suggest that the more religious people become,
the more patriotic they will be, and conversely the more devoted to the
national cause the more church-going the nation.

This public reference to politics is the obvious impact of prayer
on society. We become aware of this problem when we devise the
prayers of petition to be recited during the eucharistic celebration.
Here we suddenly realize that in writing these prayers we actually
express a particular political viewpoint and affect the social imagination of the congregation. During the Vietnam war, at a time when the
American bishops had not yet presented their public evaluation, the
prayers for peace in Vietnam were usually formulated in such a way
that no judgment was made on the war and no hope expressed in
regard to its outcome. Only when Catholics united by the same critical
spirit celebrated the Eucharist would they formulate their petitions in
a way that condemned the war and asked for the withdrawal of American troops from Southeast Asia.

In many instances, however, the political meaning of our public
petitions is hidden from us. Since we live in a common culture and
participate in the same political processes, we are often quite unable to
discover how the dreams and desires we regard as purely human and
nonpolitical are in fact expressions of our political system. Prayer is
often political in ways that escape us, and only as we observe how our
prayers sound to people who come from another cultural sphere do we
learn how deeply our own intercessions are marked by political
choices.

Let me give a simple example from Canada. In October 1970, a radical group of French Canadian separatists kidnapped two public figures. One of them was killed—some people say accidentally. This had been the first political murder in Canada in over a century. The country was shocked. The bishop of an English-speaking diocese in Canada made a public statement: "We are horrified by the violence in our midst." He then added, "Let us pray to God for unity and peace in Canada." The bishop, one can be sure, thought that his prayer was of a purely religious nature. What escaped him—and would have escaped no French Canadian—was that by praying for unity he supposed that God was on the side of confederation. Since there is a large, democratically organized separatist movement in Quebec, it would have been unthinkable to have a French Canadian bishop utter the English petition. Why should they, by praying for unity, interfere in a political issue, in which they think the church ought to be neutral? In fact the French Canadian bishops did come out with a common statement. "We are horrified by the violence in our midst," they said. Then they asked all Canadians to reflect on the injustices in their country which make such violent crimes possible. Here, then, in the spontaneous prayer for Canadian unity we have an example of a prayer that is deemed to be purely religious but is in fact a political act.

What follows from this example is that the political impact of prayer is often hidden from the praying community. What we pray for may simply reconfirm our taken-for-granted world. We will have to use more careful, analytic tools to understand the impact of prayer on society.

But before we move to the next consideration, I should mention that the church's public prayer contains a set of symbols that legitimate ecclesiastical organization and power. While we sometimes pray for God's people—especially after Vatican II—we usually specify that this people is divided into pope, bishops, priests, and the laity assigned to their care. If we read our liturgy carefully we find that the affirmation of the church as community is usually followed by sentences that verbalize the Catholic boundaries and the hierarchical structure of this church. Liturgy is the main instrument for communicating the church's jurisdictional structure to the people. Thus when we study the liturgy of marriage, we find that the special canonical status of marriage in the church finds expression in the prayers offered during the ceremony. We note in passing that the reason why some priests change the texts of the prescribed liturgy is that their theological perception of church and sacrament has changed and that they discern in the official prayers the defense of an ecclesiology they are unable to endorse.

II

On a second level prayer has impact on society through the vision of human life contained in it. Prayer is based on an implicit anthropology. As we verbalize our petitions and express our repentance, gratitude and adoration, we inevitably specify what we regard as vices or behavior to be shunned. As we study liturgical worship we must pose the question whether the implicit anthropology is in keeping with the dominant cultural ideal, or whether it is at odds with this ideal and hence leads people to a critical distance from the dominant institutions of society.

No sociologist has seen the impact of prayer and spirituality as clearly as Max Weber. His famous thesis on the rise of capitalism shows that it is impossible to render an account of the creation of the modern world without taking into consideration the Puritan ethic. While Weber clearly recognized the material factors that went into the creation of modern society—in this he was not far away from the Marxian analysis—he thought that the new work ethic and the accompanying disdain for celebration and contemplation could not be made psychologically credible unless one took into consideration the Christian spirituality of the Puritans. The work ethic was eventually mediated through secular institutions, the home, the school, the cultural ideals, and when this happened the work ethic lost its religious base. In North America the work ethic was mediated to Protestants, Catholics and Jews alike. Still, since many sections of Catholic liturgy and Catholic devotions are derived from medieval sources and/or from preindustrial cultural experiences, we do not find the same stress on efficiency, sobriety, and industry: more space is left for contemplation and feasts. Yet these same Catholic prayers derived from a preindustrial (and predemocratic) culture also promote obedience to authority and noncritical acceptance of the public order. Protestant worship expresses more clearly private judgment, conscience, and the anguish of making decisions before God. Protestant worship initiates the people to a sense of responsibility and participation in society that is unequaled in any religion. Some sociologists have asked themselves the question whether democracy can ever work in a country that has not had the experience of Calvinism.

In our present culture several images of the human person are in conflict. We have the ideal of people who fit into the prim and proper world of industry and corporations, the continuation of the Protestant ethic. Then we have the ideal of the consumer, the swinger, the person who seeks an ever higher standard of living and dreams of new ways of pleasure and recreation. In the absurd world of contemporary

North America, people are supposed to be both actively productive during the hours of nine to five and swingers spending their money on commodities in the evening. Over against this, counter-images of human life emerge. We find the ideal of the liberated person who laughs and rejoices at happiness and who weeps at what is sad, the person who can get angry at injustices, the person who seeks a new closeness to the body and finds in bodily life a source of joy that makes him/her independent of the pleasures sold as commodities.

We find another counter-type, linked to the previous or, at times, at odds with it, the engaged person, a person deeply identified with a community or committed to an historical movement: such a person acts out of a dedication that transcends personal advantage. With these images of man competing with one another and in part overlapping, where does the implicit anthropology of prayer take us? Is the Christian church generating prayer that makes us more critical of contemporary society and enables us to become people whose dreams correspond to the common good of the present world?

The folk music sung at Catholic liturgies at this time is often lacking in realism. It presents a cheerful view of life, symbolized by flowers and sunshine. Life is good, and all we have to do is discover it, open ourselves to it, and live out gently and firmly the possibilities of friendship for the moment. This view of human life underestimates the presence of sin. We actually live in a country that is divided racially and economically, and universal friendship will be available to us only if we are ready for costly social change. Reconciliation will have meaning only after we have undergone important social transformations. Some of these cheerful songs sung at Catholic masses reflect suburban bliss and suburban blindness. While modern theology has enabled us to overcome a vision of life dominated by personal sin and scrupulosity, it has also introduced us to a new dimension of sin, the injustices built into our institutions and the alienation proper to our culture. A fully Christian liturgy, in any age, should make us aware of the face of evil in our society and promise us happiness and freedom only through many conversions.

III

This leads us to a third level at which prayer affects society. Related to the preceding yet going beyond it is the symbolization of the world, expressed in private and public prayer. There are domain assumptions about human life and history that mediate the experience of reality. Since these are part and parcel of our historical existence, we usually take them for granted; we are able to detect them only

when we contrast our world with another or, better still, when we pass
through significant social change ourselves and begin to question our
own domain assumptions.

Rather than deal with this issue in a theoretical way, let me offer
two examples. The change of the liturgy from Latin to English was a
profound transformation involving a different conception of society
and a changed experience of the sacred. At the time of the Reformation, the Catholic church decided to hold onto the medieval liturgy in
Latin. Why? I suppose there were a number of reasons. The church
wanted to preserve the special unity of religion and society that characterized medieval christendom. The new emphasis on national culture
and national independence undermined the medieval vision of the un-
divided *corpus Christianorum*, the incarnation of the Christian spirit
in society. The church clung to Latin, moreover, to protect the humanistic spirit of classical antiquity and the Renaissance against various
anti-intellectual movements, action-oriented or other-worldly, that
threatened the ancient heritage. Since the vernacular was regarded as
lowbrow at that time, the church insisted on the elevated language for
the celebration of the Eucharist, and by doing so also defended the
special prerogatives of the ordained clergy. The special language legiti-
mated ecclesiastical power. Later, when the vernacular assumed
greater importance and Western culture distinguished more clearly between the sacred and profane, Latin became the sacred language, separated from ordinary usage, and hence gave expression to a special type
of religious experience. In some religions the sacred appears as the
separated holy, distinct from the profane and unreconcilable with it.
This experience always demands a holy temple and with it a holy
priesthood, superior in power and prestige to secular leadership. The
Latin liturgy promoted this sort of experience of the sacred. It mediated a living contact with the divine that left intact the church's hierarchical structure.

The vernacular introduced by the Reformation had a profound
effect on society. It inevitably introduced greater democratization into
the ecclesiastical organization. Since all understood the language of
worship, all felt responsible for the church and sought a structure
where this new responsibility could be expressed. More than that, the
liturgy in the vernacular fostered a new experience of the sacred, one
that was not separated from the profane but in the midst of it. In the
Middle Ages there was no strict distinction between the sacred and the
secular; the entire world was believed to be raised to the sacramental
order. The separation between sacred and profane became more intense through Renaissance and Enlightenment. In the Reformation

cultures, the sacred moved more and more into the inward sphere, but it was an inwardness that produced action in the world. Over the last decades, we see the emergence of a new piety where the sacred is the depth of human existence that is revealed in Jesus and the whole of biblical history, and emerges, at least for believers, in the important experiences of human life. To move from Latin to the vernacular in the present century signifies the passage from the experience of the separated sacred to the experience of God in the midst of life, in the significant moments of man's humanization.

What does the shift from Latin to the vernacular liturgy mean from a more sociological point of view? I suppose it means that after centuries of expansion to continents beyond Europe, the Catholic church has finally abandoned the dream of christendom. It may mean, moreover, that the church is no longer afraid of ethnic and national self-affirmation. The bishops may feel that the aggressive stage of nationalism of the nineteenth and the first part of the twentieth centuries has been overcome and that today the ethnic and national loyalties are humanizing forces that enable people to resist the conformity and homogenization imposed on them by technology, bureaucracy, and international industry. But by accepting the vernacular liturgy, the Catholic church reversed the centuries-old trend toward centralization of ecclesiastical life in the papacy. The future priests may no longer be able to understand Latin; even bishops may no longer be fluent in that language: what will happen is that the regional hierarchies will find it ever harder to understand the Roman mentality that still thinks in terms of uniformity and universal rules applicable in all parts of the church. The vernacular in the liturgy makes the success of a common law book in the church almost an impossibility. What the regional churches worshiping in the vernacular will demand is the authority and freedom to plan their ecclesiastical life in keeping with the needs and aspirations of their culture.

Will the change from Latin to the vernacular in public prayer make the Catholic church imitate the churches of the Reformation? While we observe many similarities between the two separate but interacting traditions in our day, the Catholic church may not follow the Protestant journey. The major Protestant churches have been identified with the successful nations and with the more affluent classes in these societies, while the Catholic church has been strong in the less successful countries, and in North America was largely identified with the later and therefore poorer immigrants. The Catholic church is the only Christian church that is still profoundly rooted among the dispossessed, especially in the Latin world of Italy and Spain, of Latin

America, and of the Spanish-speaking peoples in the United States. It is possible, therefore, that the characteristic Catholic experience of the future will be mediated by a post-bourgeois perception of society. In particular, if the Catholic tradition of contemplation and community becomes creative in new social conditions, it may give rise to a Christian ethos and a Christian style that differ considerably from Reformation Christianity.

Let me offer another example of domain assumptions implicit in prayer and spirituality. In the history of Israel and the preaching of Jesus we find a central theme summarized in the words, "the first shall be last." The order of God is the inversion of the order of the world. The real order which God comes to establish is the inversion of the order which human power and ambition have created. "The poor shall be filled with good things, and the rich shall be sent away empty." Yet there are also other scriptural themes. Opposed to the previous theme is the famous though untypical dictum of St. Paul in his Epistle to the Romans, "There is no authority except from God, and those authorities that exist have been instituted by God." The people who are presently in positions of power in society are there according to God's will and however uncomfortable this may be and however great their injustice, they shall remain there. The first shall be first. The order of God is not inversion but stability. While the Bible contains both these themes, the question is which of these forms the basic symbolic structure of a person's prayer and spirituality. These are symbols implicit in prayer that have social impact. If Christians identified with the successful classes adopt "the first shall be last" as their primary symbol, they give this phrase a highly spiritual interpretation and understand it as referring not to this world but to the next. It is after this life, in heaven, that the world shall be inverted. But if "the first shall be last" is adopted as the principal symbolism by Christians in situations of social exploitation and humiliation, it may generate a social movement for freedom and justice. We have examples for this in countries like Ireland and Poland which were for centuries controlled by foreign powers; and we have examples among German Catholics, unwilling to be submissive citizens of Prussia, who produced a social, anti-capitalist Catholicism, which after World War I formed the left-of-center Center Party in Germany. And we have examples in the social gospel movements in the United States and Canada.

We conclude that in order to study the social impact of prayer and liturgy it is necessary to examine the basic symbolism that defines people's approach to the society in which they live. Again in most instances this symbolism will be unconscious. It is the task of critical theology to make these hidden assumptions in prayer conscious. Only then can we make a responsible choice. The prayer of the church should have an impact on social reality that corresponds to its deepest reflection on the gospel.

IV

Finally we come to the political meaning of the God-image in prayer. The social and human implications of the doctrine of God and in particular of divine transcendence have become an important issue in contemporary Christian theology. How shall we symbolize the God who created us and redeemed us and is present to us as Spirit? A growing number of theologians, affected by sociological reflection, have come to see that if God is symbolized as the king of kings ruling the world from his heavenly abode, then the conversion to this God in our hearts is at right angles to the flow of history and hence independent of the historical struggle. What counts, then, is to turn one's back on history and seek this God in the heart or in the sacred temple. If God's transcendence is understood as God's radical independence from human life, the really real in human existence is independent of the political order. Then conversion to God has no political implications. Then Christians are not moved by their faith to transform the world. They will look upon authority as divinely instituted and submit themselves to it. God then becomes the guardian of the present order, the legitimator of governments, the support of the rulers of the world. Religion then becomes the ideology of the successful classes and the otherworldly consolation of the poor.

This dualistic theism, some theologians insist, expresses a dualistic consciousness according to which there is a radical break between spirit and life. Spirit regards itself as superior to the rest of life, towering over life and ruling it from above. Order in human life must be imposed by the superior spirit. It is this divided consciousness that allows men to identify themselves with the spirit and project the image of the lower faculties unto women. By doing so, they justify the creation of order through the male domination of women. Women theologians have often insisted that it is this split consciousness of traditional culture that has led to the subjugation of women and to the dualistic understanding of God. The God-image as ruler over the earth appears as the guardian of all dominations in history, including the male domination of women. But what we should desire, according to the highest vision of our tradition, is not split consciousness which regards spirit as the trump card against life, but rather a unifying consciousness that allows us to experience the spirit as emerging from life, in communion with it, and moving it forward in history. Both men and women share in this unified consciousness and hence they cannot be assigned essentially different roles in history. Even God's transcendence can no longer by symbolized as spirit ruling over the flesh nor as the king over people nor as the husband over the wife. There must be other, more reconciling ways of speaking of divine transcendence.

The Bible and the Christian tradition record many ways of speaking of God. God is not only lord and king; God is also source, river, matrix, ground of life, way, horizon, promised future. In other words, there is a traditional language that speaks of God not as "over and above," but as "in and through" life and history. Yet we note that in the Christian tradition the mode of the divine immanence is never understood as one of identity (as we find it in pantheism—with immobilizing political consequences) but one of transcendence. God is present in life as creator, redeemer and sanctifier, as tension between what things are and what they are meant to be, as matrix, vector and horizon, as redemptive passage or passover, as critical word and life-giving spirit, etc. God is the life of our life that carries us forward toward our promised destiny. It is possible, therefore, to speak of God, and even to address oneself to the transcendent divine mystery, not as a super-person or super-king in heaven but as the divine source, word and spirit operative in history.

God is present in history as *transcendent* mystery. By this is meant 1) that God is never confined or exhausted or defined by this history, that God remains sovereign in regard to this history, and 2) that God's presence to people's lives enables them to transcend the inherited concepts and structures that no longer comprehend their lives. This second point is rarely made. God's transcendence makes us transcending! If Christians understand God as the lord and king, they usually make him the supreme authority protecting stability on earth. Christians attached to the transcendent God conceived in this manner will tend to defend the inherited categories. But if God is transcendent as sovereign mystery operative in people's lives and human history, then God's transcendence is the enabling, redemptive power that liberates us from the inherited prisons and makes us move toward a more gracious future. In this perspective it becomes clear that it is impossible to separate divine transcendence and human liberation. It is impossible, in other words, to choose between divine transcendence and human liberation. For by surrendering ourselves to divine transcendence we are carried forward toward greater humanization, and conversely by dedicating ourselves to human liberation we are in fact under the influence of the divine mystery conquering our blindness, our passivity, our attachment to the past, our easy ways of compromising with injustice.

What is the image of God that predominates in the Church's prayer? The above paragraphs have shown that this image has an impact on society. In our religious tradition we have a multitude of names that refer to the divine. Since all divine names are inadequate, we must have many names so that one may correct the false impression created by the preceding. It would be lacking in good sense to expect that any liturgy or any prayer confine itself to a single language about the divine. Still, we are able to ask what God-image predominates in a worship. Is there a readiness to let the lord and king language determine the style of prayer? Or is there a multiple language that accompanies the male language of father with the female language of matrix and corrects an overly unhistorical view of the divine transcendence with an emphasis that God is, in the terminology of the fourth gospel, love, light and life. In this way, by drawing upon the richness of the Christian tradition, we can assume responsibility for the social impact of prayer.

4.
The Nature and Function of New Testament Christology

Reginald H. Fuller

In traditional theology Christology has always preceded soteriology. Reginald H. Fuller confronts this model and suggests that the opposite approach would be more appropriate. He then considers what such an approach would mean to religious educators, emphasizing that the irreconcilable Christologies of the New Testament would be allowed to surface intact and the integrity of the humanness of Jesus would be preserved.

Christology asks questions about Jesus Christ. Who was he? What was the source of his authority and of his being? Who is he today? Traditional dogmatic theology dealt with Jesus Christ in two chapters: one on Christology and the other on soteriology. Christology was concerned with elucidating the *person* of Jesus Christ, soteriology his saving *work*, both in its objective and subjective aspects. That is to say, soteriology embraced both what Jesus had done in his earthly life and its continuing effect in the life of the believers.

The kinds of questions which traditional Christology sought to answer were: What is the relation of the eternal person of the Son of God to God the Father? How can he be distinct from God the Father, yet share the divine nature? Properly speaking, this aspect of Christology was part of the doctrine of God, namely of the Trinity. Then there was Christology proper, which sought to define the distinction and relation between the divinity and humanity of Jesus.

On the first aspect of Christology, the relation of the eternal Son to the Father, the church hammered out its faith in the words of the Nicene Creed (325 A.D.):

> God from God, Light from Light,
> true God from true God,
> begotten, not made, one in Being with the Father,
> Through him all things were made.

It was the Council of Chalcedon (461 A.D.) which in turn hammered out the doctrine of the divinity and humanity of the incarnate Son, and it did so in the following terms:

Therefore, following the holy Fathers, we all with one accord teach men to acknowledge one and the same Son, our Lord Jesus Christ, at once complete in Godhood and complete in manhood, truly God and truly man, [the definition expounds the Godhead by repeating the Nicene definition on the eternal Son and adding to the clause on the incarnation the title of "God-bearer" (theotokos, often not too accurately rendered as "Mother of God") for the Virgin Mary. It then proceeds:] one and the same Christ, Son, Lord only begotten, recognized in TWO NATURES, WITHOUT CONFUSION, WITHOUT CHANGE, WITHOUT DIVISION, WITHOUT SEPARATION. [Finally, it elaborates on the two natures:] the distinction of natures being in no way annulled by the union, but rather the characteristics of each nature being preserved and coming together to form one person and subsistence (hypostasis) not as parted or separated into two persons, but one and the same . . .[1]

Soteriology was concerned in its objective aspect with the saving significance of Christ's death. It sought to explain how that death saved mankind from sin, from death and the devil. This was commonly known as the doctrine of the atonement. No official definition of the doctrine of the atonement was ever produced by an ecumenical council. Theologians were free to produce their own interpretations. The main interpretations are associated with the names of Athanasius,[2] Anselm,[3] and Abelard.[4] For Athanasius, Christ's death was the victory over sin, death and the devil. For Anselm, it was the satisfaction of the righteous demands of God. For Abelard, it was the noble example inspiring us to righteousness. Reformation theology took Anselm's theory further: Christ's death was the satisfaction of the wrath of God.[5]

In the dogmatic systems of the past Christology has always come before soteriology. You had to know who Jesus was before you could understand what he had done. He did what he did because he was what he was. The saving significance of his work depended upon his divinity and humanity. Karl Barth expressed the traditional view of the matter in his criticism of Rudolf Bultmann:

Bultmann's general intention—in traditional terms—is to understand Christology and soteriology as a unity, and the New Testament kerygma as a proclamation of this unity. In this general intention I can follow him. But I fail to understand how one can help conceiving this unity, the event of Christ, as a differentiated unity in which Christology without thereby being separated from soteriology, precedes, whereas soteriology must follow.[6]

This is a typical reaction from a dogmatician. The order of presentation is doubtless correct. In dogmatics, and from the standpoint of Christian faith, the being of Christ precedes his action. But for the New Testament it was the other way around. The earliest Christians first experienced what Jesus had done and then drew their conclusions from that about who he was.[7]

A corollary of the traditional position is that it leads to thinking of revelation in propositional terms. Revelation becomes a process in which a body of truths is conveyed. We can see this from the way in which Christology was thought to be based initially on the direct teachings of Jesus about himself. He claimed to be Son of God and Son of man. This was the basis for the doctrine of the two natures, Son of man indicating his humanity, and Son of God his divinity. The explicit claims of the Johannine Christ, "I and the Father are one" (John 10:30); "he who has seen me has seen the Father" (John 14:29); and "Before Abraham was, I am" (John 8:58) clinched the matter. Thus the christological definitions of the councils, supported by the words of Jesus in the fourth gospel, came to be treated as presuppositions. In the process, everything else about Jesus' earthly history had to be squared with these presuppositions. This led to problems with the text, some of them from quite early days, others from the rise of historical criticism. If Jesus was divine, he must have known all things. How then could he say a thing like "But of that day or that hour no one knows, not even the Son, but only the Father" (Mark 13:32)? Or in the light of modern critical knowledge, how could he have attributed the psalms to David: "David inspired by the Holy Spirit declared . . ." (Mark 12:35)? How did he come to think Jonah was a historical personage, rather than a fictitious character in a novel, when he spoke of his having been in the belly of the whale three days and three nights (Mathew 12:40)? Such are the problems posed when we use traditional dogmatic formulae as a presupposition for interpreting the gospels, or when we take the view that in the New Testament Christology precedes soteriology.

In the nineteenth century liberal Protestant theologians broke with the traditional approach (Ritschl, Harnack, Sabatier et al).[8] They attempted to retain the traditional christological dogmas but to reinterpret them within the framework of their own liberal theology. They still believed that Jesus was God incarnate but they affirmed that faith on the basis of their assessment of Jesus' human personality. Jesus was a teacher of the most sublime truths ever attained by a human being, for he taught the Fatherhood of God and the community of men and women. Because of this Ritschl could say "Jesus has for us the value of God." In other words, so sublime was his humanity that it was divine. Such a position represented one gain over the older orthodoxy. It had at least discovered that Christology was essentially a confessional response to an encounter with a particular history, not the playing back of already revealed doctrine previously disclosed in the act of revelation. But its mistake was to locate the historical data to which Christology is the response in Jesus' human character as reconstructed by the so-called old quest of the historical Jesus. That reconstruction was a figment of the critical imagination.

As such it was destroyed by a series of fatal blows from Martin Kähler,[9] Johannes Weiss,[10] and Albert Schweitzer.[11] Kähler showed that it is impossible to get back behind the witness of the apostles, "the preached Christ" as he called it. The Christ attested by the original witnesses was not a human teacher of spiritual and moral ideals, but the savior of humankind from sin. In the same year Weiss discovered that the central message of Jesus was not the Fatherhood of God and the community of men and women, but the kingdom of God. This kingdom moreover was not an ideal utopia to be built by human effort or an inner state of the soul, as the liberal Protestants variously supposed, but the apocalyptic goal of cosmic history, effected by the miraculous intervention of God. No wonder the Catholic modernist Loisy quipped that "Harnack looked down a well to find the historical Jesus and saw the reflection of his own liberal Protestant face"!

Meanwhile, historical-critical method, which had been applied to the biblical text, had demolished the pillars of traditional Christology. By the end of the nineteenth century it was commonly agreed that the fourth gospel did not contain tape recordings of the *ipsissima verba* of Jesus, but consisted of a series of meditations by the author placed upon the lips of Jesus. You could no longer defend Christ's preexistence by quoting "before Abraham was, I am," or his divinity by quoting "I and the Father are one."

Between the two World Wars, British and American Protestant scholars[12] sought to do justice to the strange character of Jesus to which Weiss and Schweitzer had called attention and yet, like the older liberalism, to maintain the traditional creeds. Like the liberals, these neo-orthodox scholars were aware of the difficulties posed for traditional Christology by the results of historical criticism. The dogmas of Christ's divinity and preexistence could no longer be maintained by an appeal to the fourth gospel. Nor could the apocalyptic message of Jesus be transposed into modern humanistic terms. What could be done about the data of the real Jesus as portrayed in the synoptic tradition? He called himself Son of man and Son of God. But this did not mean that he was claiming humanity with the one and divinity with the other. "Son of man" was an apocalyptic term derived from the Book of Daniel or from later Jewish writings. It meant not the humanity of Jesus but the supernatural agent of judgment and redemption who was to appear at the end of history. You could almost say that Son of man represented the divinity rather than the humanity of Jesus. On the other hand, Son of God was a title used for human beings in the Old Testament and in pre-Christian Judaism. Israel in its corporate capacity was the Son of God ("Out of Egypt have I called my Son," Hosea 11:1). So, too, the king as the people's representative could be called the Son of God. The evidence suggested that Son of God stood for the humanity of Jesus!

Accordingly, the neo-orthodox sought other support for traditional Christology, in Jesus' filial or messianic consciousness. Jesus called God Abba, and by implication himself the Son of God, not in the sense of the Davidic king but as an expression of intimate relationship. A favorite view of the neo-orthodox was that Jesus expressed his messianic consciousness by combining in his self-understanding the two figures of the servant of Yahweh (Isa. 42, 49, 50, 53) and the Son of man (Daniel 7:14). Jesus believed that it was his destiny to attain to the glorious role of the Son of man by first passing through the humiliation and rejection, the suffering and death of the servant of Yahweh. This view represented a great advance on the older liberal Protestantism. The strangeness of the thought-world of Jesus was given full recognition. It was also an advance on traditional Christology—and this it shared with the liberals—in that it made no attempt to impose upon Jesus the metaphysical categories of person, nature and substance. It also shared with the liberals the insight that Christology was a response. And yet it had its own shortcomings. It ignored the implications of the rise of form criticism. This new method of gospel study[13] sought to get back behind the written gospels to the shaping of the gospel material during the period of oral transmission. For our present purposes its most important result was the establishment of criteria of authenticity for the Jesus tradition. First and foremost, there was the criterion of dissimilarity, according to which a saying is authentic to Jesus if it differs both from contemporary Judaism and from the teachings of the post-Easter church. It is possible to criticize the use of this criterion, but it is useful as a starting point in recovering an assured minimum of Jesus tradition. This means that it is unlikely that Jesus used the Son of man as a self-designation or operated with the suffering servant as a framework for his self-understanding.[14] There is growing agreement that Jesus' activity, his message and his teaching, all *implied* a Christology. When he proclaimed that the kingdom of God was near, its coming was intimately bound up with his own person.[15] When he spoke, he dared to speak in place of God.[16] When he acted, he acted for God.[17] It was only after Easter that the implicit Christology became explicit in the response of the earliest Christian community to the overall impact of Jesus' history from his baptism to his resurrection.

For us today, therefore, an authentic encounter with Jesus is not with his human personality and character, nor yet with his teachings, considered as purely human instruction. It is with Jesus preached by the church as the salvific act of God. This encounter, when it evokes faith, issues in a confession of faith. Confession is framed in the language of Christology.

In the New Testament times such christological response availed itself of many different christological images, titles and patterns. So we should speak rather of "Christologies" than of Christology, for the church picked up the language for its response from the constantly changing environment in which it found itself as it moved from Aramaic-speaking Palestine to the Hellenistic Jewish communities of Palestine and Syria and the diaspora to the Gentile world of the Eastern and central Mediterranean. Ultimately this spread of the gospel brought the church in contact with the metaphysical thinking of the Greco-Roman world. The story of the development of Christology from the earliest days in Jerusalem to the councils of Nicea and Chalcedon was a story of trial and error, or at the very least, of the discarding of inadequate or outmoded expressions. But amid all the change, the basic faith remained constant: God had acted, was now acting, and will finally act salvifically at the consummation of world history in the person of Jesus Christ. Images and titles, concepts and terminologies were pressed into service from popular messianic expectations in Palestine (Messiah, Son of God, and Son of David); and from more sophisticated expectations—such as the eschatological prophet like Moses, and the apocalyptic Son of man—Hellenistic Judaism provided the church with the concept of the divine wisdom, a heavenly being who sought to become incarnate in a succession of human lives. The mystery religions and the emperor worship of the Greco-Roman world furnished the title of *kyrios* (Lord), and popular Hellenistic religiosity the concept of Jesus as *theios anēr* (the divine man or miracle worker). Finally, the church adopted from Greek metaphysics terms like "nature," "person," and "substance."

All this suggests that the church was trying to find the most satisfactory language in which to respond to the mighty acts of God. This response was made in preaching, worship, and in the baptismal profession of faith.

Once the nature of Christology as response is realized, it need not surprise us that some of these responses are difficult to reconcile with others. For the people who made them were not seeking to build a coherent system but to confess their faith in concrete situations. Thus, as Bultmann[18] pointed out, the title of Messiah represents a different Christology not immediately reconcilable with that of the second Adam. The kenosis (self-emptying) Christology of the pre-Pauline hymn in Philippians 2:6-11 cannot without difficulty be reconciled with the gospels' presentation of the miracles as proof of Jesus' messianic claims or as epiphanies of his divine glory. Or again, the virginal conception of Jesus is hard to square with his heavenly preexistence. Such difficulties arise when we treat confessional responses as ontological statements or as propositions to be used to interpret every part of the New Testament without discrimination.

This means also that the images and titles, patterns and concepts are in principle replaceable by others. This is what Bultmann meant by demythologizing. It should not mean eliminating anything from the New Testament witness to Jesus Christ but interpreting it for today. After all, this is nothing new, for it is just what Nicea and Chalcedon did, when it translated the mythological titles of the New Testament into the abstract language of philosophy.

We can now see why for the New Testament soteriology comes before Christology. The point was clearly put by Martin Dibelius some forty years ago:

> The faith of the early Christians was centered not on what Christ was, but rather on what he had done for mankind. The New Testament contains practically nothing about the person of Jesus Christ in his ontological significance, nothing apart from his relations with mankind.[19]

In a footnote, Dibelius notes two partial exceptions, Philippians 2:6-11 and John 1:1.

What are the practical implications of all this for Christian education? Perhaps the most important thing is that in studying the gospels we should always start with the presupposition that Jesus was
fully human. We should not start with his divinity, and then try to
square his humanity with that. If we do, we shall end up by treating
him as something less than human, not more, and so fail to take
seriously what John 1:14 says about his flesh and what Nicea and
Chalcedon were talking about in the *vere homo* (truly man). Only
then, when we have encountered him in his full and complete humanity, shall we discover "God's presence and his very self."

Does the New Testament call Jesus God? It does so unam-
biguously in one place, in Thomas' postresurrectional confession
(John 20:28). There are two other places which are ambiguous, de-
pending on the punctuation or interpretation of the Greek text.[20]

It *is* possible to call Jesus God, but only with careful nuances and
qualifications. He is God in a certain way. That is what the tradition
meant when it called him God the Son in distinction from God the Father. He is *deus pro nobis*, God for us. In him we encounter God
turned to us in revelation, love and grace. It is to confess the experience of that encounter that Christology was designed, and Christians
would seek to confess that same faith today in preaching, worship and
daily life. To lead men, women and children to that confession is the
task of Christian education.

Notes

1. H. Bettenson, Trans., *Documents of the Christian Church* (Oxford:
U.P., 1943), p. 73.

2. Athanasius, *c.* 296-373. His work on the atonement is entitled *De In-
carnatione* ("On the incarnation").

3. Anselm of Canterbury, 1033-1109. His work on the atonement is entitled *Cur Deus Homo?* ("Why did God become man?").

4. Abelard, 1079-1142.

5. Luther's favorite text on the atonement was 2 Corinthians 5:21.

6. K. Barth, "Rudolf Bultmann, an Attempt to Understand Him" in
Kerygma and Myth, vol. 2 (London: SPCK, 1962), 83-132, esp. 96.

7. For an account of biblical criticism see the *Jerome Biblical Commen-
tary*, ed. R.E. Brown, *et. al.* Englewood Cliffs, N.J.: Prentice-Hall, 1968), II, 8-
20.

8. The most popular and readable exposition of the liberal Protestant
position was A. von Harnack, *What is Christianity?* (London: Williams and
Norgate, 1901).

9. Kähler's epoch-making essay was first published in 1892. It was
translated into English and published under the title *So-Called Historical Jesus
and the Historic-Biblical Christ* (Philadelphia: Fortress, 1964).

10. Johannes Weiss' slim volume *Die Predigt Jesu vom Reiche Gottes*
(1892, "Jesus' preaching of the Kingdom of God") has been translated at last:

NEW TESTAMENT CHRISTOLOGY

Jesus' Proclamation of the Kingdom of God (Philadelphia: Fortress, 1971).

11. A. Schweitzer's famous book *A Quest of the Historical Jesus* (London: Black, 1910) originally appeared in German in 1906.

12. E.g., T.W. Manson, *The Teaching of Jesus* (Cambridge: U.P., 1931); W. Manson, *Jesus the Messiah* (London: Hodder & Stoughton, 1943); J.W. Bowman, *The Intention of Jesus* (Philadelphia: Westminster, 1943).

13. The pioneering works were written by K.L. Schmidt and Dibelius in 1919 and by R. Bultmann in 1921. Two of them are available in E.T.,: M. Dibelius, *From Tradition to Gospel* (London: Ivor, Nicholson and Watson, 1934); R. Bultmann, *The History of the Synoptic Tradition* (Oxford: Blackwell and New York: Harper & Row, 1968). This is a revision of the unsatisfactory translation published in 1963.

14. On Jesus and the Son of man see R.H. Fuller, *The Foundations of New Testament Christology* (London: Lutterworth and New York: Scribner, 1965), pp. 119-25. On the Servant of Yahweh and Jesus' self-understanding see M.D. Hooker, *Jesus and the Servant*, (London: SPCK, 1959).

15. See Mark 1:14; Luke 11:20.

16. See Jesus' "But I say to you" in the antitheses of the Sermon on the Mount (Matthew 5:21-48).

17. Luke 11:20 is again evidence for this. Also the parables of the lost, which interpret (Luke 15) Jesus' conduct in eating with the outcast as God's search for sinners occurring in his (Jesus') ministry.

18. See his essay "New Testament and Mythology" in H.W. Bartsch, ed. *Kerygma and Myth I* (London: SPCK, 1953), pp. 34-35.

19. M. Dibelius, *Gospel Criticism and Christology* (London: Ivor, Nicholson and Watson, 1953), p. 86.

20. Cf., Rom. 9:5 RSV with RSV margin and Titus 2:13 RSV with RSV margin.

EXTENDING MODELS

Maria Harris
John A. Swartz
Martin A. Lang

5.
Isms and Religious Education

Maria Harris

Maria Harris examines the paradox that we seem to need a particular "ism" in order to extend ourselves beyond it. And yet, if we have not moved beyond one struggle we may not have been engaged in that one at all. She proposes several changes in curriculum design and metaphor which would move religious educators towards a more experiential inclusion of all persons.

Racism. Sexism. Ageism. Clericalism. Terrorism. Pacifism. Individualism. Feminism. Heroism. Judaism. Ecumenism. Our language is filled with isms. What do we mean when we speak of an ism? How might a study of isms inform religious education? What could such a study tell us about ourselves?

An ism is a distinctive doctrine, system or theory. If added to a noun it may indicate an action, practice or process; for example, terrorism or favoritism. It may indicate a state or condition of being; for example, pauperism. It may mean a characteristic behavior or quality, such as heroism or individualism. When the word *ism* is used alone, it is generally thought of as something negative. However, if we reflect on some of the isms noted above, we realize that an ism may be negative, as in ageism, sexism, and racism; or positive, as in Judaism, heroism and ecumenism. More often, it is paradoxical—as in pacifism, feminism, communism, or individualism.

I should like to reflect first on the paradoxical quality of an ism, that quality which causes something to have apparently contradictory aspects which are both nonetheless true.

As a white woman in United States society today, I find myself committed to feminism, a doctrine or theory through which I may both articulate and live my conviction that women and men each embody the totality of human personhood and that there are both masculine and feminine elements in all human beings that need to be acknowledged, accepted and affirmed. As a feminist, I have become aware of sexism operating in the society, particularly in its institutions, language and customs, to the point where sexist language leaps at me from the pages of a book I might be reading. Conversation that refers to "men" rather than "boys" while at the same time calling women "girls" dismays me with its frequency. Statistics about unequal pay for equal work push my frustration level to a new low. However, I must admit a peculiar, though somewhat embarrassing, autobiographical note. It was not always so. There was a time in the not too distant past, where I too used only the masculine pronoun. I too referred to women as "girls." Questions of equity did not even occur to me. I suspect it had something to do with the way I was socialized and the way I was educated. Now, however, that I have been resocialized and reeducated, a peculiar thing has happened which brings me to the paradoxical quality of an ism. I have begun to realize that although discrimination concerning women and girls leaps at me from the surrounding culture, I am far less sensitive to the other discriminations in society that separate people on the basis of race, or age, or religion, or national origin. I am only beginning to be aware, with a personal as distinguished from an intellectual awareness, of the systematic exclusion of the black, the Indian, the oriental experience that is obvious in, for example, much curricular material and church practice; the frightening patronization of both the young and the old in daily life; the terrible blandness that pervades an essentially white, middle-class society. What is paradoxical for me is that had I not focused on one ism, namely feminism, I would probably not have become aware of the other divisions. Thus I, and those like me, are nourished and empowered by conviction in one area. But that commitment, if it is genuine, pushes us out to an embracing of the struggles of our sisters and brothers with other emphases and other equally urgent concerns. The paradox quite simply is this: we need a particular ism in order to go beyond it. If we have not moved beyond one struggle, we may not have been engaged in that one at all.

There is a more social application of the awareness of an ism, however, and it again incorporates a somewhat paradoxical note. As Jill Ker Conway remarked in her inauguration address as first woman president of Smith College,[1] movement toward providing educational, economic and cultural equality of opportunity for persons previously discriminated against in the wider society has often, if not always, been based on the principle of justice. The principle invigorating the movement has been a realization of what some groups did *not* have. But what is not always noted, and what seems to me to be a particular concern for religious educators, is the need for inclusion of previously excluded persons on the basis of what they *do* have. Our society has systematically been starving itself by refusing to acknowledge its need not only for the range of humanness all people possess, but for the access to feeling and interpersonal communication that has been so well developed in women; for the grace of negritude, the experience of the holy, the communal church life and sisterhood/brotherhood so evident in our black communities; for the spontaneity of childhood and the wisdom of old age; for the appreciation of and oneness with the earth cherished by the North American natives; and for the power of redemptive suffering evident nowhere so much in this century as in the lives and deaths of Jewish people.

We have reached a time where we need, simply in order to survive, the combination of the minds and hearts and wisdom of all peoples. Somehow, while loving those nearest and dearest to us, we must place our family and our intimates in the same category as all humans. Politically, we need a complete desovereignization of nations. Patriotism, once viewed positively, has become a liability, if it means that my love for one country limits my love for the peoples of other nations. As each new child is born we are asked the question: shall we teach her or him, with all this love to give, to give to everybody? Or shall we help her or him learn to be selfish?

Which brings us to the religious task, the educational task, and therefore, the task for religious educators. With reference to the religious task, as Roger Hazelton has recently pointed out, contemporary theologians and reflectors on the religious are engaged in an attempt to "relocate transcendence by extending its scope of meaning on the one hand and by seeking to restore to theology its traditional dialectical balance between transcendence and immanence on the other."[2] Hazelton goes on to suggest that the work of those who would call themselves religious, their liturgy, if you will, is to explore the "*theos* of *logos*—in short the transcendent horizon of all human meaning."[3] All human meaning can only be explored, however, if there is acceptance of all human beings, regardless of race, sex, or age. The transcendence which is constitutive of our experience, rather than the object of our experience, is that of all of us, or of none of us. Either all of us are "absolutely open upwards," in Rahner's phrase, or none of us are. The question of God is irrevocably bound to the question of our relationships with one another; we do not get rid of God by concentrating on humanity, but it may be true we shall lose God if we do not.

The task of education, which is logically, although not really, distinct from the religious task, is similar. For the educator's task is to create an environment where one can first come to know limits and boundaries and then begin the lifelong enterprise where the boundaries and limits are constantly being widened outward toward all realizable reality. Again, paradox. We must come to know first our primary community, then ourselves, our religious tradition, our "people" and our nation, if we would come to community with our planet, our universe, our God. One partakes in an ever-widening horizon; but does so while rooted in a particular time, a particular race, a particular culture. The educational question is whether one affirms both the particular and the universal at the same time, and whether, in the process of learning, it is a given that education means affirmation. One cannot create a new world if there are good people and bad people, where some of those persons are disaffirmed. One can attempt to create a new world only if all of us are affirmed. For this reason, educators might do far better to use "horizon" rather than "content" or "process" as their central metaphor.

If this is true, then religious education becomes the field that helps us hold on to immanence and transcendence at the same time, while constantly pushing forward the horizons of human life. For this reason, religious education needs to be characterized in the first place by the word human. If something is to be defined as human, in this case religious education, then it needs to have the same characteristics as the human. It needs to be fleshly and organic; it needs to be alive; it needs to be situated in time, and especially, in space. At the same time, however, it needs to recognize that what constitutes the human is always to be discovered, particularly as the living experience of previously ignored peoples is incorporated. Ultimately, it needs to be an acknowledgement of the religious mystery of the presence of God in our midst, where the human and the divine are never separable. With reference to boundaries, it must be a movement toward the stage in life which Fowler speaks of an "universalizing," where persons' "love for and communion with God seems unselfconscious and fully integrated into a life of activity, responsibility and generative practical concern for the fulfillment of what Jews and Christians call the Kingdom of God."[4] It must be a movement toward the stage where the community of persons is "universal in extent."[5]

It is my contention in this paper that religious education has been hindered in the past from moving toward a community that is universal in extent through failure to consider certain divisions or isms that preclude universality, because they preclude the understanding or incorporation of some peoples. Among us are those who are still guests in the culture. Here let me limit consideration to the three areas of sexism, racism, and ageism with the hope that by examining some of the ways these appear in religious education, we will discover other separations where they exist, and move toward the eradication of all of them.

Some Areas of Concern

The first instance where we, as religious educators, have been remiss has been an unexamined attitude to the nature of human power. Religious educators are very often uneasy when questions of power are raised; power is too often looked upon as force. Yet genuine power is the fullness of human energy directed toward the betterment of the universe, the power of the heart surgeon, the poet and the saint. If powerless peoples are to share their gifts as well as receive the gifts to which they are entitled, there is need for those in positions of visibility and power to be coadvocates. We need to be engaged in direct advocacy in considering nondiscriminatory materials, programs and attitudes among the people with whom we work. We need to design environments leading to the self-advocacy of women, racial minorities, the young and the old.

A teacher, a clergyperson, a DRE, a Minister of Christian Education, is by definition a person in power. She or he is one who influences, or seeks to influence others. Do we use our human power reflectively, in a conscious attempt to marshal energies that will break down negative attitudes, particularly negative stereotypes, when they are encountered? Do we encourage participation on our decision-making boards by women and members of racial minorities? More difficult to answer, do we encourage and move actively for the presence of old people and of children? Response to this last question may help to surface some of our own stereotypes with reference to age. Where we have moved to awareness of sexual and racial bias, we may as yet be unaware that we possess negative stereotypes toward children and young people. Would we exclude children from a board, the same children who can organize and run committees and communities of their own quite well, because we have stereotypes of young people as incompetent? Can we even address the question of whether these are stereotypes?

It may be possible that in reflecting upon such questions, we uncover something of our own inappropriate attitudes to power. We may find what some men have begun to acknowledge in facing the question of ordination of women. We resist, as human beings, any diminution of our power. We like to be in control. We forget that letting go and living in faith is a primary religious stance.

The use of power can, of course, become a form of oppression, and there is always the danger that it will become domination. Thus, religious educators might do well to periodically examine their attitudes toward power, ready to bow out when they are no longer needed.

A second area of consideration might be our preference for time over space in both our religious and our educational thinking. Western theology has developed with a preference for history, where an understanding of an original revelation made at some point in time takes precedence over understanding religious life as rooted in a particular place, and dependent on that place for its unique and special character. If we were to shift from temporal to spatial concerns in religious education, we would have to see revelation not so much in the period of time it occurs, but in the place where it occurs. The radicality of such a change in worldview cannot be minimized. It calls into question the universality of truth as well as the missionary activity of churches. Vine Deloria asks,

> Can (a religion) leave the land of its nativity and embark on a program of world or continental conquest without losing its religious essence. . . . Are ceremonies restricted to particular places, and do they become useless in a foreign land? . . . These questions have never been raised in a fundamental manner within Western religious circles, because of the preemption of temporal considerations by Christian theology.[6]

Concern with time over space also colors our thinking about education. It is basically a temporal orientation that speaks in terms of goals, objectives and end states. Therefore, "Changing the conception of religious reality from temporal to spatial terms involves severely downgrading the teaching/preaching aspect of religious activity. Rearrangement of individual behavioral patterns (a temporal concept) is incidental to communal involvement in ceremonies and the continual renewing of community relationships with the holy places of revelation."[7]

The fact that our theology has been written almost exclusively by white, Western, male clergymen has almost certainly kept us from examining such considerations until now. This is mentioned not to denigrate white Western male clergymen, but to point out how limited our theology has been, coming as it does from one sex, one race and generally, one profession. Theology would be different but it would be just as limited if it had been written by, say, black female African midwives.

If we begin to incorporate the experience of all peoples in reflecting on our religious questions, however, there would certainly be a shift from time to space as fundamental in religious understanding. I think it is safe to say that women are more oriented to space than to time, not only biologically, but through a more developed sense of feeling which deepens their sense of both inner and outer space. Children too are more at ease with space, developing a sense of time only in later childhood. But most notably, the American Indians have developed space as the metaphor central to religious understanding. Young Chief, a Cayuse, refused to sign the Treaty of Walla Walla because, he felt, the rest of the creation was not represented in the transaction:

> I wonder if the ground has anything to say? I wonder if the ground is listening to what is said? I wonder if the ground would come alive and what is on it? Though I hear what the ground says. The ground says, It is the Great Spirit that placed me here. The Great Spirit tells me to take care of the Indians, to feed them aright.[8]

Deloria, commenting on Young Chief's attitude toward creation as a religious doctrine, continues, "The similarity between Young Chief's conception of creation and the Genesis story is striking, but when one understands that the Genesis story is merely the starting place for theological doctrines of a rather abstract nature while Young Chief's beliefs are his practical articulations of his understanding of the relationship between the various entities of the creation, the difference becomes apparent."[9]

A third area that needs attention, an area where many religious educators spend the bulk of their time, is in curriculum design. Three aspects of curriculum design that need consideration are (1) the way curriculum is understood in the actual learning situation; (2) the selection of materials; and (3) the choice of teachers.

(1) The understanding of curriculum determines in large part the way it is used. Religious educators would do well to examine whether their notion of curriculum is too narrow, and if the word is equivalent for them to the academic resources used—at the least significant level of meaning, the textbook series. A teacher, it is to be remembered, is an agent or a community which structures the environment in such a

way that persons can get in touch with their own resources and the resources around them, toward the future. The concern with structuring the environment is the critical element. Another way of saying this is that a teacher or educator is one who uses curriculum. The caution I mention above, however, is the myopic view of curriculum that still pervades the understanding of many of us in religious education. In most settings where the term curriculum is used, it generally is in a sentence such as, "If we could only find the right curriculum," meaning in practice, "Shall we use Uniform Lesson Plans, the Judson Press series, Shalom, Benziger or Paulist?" This notion of curriculum focuses on its least important aspect, and the one that is last in order of importance. For curriculum has at least a five-fold meaning: (1) the physical environment itself, based on the belief that *where* people learn determines to a great extent what and how they learn; (2) the interaction curriculum, that is, all the relationships impinging on the learning situation, such as: administration-teacher; teacher-administration; teacher-teacher; student-teacher; teacher-student; teacher-students; teachers-students; student-student; and students-students; (3) the private curriculum; that is, the *inside* of both teacher and student, the presuppositions, convictions, moods, prejudices and prior experience they bring to the situation; (4) the community curriculum, that is, the kind of community from which the persons come, the community existing in the learning situation (if any does in fact exist), as well as the wider local, state, national and world community; and (5) the academic or knowledge resources that assist in the entire process; for example, the texts, films, materials and machines. It is this much, at least, which is incorporated in the idea of curriculum, and it is evident that all of these elements are related to ageism, sexism, and racism.

From such a perspective on curriculum, we need to examine carefully what can be learned from newer educational patterns. One example is family clustering, where members come together on other bases than segregation by age. (I find myself engaged at present, for example, in a Family Cluster at Cambridge where the youngest of us is two, and the oldest of us is seventy. It is amazing, first, how easily we all get along, and secondly, how many curriculum suggestions made by the four-year-olds make sense to those of us in middle age.) We need also to devise situations where the religious experience of participation in black churches causes us to realize, among other things, that preaching need not necessarily be one-way communication, and that there are richer variations on the theme of speaking the Word than many of us have yet experienced.

Perhaps the most important thing religious educators might do, however, and the easiest, is to listen. One intelligent and articulate senior citizen, recently speaking of discrimination toward older persons in religious education, commented that, as an older person, she was offered bus rides where interesting sights were pointed out to her, dances which she could watch, classes in ceramics, but very little for her *mind*. She then added that what she found most difficult was that she seemed to be seen, even by well-intentioned educators, solely on the basis of her age. "What I really would like is to be seen as a person, and treated with respect, not because of my age, but because of the person I am." How familiar that request will seem to blacks and to women!

Speaking of the needs of black people, Peggy Ann Griffen makes this curriculum suggestion:

> A cadre of churchmen need to visit the ghetto areas of the city and the remote rural areas of the country providing a communication network ministering to the basic needs of people. We need to be concerned about attendance—not of people in church, but the attendance of the church in the day to day existence of people.

> The cadre of churchmen need to visit prisons, old age homes, rest homes, hospitals. . . . Members of the family that have been put away from society need to be brought home. All of these actions are part of religious nurture because children can be involved in them. Involvement of children in these activities far exceeds the memorization of verses or reading stories that do not relate to their lives. Involvement in these immediate experiences will have more lasting effects than hearing about the experience of another person.[10]

(2) The selection of curriculum materials involves a number of factors. Of crucial importance is a realization of what has been left out. This requires some degree of awakened consciousness that has not always been developed, or has even been systematically and purposely *not* developed. Do we find in curriculum materials, whether for children or adults, the incorporation of statements such as the following, from the National Committee of Black Churchmen:

> White theology sustained the American slave system and negated the humanity of blacks. . . . Black Theology, based

on the imaginative black experience, was the best hope for the survival of black people. This is a way of saying that Black Theology was already present in the spirituals and slave songs and exhortations of slave preachers and their descendants. . . . The message of liberation is the revelation of God as revealed in the incarnation of Jesus Christ. Freedom IS the gospel. Jesus is the Liberator! "He . . . has sent me . . . to preach deliverance to the captives." (Luke 4:18). Thus the black patriarchs, and we ourselves, know this reality despite all attempts of the white church to obscure it and to utilize Christianity as a means of enslaving blacks. The demand that Christ the Liberator imposes on all men requires all blacks to affirm their full dignity as persons and all whites to surrender their presumptions of superiority and abuses of power.[11]

Are we able to hear such statements?

Another question arises in considering what may have been left out. In teachers' manuals, is there, as a matter of course, a reminder to all teachers that it is different to grow up black, or red, or oriental, or female, in a white male culture; that a black child is born a human being and gradually discovers in this society he or she is black, which often is conveyed and interpreted as "inferior"? Are white teachers, female and male, aware that a nonwhite child grows up understanding the dominant culture, because living in it, an advantage the teacher may not share in reverse?

A further question in selection of material is whether religious educators are sensitive and alert toward the values being conveyed. Much curricular material on the market today needs to be questioned in terms of the values portrayed, again especially for black students. Peggy Ann Griffen comments that the oppressive system to which many black children are exposed "has used the church to teach us white standards and values which cause us to accept circumstances that infringe upon our human rights."[12] She adds that although the black church holds *people* and *land* as its two most fundamental values, it has been negatively influenced by white society.

On an organized level the participation of the church in economics has produced many negative results. When we weigh some of the practices of the Black Church against a people oriented value system, we can understand why we are not independent. Some of these practices are: giving the Church

School banner to the class that brings the most money, awarding medals to servicemen who have engaged in the destruction of human lives; purchasing status symbol cars; traveling to annual conventions and purchasing old buildings at a price that far exceeds the worth of the building.[13]

Griffen is also of help to religious educators in considering some of the aspects of family education that are not always emphasized in a program where a more typically white style of life is the dominant image. She writes:

Relating to the family in the Black Church includes acknowledging the strength of the Black female. The Black female has to acquire strength because of the persecution of the Black male. The Black Grandmother had the task of religiously educating both Black and White children. Her deep feelings and facial expressions communicated non-verbal messages. Her message told the Black child that he must struggle to be free. Her message to the White child was that he should not grow up to be another oppressor. As a result we have two groups of revolutionaries today. One is trying to overcome his past history of servitude while the other is trying to reject his past history of dominance.[14]

Finally, with reference to academic resources, mention needs to be made of the ongoing task for religious educators as they review materials for evidence of various isms. *Joint Educational Development* is engaged in this task with great seriousness. A number of denominations have created task forces to deal with the issues of sexism and racism in published materials: hymns, prayers, liturgies, books. The ordinary procedure is to examine these materials by noting pictures, language, situations and roles in terms of: how many males; what are the males doing; how many females; what are the females doing? A simple count provides enough evidence to realize the message being conveyed: one sex and one race is superior to the rest of us. Though they may naturally call forth defensiveness when cited, the statistics are impossible to contradict.

Much more still needs to be done, not only by denominations that have not as yet addressed these issues, but also by those who, alerted to sexism and racism, have now turned to ageism, classism, nationalism and clericalism as well. One corrective: appropriate language and images may be the point of departure as they have been until now, but one needs to entertain the possibility that knowing how to speak inclusively of women and men, all races, and young and old is only the beginning. Unless the attitudes underlying sexist, ageist and racist language have not changed, we still may be at point zero.

(3) The understanding and examination of curricular materials needs to go hand in hand with the selection of teachers in our religious education programs. Churches and other agents of religious education tend to mirror a teacher selection pattern that is entrenched in the society as a whole. With preschool and elementary children, the majority of teachers are female. This is a bit less true at the high school level. Once one reaches the college, university and seminary level, however, a reversal in the pattern becomes marked, and solidified at the decision-making and official level. The majority of persons at the official teaching level are male. In the Roman Catholic church, for example, *all* officials are male. No one needs to say anything verbally about this pattern, for the message is clear. Women's appropriate province is a relatively passive one, best spent with young children; men's appropriate province is a decision-making one, best spent with adults. As long as this pattern continues, the young people growing up in our churches and institutions receive several clear messages, not just about adults but about themselves as girls or boys. This is attested to by the following autobiographical reflection of a young woman seminarian in 1971:

> I have discovered that for years, I had been waiting 'to be moved'—by a man, to faith—waiting for something to prod me, to tell me where to go or what to do. In attempting to be 'feminine' all these years, I had lost the courage to shape my own life. I had waited passively for some man to do it for me. I had waited passively for my denomination to ordain me. Waiting, waiting; dropping in and out; hesitant to plunge headlong into any vocation; lurking by the phone; reluctant to speak out in classes; afraid of not measuring up to the standards of 'masculine intellect.'[15]

This particular seminarian then goes on to speak of the frustration that occurs when one turns to the tradition for sustenance.

> Sooner or later any seminarian turns to the Bible for answers to their deepest questions. But for a woman to turn to the Bible in search of a new and liberating identity is often an exercise in frustration. Take 1 Timothy 2 for example. It is not

so bad to be chided into sobriety and modesty—the author of
1 Timothy expected these qualities from Christian men and
women. But to be indicted for the very presence of sin in the
world is to be given a burden we cannot bear. "Yet she will be
saved through motherhood—if only women continue in faith,
love and holiness with a sober mind."[16]

This particular passage helps in consideration of the question of
teacher selection for several reasons. The first has already been alluded
to. As long as teacher selection continues as it does now, at the volun-
teer level particularly, with no notable move to change the pattern, sex
role stereotyping will continue and nothing needs to be said about the
role expectations of our society. Religious educators will continue to
confirm these expectations by their silence. But consideration also
needs to be given the resistance to verses such as the one cited from
Timothy, "yet she will be saved through motherhood," because many
women who are teaching in our programs hear this kind of resistance
as a subtle put-down of their present chosen life-style as mothers.
They are not always aware that raising the question is an inquiry into
whether woman's sexuality reduces her own vocational possibilities to
one—that of motherhood—thus limiting her identity and her contributions to her function as a sexual being. More important still, reinforce-
ment of teacher selection patterns on the basis of sex tends to con-
strain the asking of the religious question, which is not "What does it
mean to be male?" or even, "What does it mean to be female?" in
the society, but, "What in God's name does it mean to be human?"
Returning to the thesis stated in the opening pages of this paper, the
humanity of all of us is narrowed when the humanity of any of us is
denied its fullest expression. The reader may be interested to note that
the seminarian quoted above, writing in 1971, was Carter Heyward,
who in July of 1974 was one of the first women ordained to the Epis-
copal priesthood. Thus one can overcome the stereotypes, but how
much more fruitful for the religious task it would be if the entire community worked together to do this.

A Change in Metaphors

I suggested in my introduction that religious educators might do
their work better by choosing "horizon" rather than "content" or
"process" as their central metaphor. I would like to reflect now on a
number of other categories or lenses through which we might view the
work of healing the divisions of peoples so evident in our society. To
this time, our concentration has been on such foci as scripture, tradi-

tion, morality, doctrine and liturgy. However, these concerns might be better served by using more inclusive categories which will help us concentrate on what we *do* as educators rather than what we *convey*. More inclusive categories are needed; they are also available. I shall propose six.

(1) The first is *Grounding*. An emphasis on grounding would lead the educator to begin with an awareness of roots. Not just her or his own roots, but the roots of the individuals and the groups who are the educatees. To conduct an educational enterprise, we need to know our own and others' personal roots, to accept them, and more importantly, to articulate them. When and if persons learn together, there needs to be discovery and affirmation of where all of us are from. We also need the sensitivity to realize that society has sometimes torn people from their roots, as was the case with black slaves and the North American natives. Only from this point can we move on to a religious grounding, one that puts us in touch with the roots of our tradition, the sense of where we come from at a more universal, more cosmic level. Often, such attention to grounding is ignored, and this may be the reason we do not move either as fast or as far as we would wish.

(2) A second activity is *Probing*. Probing can of course carry a negative connotation in education, particularly if it is thought of as a psychological or manipulative incursion into the private awareness of persons, which is their special and unique province. Here, however, I should like to suggest probing as the attempt to get at the basic intentions of our peoples, our churches, our scriptures, our creeds, ourselves. More important for the purposes being articulated in this paper, however, we need to probe our differences, particularly in the way we view reality. Before I, or any educator, can ask you to try to see things the way I do, I need to ask you why you view things as you do, and I need especially to listen to your answer. The question we often have as children, "Why is this so?" is too little asked in later life. The question of young people, "Why do we have to learn this?" is too seldom answered. Together we need to raise probing questions, not only with reference to published materials, but at far deeper levels. Why *do* we believe what we do? Why do we want to hand on a tradition? Why are we "in" religious education? Are there some of us who decide the essence of tradition and then use that as a determinant of human experience, or do we use our communal experience as a shaper of the tradition? Are tradition and experience always engaged in conversation? Finally, when we reach the question of isms and ask, "Why are some people left out?" it may be important not to concentrate too much on some impersonal "They." We may discov-

er that there is an answer here, in the "We" and in the "I."

(3) A third activity called for today is *Symbolizing*. A number of considerations emerge here. One is the need human persons have for universal religious symbols, as well as for the symbols of their particular traditions. Children particularly need some kind of grammar, some semantic, that will help them incorporate, take into their bodiliness, the meaning conveyed by their experience. This would undoubtedly include the entire range of artistic symbolism. But symbols are also problematic. For there is need today both to form and reform symbols as revelation continues. Not all symbols—the king, shepherd, the monarch, brotherhood, for example—are as adequate today as they once were. The question is not so much "What is wrong with them?" as "What is there about them which is no longer appropriate for everyone?" Obviously, women are having more and more difficulty articulating religious understanding through male symbols or symbols reflective of another culture and their greatest source of new symbols might be those which are spatial rather than temporal. More troubling is the equation of a symbol with that toward which it points, an association that sometimes causes people to be unaware that rejection of the symbol *for* a reality is not equivalent to rejection of the reality itself. Here religious educators need to be sensitive to the genuine difficulty many persons have today in finding expression for their deepest convictions. It is not always the conviction that is the problem; it is the finding of suitable images, metaphors or symbols that embody it.

(4) Symbolizing is related to a fourth activity, *Envisioning*, and envisioning is the refusal to leave the future to chance. It is the action linking the already to the not yet. It is the sign that people have dug their heels solidly into the now and the here, this *place*, despite all the prophecies of doom, working as if everything depended on them, while praying as if everything depended upon God. It is the work religious educators have engaged in more and more recently as questions are asked about 1980 and 1985 such as, "What is possible?" "What is probable?" and "What is preferable?" Envisioning is a harnessing of energies toward what is preferable, a very practical activity that includes dreaming, articulating assumptions, and deciding what is needed, what is to be discarded, what is to be conserved. It is the stance of the person who lives in hope, in striving and labor, not an ephemeral or somnabulant state. At best, visionaries are the ones who dream, but not in retreat. True visionaries dream until their arms ache and the sweat runs down their faces.

(5) A fifth activity is *Integrating*. For religious educators, in-

tegrating is the task where they analyze critically any discrepancies between the vision their churches, institutions and they themselves affirm, and the behavior concurrent with this affirmation. It is, with reference to the divisions of people, the prophetic task, the open response to Dr. King's *Why We Can't Wait* or to Vine Deloria's *We Talk, You Listen*. It includes the tasks of penitence, confession of sin and reparation, as well as the tasks of building, liberation and teaching. It is the bringing together of one's espoused theory and one's theory in use, integrating words and deeds as they flow from a center that is moving toward wholeness, at-oneness and integrity.

(6) The final activity is *Professing*. Several years ago, writing in the London *Times*, Bernard Levin was quoted as saying of the sixties: "Certainty had vanished, conviction was vanishing, will itself was crumbling, and those behind cried 'Forward!' and those before cried 'Back!' and both cries were constantly drowned by a mysterious muttering of 'Sideways, Sideways,' which came none knew whence."[17] Levin's analysis of the times still appears valid. There are few if any absolute certainties. However, there are some probabilities, and some relatively absolute convictions that are as old and as true as Deuteronomy. The first is the loving of God with one's whole heart and soul and mind and strength; the second is the loving of one's sisters and brothers as oneself. At the evening of this life, it is still these two commandments on which we shall be judged. The profession of educators need not be extensive; but it will be all-inclusive if it does these: love God, love others, love oneself, love the earth. It is this professing that needs to be embodied in our lives. For it is still deeds of love which make God credible.

Conclusion

There is a line in a poem of W.H. Auden that goes something like this: "For men and women are love as God is love, and every kindness to another is a little death into the divine image." We are baptized, by being born human, into kindness. Most of us do believe that it is in kindness to our sisters and brothers that we find God. The work of religious education, and the taking up of that work by particular persons, is the affirmation of that belief. "For men and women are love as God is love, and every kindness to another is a little death into the divine image."

But there is another 'other'; the other part of ourselves. Society and our culture say that some of us are strong and some are weak; some are advantaged, some are disadvantaged; some are rich and some are poor; some are children and some are aged; some are black and some are white. That, however, at the deepest level of our experience is *not* our experience. For our experience is that we are an entire range of human possibilities, each and every one of us. In each of us there is a child and an old person, masculine and feminine. In each of us there runs a relationship in blood that makes us sisters and brothers far beneath the pigmentation of our skins. Genesis reminds us of the archetypal image in which we were all created. Our kindness to ourselves then, is to the other within ourselves, to all those human elements within us we have yet to reclaim, but which we see mirrored in those around us. As women, for example, our kindness needs to be toward our strength, our independence, our rationality; as adults, for example, our kindness needs to be to the child within us now as well as toward the aged one waiting within our future. As human beings, our kindness needs to be to the earth of which we are formed, the earth and the land and the place that make us ourselves, toward that nonhuman nature that is very much part of us.

Possibly the reason we are separated from one another in the wider society is that we have not yet overcome the separations within ourselves. Possibly the divisions and separations that continue to keep hate alive in the world are the result of our not accepting the hidden, forgotten and 'other' parts of ourselves, the entire divine image within us. As religious educators, our primary personal and professional vocation may be not to be distinct from everyone else, but to be one, to dwell in the Omega Point of which Teilhard has spoken so well and with such intensity.

"For men and women are love as God is love, and every kindness to another is a little death into the divine image." When the racism and the sexism and the ageism are gone, we may find that we too have died. Let us hope that it will be a death into the divine image.

Notes
1. Smith College, Northhampton, Massachusetts, October 19, 1975.
2. Roger Hazelton, "Relocating Transcendence," *Union Seminary Quarterly Review*, Volume XXX, Winter-Summer, 1975, pp. 101-109.
3. *Ibid.*, p. 102.
4. James Fowler, "Toward a Developmental Perspective on Faith," *Religious Education*, Volume LXIX, pp. 217-218.
5. *Ibid.*, p. 218.
6. Vine Deloria, *God is Red*. New York: Grosset and Dunlap, 1973, p. 83.
7. *Ibid.*, p. 81.
8. *Touch the Earth*, compiled by T. C. McLuhan. Outerbridge and Dienstfrey, 1971, p. 8.

9. Deloria, *op. cit.*, pp. 95-96.

10. Peggy Ann Griffen, "The Educational Mission of the Black Church," n.d., n.p., p. 11.

11. "Black Theology," a Statement of the National Committee of Black Churchmen, Atlanta: Interdenominational Theological Center, 1969.

12. Griffen, *op. cit.*, p. 3.

13. *Ibid.*

14. *Ibid.*, pp. 7-8.

15. "Alternatives to Submission," in *The Tower*, New York: Union Theological Seminary, Spring, 1971, p. 5.

16. *Ibid.*

17. In *The Critic*, Chicago: Thomas More, February, 1972, p. 8.

6.
Jung, Comic Strips and Where Do We Go from Here?

John A. Swartz

Working out of the Jungian framework John Swartz locates and extends certain key hero symbols through the mythology of the Winnebago Indians and some central figures of the Old Testament, as well as some of the characters featured in popular comic strips. He offers concrete strategies which would enable religious education students to make similar creative connections with the Bible, the comic strips and their own unconscious.

No one dreamed in 1896 that the introduction of a color page of comics would revolutionize the newspaper industry, but it did. Richard Outcalt, the creator of "Yellow Kid," was jockeyed back and forth from the *New York World* to the *New York Journal* in a circulation war between Pulitzer and Hearst. The victory in the war was determined by the amount of money paid at a given time to the cartoonist. And the importance of the victory was implied in a statement made thirty years earlier by the editor of the *New York Herald*, James Gordon Bennett:

> Books have had their day—the theatres have had their day—
> the temple of religion has had its day. A newspaper can be
> made to take the lead in all of these in the great movements
> of human thought and of human civilization.[1]

This was an arrogant statement. But it was followed by an even stronger one which said that the newspaper saves and damns more souls than all the churches in New York. The importance of the medium could be found in the invective of the 1920s. There appeared article after article damning the comic strip as a corrupter of youth. The comics are still with us; and they will be with us a long, long time.

A nation's mythology does not die easily. And in every age, the tradition is carried on so that the young will have the best of their past. The great psychologist, Carl Jung, says that all mythical figures correspond to inner psychic experience and originally sprang from them. Could it be that the comic strip is merely the medium for the dreams of the American mega-community?

At about the time the comics began to appear in American newspapers there was published a mythology passed on for years by the Winnebago Indians of Wisconsin. When Carl Jung was asked to comment on the material, he pointed out the similarity between the Winnebago hero symbols and the universal hero symbols of men and women. It seems inexplicable that all societies should engender the same symbols. Jung's explanation is that these symbols are reflections of the "Collective Unconscious."

The "Unconscious" is a grab bag of reactions, sensitivities, experiences, impressions, and images which are momentarily obscured from consciousness but which at any time can emerge in consciousness.[2] The concept explains startling revelations, memory lapse and recall, the experiencing in height emotion what was originally experienced in an only semiconscious way.

The "Unconscious" can involve the collective experience of humanity, Jung maintains, so that what is recalled is the experience of one's heritage. This concept explains the common symbols used in different mythologies.

The kind of myth which concerns us is the hero myth in the Winnebago stories. And we are reminded by the Jungian disciple, Joseph Henderson, that the hero myth is the most common and best known myth in the world.[3] What often frustrates the observer is the multiplicity of symbols. How does one sort them out? Is there a thread which holds them together?

Dr. Paul Radin sorted out the myths and investigated them as four hero cycles, the Trickster, the Hare, Red Horn, and the Twins.[4]

The Trickster is undifferentiated as a person. He assumes animal characteristics and yet is a human being. He lives a whimsical life of sense gratification, preoccupied with self, but incapable of delineating what that self might be. He is constantly involved in some trickery, at times deceiving and at others deceived. His own loss physically at times brings benefits to humanity. While he is purposeless, he was supposed to remove the obstacles to men and women, killing all which would molest them. And he brings to humanity countless plants through the loss of his genitals.

The Hare has unique origins, born of a virgin who dies shortly after his birth. Hare is taught by his grandmother who is fluidly described in the myth narrative. At times inimical to humanity, she becomes friendly to it through the intimidation of Hare. Hare becomes the great benefactor of men and women, killing the evil spirits which harass them. He brings food to men and women, and leads them from oppression through the sides of an engulfing animal to freedom. He generally works victory from his oppression, and restores to his grandfather the scalp which had been lost. He is rewarded; but through a character flaw he does not use his newly gained power in the right way and loses for humanity the ease which should come in its work. His purpose is to better humanity's condition in a world populated by animal monsters as well as human beings. The self, here, is imperfectly differentiated, unlike the self in the Trickster cycle, which does not seem differentiated at all.

Red Horn is the last of ten brothers, all of whom compete in a race for the daughter of the chief. Red Horn, the last, becomes the first and gives the chief's daughter in marriage to his oldest brother. He is a healer and in each healing is rewarded with a woman whom he rejects and gives to his brothers in marriage. He accepts challenge after challenge, but with the help of his "beyond this world" friend, Storm-As-He-Walks, a Thunderbird. He usually wins, but in the wrestling with the giants, he is defeated and killed. He is revived by his two sons, and rewards them with the understanding that they are now his equals. His need for outside help makes it clear that the self is well delineated. And his purpose is healing and victory, not for himself, but for others.

The Twins survive the sacrificial killing of their mother by her father-in-law. One, named Flesh, is passive and obedient; the other, Stump, is active and rebellious. Flesh eventually adopts the way of Stump, and both so intimidate their father that he tries to run away. They are in control of his wandering; they seem to control everything. They even try in their journeys throughout the four worlds to control the guardian of the book of life, Heregunina. In assuming to be the sole arbiters of their fate, the Twins have overstepped their bounds. They are led, through intimidation by Earthmaker, to an acceptance of their limitations. They are to live in the Hills of the East and they are to recognize their own position in a world ruled by Earthmaker. The Twins have integrated the self, journeying to find their place and their limits, through an apparently limitless adventure.

These story cycles grew and filled a need in the Winnebago community. Indirectly they betray a latent understanding of the development of the individual.[5] They provide hero symbols with which the growing person could identify at any phase of his or her life and move on to greater integration of self.

Individuals could find themselves in the Trickster, could laugh at themselves and their incapacity to determine their own way; they could identify with Hare who learns from others the way to adventure and to courageous enterprise on behalf of his fellow men and women. They could find their need for outside forces expressed in their identification with Red Horn, who finds his way to victory and life through the Thunderbird and, in turn, through his own sons. And finally, they could reach maturity by standing with the Twins against all that defines and limits in order to determine the true limits and to come to better grips with the self.

These symbols served the Winnebago Indians in their individuation. But people throughout the world are not that different. All people need those symbols, although at times the symbols may be wrapped in a cultural clothing quite foreign. In these Winnebago symbols can be found symbols universally valid for all men and women.

The four cycles can be found mirrored in the biblical heroes of ancient Israel. Jonah and Samson are much like the Trickster since they live by whimsy and the moment's self-gratification. Both seem preoccupied with themselves and the concerns of the moment. Jonah is trapped by the fish and freed; Samson builds a world of trickery through fables told about lions, events involving the frenzied chasing of foxes, and manslaughter through a weapon made of a donkey's jaw. Jonah is deceived in the process of attempted deception; Samson is rendered powerless by deceit when he seems to be most powerful. But Samson moves into the Hare cycle when he acts as warrior to bring his people to freedom. His origins hint at the Hare cycle. Born of a barren woman, he vacillates between the two cycles, at one time greedily pursuing his own bodily needs, at others saving others through his warrior tactics.

Moses fits well in the Hare cycle. Again his origins are unique. He brings about the development of his people by leading them to freedom from oppression. He provides them food on several occasions. But he, too, has a flaw in his character. He refuses to accept a decision of Yahweh. He is punished and faces death outside the land of promise. He finds his way to survive in his vicarious leadership through Joshua. Samuel also has unique origins, born of a barren woman. He, like Hare, is given to a guardian for education and socialization. He frees his people from oppression and provides them a leader, to his own chagrin.

Jacob has origins like Red Horn's. He is the last who replaces the first, Esau. He prays that he will live on through the two sons of Joseph. These grandsons become his sons through a blessing. He struggles with the powers beyond, wrestling with God, always aware that the power beyond is a friend whom he needs. After replacing his brother, he shares his goods with his brother as did Red Horn. He seems defeated when dying in a strange land, but his bones are brought back to the land of promise.

Adam and Eve play the role of the Twins in their attempt to make the rules, to decide for themselves. They are led to assume they do not need God. When they face their God as the Twins faced the Earthmaker, they find that the limits are drawn for them. They are given a place in which to live; they will not decide for themselves. Job, also, becomes the integrated personality who must at first determine where to go when his experience leaves him naked as a newborn child. A kind of orphan, rejected by his friends, he is asked by Bildad, Zophar and Eliphaz to acknowledge his guilt. They try to establish his limits, but they cannot. Youth in the form of Eliu also tries to establish the limits of Job. His wife suggests he take a stand against God and be wiped out. God, himself, intimidates all through the monsters Leviathan and Behemoth. After this, everyone knows his limits. Job is rewarded for speaking truthfully about God. He finds his place as one who stands in awe before the mystery of God. God will delineate; God will set the limits.

The hero cycles are much the same in the Winnebago and biblical stories. But neither provides the cultural resonance to reach the student of today. The greatness of the first is its ability to provide identity symbols for the Winnebago Indians, and the beauty of the latter is its ability to provide identity symbols for ancient Israel. But both need the work of a translator who will find the cultural equivalents of those symbols in the world of today.

When the translation is not done, or poorly done, teachers fail and evolve a despair theology. Often the solution is to reduce the religious education program to a social action and evening social package with an occasional liturgy or paraliturgy. It is conceded that the informational, doctrinal and content dimension were a grand dream, but practically impossible.

The real issue is not whether students at any given age are teachable. The real issue is "how" are they teachable. While there may be impossible students in a given situation, the teacher can expect some students who are "Jesus people" and open to cultural heroes and transcultural heroes. And at the same time he or she can expect some students capable of stripping a moving car. Somehow these must be reached also.

The real issue then is whether there are symbols which can move today's youth. Have the heroes all died? The popular arts people are hardly willing to admit this. When people will stand in line to watch Robert Shaw battle the *Jaws* monster—he really lives out the Hare cycle—and when they will gladly watch Woody Allen get himself together in *Love and Death*—he is acting out the Trickster cycle—they are acknowledging the meaning of hero symbols in their lives.

The films supply many hero symbols, but comic strips, through their accessibility, offer the teacher many more possibilities. And the history of comic strips reveals a marked tendency to reintroduce old heroes when the needs recur. "Bringing Up Father" is making a comeback, as is "Prince Valiant." "Little Orphan Annie" has returned in book form and in the comic strip medium. There may be a time in the near future when "The Katzenjammer Kids" will again surface.

How, then, do the comics provide these hero symbols? Which of the hero symbols can be found in the different strips? Dagwood seems to be the Trickster, undifferentiated, more often the loser than the winner. Preoccupied with his bath, newspaper, sandwich and the relaxing chair, he is a lot like Wimpy of Popeye fame, whose whole world is a hamburger. Jiggs of "Bringing up Father" spends most of his time either dreaming of or sauntering to Dinty's for that proverbial corned beef sandwich. And Andy Capp never gets beyond this stage as he makes the hourly trip to the local bar for a drink. They don't seem to be able to get beyond physical needs. (*See* p. 67.)

Rodney of the "Wizard of Id," however, brings us to the Hare cycle. Much like Don Quixote, he chases his windmills and shows his basic concern for his fellow human beings. From time to time he helps one of the oppressed, or through some ruse saves the day for the king. He is willing at times to face the monster, whether dragon or Black Bart, although he seldom finishes a St. George. He tries to better the lives of those he meets, even if only improving the swill of the prisoner in the last cell. Maggie, Jiggs's wife, has much of the aggressiveness of Hare. She is a dreamer who hopes to find the meaning of life in her newly gained affluence and status. Humanized through her society calendar, she tends to forget her past and would have Jiggs live the better life "too." Dick Tracy also will socialize his fellow men and women. He will right the wrongs and bring victories from oppression. At times he puts his life on the line to restore what has been lost. He kills those who abuse their fellow human beings and brings all to the service of law and order.

Little Orphan Annie is the Horatio Alger of the female set. She faces one challenge after another, hoping in some way to overcome wrongdoing and to undo corruption. A Red Horn heroine, she needs power from outside to help her solve the many problems she faces, and the power is usually found in Daddy Warbucks. A reject of society, Annie becomes one of society's most respected members. Popeye, too, is a Red Horn hero. He comes to the rescue of the Oyl family and his kindness and power make possible many a success. But he also needs outside help. His power is to be found in "supernatural" spinach.

The rare comic strip character who lives out the Twins cycle is Lucy of "Peanuts." She is the self-possessed individual who rules all people and all things. She is so much in control that she sells her counselling time at the local "Psychiatrist's booth." She makes demands of everyone; she knows no limits. She awaits at times a day of reckoning. And yet the superior force never seems to be available to define her limits for her. She usually gets what she wants by intimidating Charlie or Snoopy. And her only unfulfilled aspiration is the control of Schroeder. Beethoven may be her nemesis. Perhaps this is the superior power which will help her find her place.

If there are symbols for today's youth to be found in the comic strip, then the teacher's task is to determine how they can be used in the teaching situation. One process flows from our research into the hero cycles.

The teacher could give to the students a large envelope filled with different comic strip characters cut from the Sunday newspaper. Students would be asked to find the one they liked best or the one they identified with. Each then would be asked to explain why he or she liked the character, or why he or she identified with it. Students with the same identity symbol could be paired up to determine what they have in common. The comic strip symbols could be lined up on a board, and the group could attempt to find the biblical parallels. The group could then move into the biblical text itself.

The teacher could also approach the comic strip as a unit. Any number of comic strips yield messages which parallel those found in the parables. And the students could learn how this medium and the parable genre convey their messages. At the same time the students will be thrilled with the insights gained from others on a strip which they have read again and again superficially.

The teacher can also suggest the reediting of the single comic strip in such a way as to change its message. This study could be a prelude to an analysis of the editorial purpose of Matthew and Luke in the parable of the talents.

Several comics strips could be cut in segments and reedited to yield altogether different meanings. The students could be grouped and asked to create a completely new comic strip from several "Wizard of Id" frames. After they have created new ones, the different groups could share these with one another. Afterwards, the teacher could show how the material in Matthew's Sermon on the Mount is edited by Luke throughout his journey narratives in chapters 9-18.

The characters from different strips could be given to individual members of a group. Each of the members would be asked to role-play the character in a meeting between any two. A third person might be asked to suggest the situation. After several of these acts, the students could observe the different ways in which Jesus reacted to different kinds of people. They could notice how Luke's Jesus is constantly reacting atypically to sinners and rejects of society.

The strips could be studied to determine the audience they are directed to. Is "Ponytail" a teen comic strip? Does "Prince Valiant" appeal to the twelve-year-old boy? Does the college student enjoy "Nancy"? After discussion of this, the group could analyze the genealogies of Jesus found in Matthew and Luke to determine what audience they were directed to.

The comic strip could also provide the setting for liturgy or paraliturgy. Cutting out characters from cartoon strips on overhead transparencies, the students can suggest the meanings of the readings by rear projection on a white cloth backdrop. Responses for the participants could also be presented there, as well as themes and prayers.

Russell Nye in outlining the importance of the comic strip quotes Milton Caniff, author of "Steve Canyon" and "Terry and the Pirates": "Whatever it is that makes a popular art effective—escape or appeal to basic emotions, or audience identification—the funnies have it, and they have more of it than any of us ever suspected."[6]

The comic strip has been a force in American life since 1896. And some comic strips have reached more than one generation. "Katzenjammer Kids," under some four different titles, reached three generations of readers. "Blondie" has been circulated in as many as 1,500 newspapers. "Pogo" before its demise had an audience of 60,000,000 people a day. And the good thing about the strip is that it can be relevant if not contemporary!

The comic strip can be a very effective instrument in the hands of an imaginative teacher. But the strip is only effective because it reinforces a hero symbol already meaningful for the young. The student needs to find the "significant other" with whom to identify in his or her path to individuation. The student may find the significant other in a parent, a peer, or hopefully in an honest, sincere and truly Christian teacher.

There is no substitute for teachers who live an authentic life. They will know it, and the students will know it. And no use of media, no use of the popular arts, will substitute for character in the classroom.

However, authentic teachers, imaginatively using the resources of film, sound, television and the comic strip, will find that the students will find Christ in them, in the Scriptures and in the media. The American poet Sam Walter Foss put it this way:

"He is the greatest poet, who will renounce all art,
And take his heart and show it to every other heart."[7]

Notes

1. Eric Barnauw, *Mass Communication*. New York: Rinehart, 1956, p. 7.

2. Carl G. Jung, *Man and His Symbols*. New York: Dell, 1975, p. 18.

3. *Ibid.*, p. 101.

4. Paul Radin, *The Evolution of an American Indian Prose Epic, A Study in Comparative Literature*, Parts I and II. New York: Bollingen, 1956.

5. Paul Radin, *Winnebago Hero Cycles: A Study in Aboriginal Literature*. Baltimore: The Waverly Press Inc. 1948, p. 15.

6. Russell Nye, *The Unembarrassed Muse: The Popular Arts in America*. New York: The Dial Press, 1970, p. 236.

7. Sam Walter Foss, *Back Country Poems*. Boston: Potter Publishing, 1892, p. 6.

ANDY CAPP by Reggie Smith, Daily Mirror Ltd., Courtesy of Field Newspaper Syndicate

by. Brant parker and Johnny hart

THE WIZARD OF ID

THE WIZARD OF ID by permission of Johnny Hart and Field Enterprises, Inc.

7.
Faith as a Learned Life-style

Martin A. Lang

Martin Lang explores what he describes as the basic dynamic in religious education: sharing faith. He extends the model of faith by integrating the fields of philosophy and psychology with theological data. His person-to-person theory of faith-sharing says that faith growth participates in the same dynamics that govern all human communication.

Religious education at its most basic functional level consists in sharing one's faith with another person. This occurs as a one-to-one communication even if the setting is a classroom of students with a single teacher or a congregation with one pastor. The nuclear dynamic at work involves the human interaction between two sharers.

This description seems simple enough until we begin to take each aspect of the faith-sharing phenomenon and study it separately. In doing this we discover that the individual elements,

first, the meaning of faith understood functionally

second, the sharing of that faith and

third, the sharing of that faith on a one-to-one basis are really part of a very highly integrated and complex process. This essay intends to investigate the process and in so doing, shed some light on the field of religious education.

Let us start with the functional meaning of faith. What is functional religious faith? As we understand it, it is the faith-life of people as they actually experience it from day to day. As such, it is a complex of thoughts, emotions, attitudes, initiations and responses that are directed not only toward God but toward people as well.

Faith is, of course, a total personal affirmation, therefore it goes well beyond simple mental assent. It is elemental in the lives of people and therefore ought to be understood as a form of life-style, a life-style that is filled with both intellectual and emotional content.

We cannot speak of "having faith" if we look at it in this way because faith would then be an adjunct, a thing to be possessed. People do not experience it this way, as something to be grasped; they experience it as a dimension of their lives.

Religious faith is embodied in the unity of the person. It is the whole person that is challenged to summon a response in moments evocative of faith. Many moments in the faith-life of people are responsive moments, thrust upon them unpredictably. The shocking and devastating news of an accidental death, the death of one's child, floods a person with grief, sadness, anger, unbelief—and yet, somehow, faith. One asks, why? One turns to God in both doubt and hope. One prays to understand. At this moment one calls upon all the resources of one's being. In this unitive call faith is inseparably joined to the person; it interpenetrates the personality.

Each human life is an ongoing panoply of just such moments. Not all are responsive moments and not all are so dramatic, but all are laden with feelings like fear or hope or joy or surprise. Faith inheres in life under all these circumstances.

Viewed in this light the faith-life transcends institutional designations. In the moment of death we have just described the fundamental issue of faith could be the same for the Catholic, Protestant and Jew: what is my God like? How do I relate to him in this?

On the other hand, the response of the institutional religious body to which the person belongs can vary considerably according to the tradition that has given rise to it. People participate in the particulars of their own religious group. In this case the funeral is conducted according to the ritual of the institutional faith of the deceased. Those who attend, because of the music, the prayers and even the physical setting, feel and perceive this moment in a manner that is particularized by this specific service of worship. It is part of their experience of faith resulting from this death. The faith-life, therefore, embodies intake from a variety of sources and it incorporates a full range of experiences.

Definitions of faith can be very misleading. Definitions are written with words, in cursive, logical order. The preselection of words as the instrument of investigation predetermines the findings in the cognitive mode. Descriptions have limited value when we are dealing with the nonverbal in human life. It is interesting that the recent General Catechetical Directory of the Catholic Church stresses this apprehension of faith over the more cognitive definitions of Vatican I to describe the phenomenon. The Directory says "the life of faith admits of various degrees, both in the global acceptance of the total word of God and in the explanation of that word and the application of it to the different duties of human life, according to the maturity of each and the differences of individuals" (General Catechetical Directory USCC, Washington, D. C. 1971, paragraph #30). The faith-life is a phenomenon that does not exist apart from the life-style of individual people.

Let us now turn to the second aspect of our description of the basic dynamic in religious education: sharing faith. Can faith really be shared? Is it not so personal and individual an experience that sharing is an inappropriate word to use in association with it?

In addressing this question we might keep in mind three points. The first is the unitive character of faith as we have just presented it, embracing a full range of thoughts and emotions. The second is the interpenetration of the faith-life with the personality structure. In everyday life we cannot separate out our faith like a distillate and view it apart from the expression of it in our personality. No matter how complex the problem becomes for us we must study people as unities and we must study their faith within this unity. The third point brings us to the heart of the question. Contemporary philosophical and psychological awarenesses can shed some light on the faith-sharing process. In both of these fields current insights seem to move the study of humanity along a similar path. That path is the importance of interrelatedness in determining the identity of humanity.

Let us start with philosophy. From Plato to Hegel, a human being was regarded as a thinking subject, a rational being, who as a unity defined himself or herself by his or her choices. The person was looked upon in isolation. Other people, as well as the cultural environment in which the person lived, were merely tangential to his or her basic nature. Therefore, the human being for all times and seasons, for all cultures and ages, could be defined. In this kind of monistic definition the nature of the person was static.

A different understanding takes hold in our time, an understanding that studies the human being in the plural, that is, in concert with others. Martin Buber might typify this outlook when he alerts us to the important "thou" in the life of the human being, the necessary corollary to the traditional "I." In this manner of thinking the human is a responsive being, an interactive subject who is recreated in relationship to the "thou." Buber's basic dictum paraphrases the creational statement: in the beginning is relation. This view of humanity is dynamic; it sees the person as capable of fundamental change and this is accomplished in concert with others.

In the field of psychology the insights move along similar lines. Developmental psychologists see the person as achieving his or her identity through the ministrations of caring others. As Erik Erikson points out, the human being on the path to full maturity passes through emotional stages of growth, aided in the process by parents and peers. The counseling modalities of such humanistic psychologists as Rollo May and Carl Rodgers function on the basic assumption that the human is a social being achieving selfhood only out of the commerce of loving human interactivity.

What does all of this say for the faith-sharing phenomenon? It says, as we see it, that people arrive at their self-awareness through the interactivities, initiations and responses that are developed in conjunction with others. It says that their faith-identity is inseparably bound up with their psychological identity. It says that the same dynamics that are operative in the establishment of a self-identity also participate in the faith-forming process. People arrive at their faith-identity (or nonfaith-identity) through interactivity with the revered "thou" in their lives. This revered "thou" serves as a model of faith.

The "faith-model" is an individual whose entire self-presentation as a unity is attractive to the faith-sharer. In spite of weaknesses the model is acceptable unitatively as a human being. In the commerce between these two human centers love, in one or other of its many manifestations, is exchanged. It may be the love between parent and child or the love between spouses, or simply the tempered love between people who think very highly of each other. In any case, those who love each other share each other. That is the fundamental datum in the faith-sharing phenomenon.

The Christian faith tradition derives from the paradigm of Jesus as faith-model. He was attractive initially to his followers as a person. Not only his mind but his entire self-presentation formed the basis of a relationship with them. Out of this relationship and out of his deep attachment to his friends he shared with them the sense of God that was his. His words to them were actually the outpourings of his own intense and intimate experience with God. His was truly a self-revelation. These friends felt enhanced in his presence; for them Jesus was truly a gift. In theological terms that is the meaning of grace.

It is necessary to speak of grace in connection with faith-sharing especially because we have identified the same dynamics at work in the faith-forming process as inhere in the growth of personal identity. Is God present in this process at all or is it simply reduced to a kind of secular, psychological phenomenon?

Again, we must return to the Jesus paradigm and take seriously the Christian understanding of the Incarnation. In this paradigm the transcendent God is joined to the human, and forms a unity of person in Jesus—inexplicably. In classical theological terms the "two natures" of Jesus are inseparably bound together. Only conceptually are they separable. Jesus is one whole person. What he has to give is not material because he is poor. His love, his divine awareness, his teachings are all immaterial gifts. They are transmitted in the person-to-person encounter. Jesus mediates the divine gift of love through his person. That is the character of grace as it functions in human life. While it is immaterial it is mediated through the physical. Most fundamentally it is the communication of caring love.

The smallest infant communicates with his or her mother in an intuitive center-to-center exchange. The infant senses her love, feels valued and appreciated. If the infant learns in this rudimentary way that he or she is of great value, that "being here" is good, that he or she can rely upon others with security, he or she has learned several fundamental awarenesses of the Judeo-Christian tradition. He or she has indeed been *graced* by his or her parents and has begun his or her own personal salvation history.

In this view, grace does not come from a separate God "out there" flowing through an ether of distance; it inheres in the loving interchange between persons. The Christian understanding of the Holy Spirit, the spirit of God dwelling within people communally, expresses this view beautifully. While startling, it is no less improbable than the doctrine of the Incarnation itself.

Within the Christian church the Catholic tradition has had a long history of infant baptism. This is because it seems to recognize that faith grows up with the child. In our understanding baptism is less the single ritual moment in which the Christian faith is conferred than it is the community's first celebration of an ongoing gift, given originally at birth and nourished throughout life by loved ones and friends.

But this has been a long route to explain the faith-sharing process. While we have confined our observations to information drawn from the fields of philosophy and psychology, trying to integrate this with theological data, we are not unaware of the need to incorporate sociological insights into the dynamics of human growth. We can only mark this omission at this point and save its inclusion for a more extensive treatment elsewhere.

We must now turn to the third factor in the faith-sharing phenomenon: the one-to-one character of the exchange. Our person-to-person theory of faith-sharing says that faith-growth participates in the same dynamics that govern all human communication. Now human communication reaches a peak of intensity when people care about each other. Both love and hate explode between caring people. These moments, as well as less intense but still significant experiences, constitute landmarks of self-awareness in human life. Of all the interactional moments in an individual human life, the vast majority are forgotten. A relatively small number are preserved. Out of this number people repeat the stories and incidents they consider most descriptive of who they are. These landmark experiences become the working vocabulary of self-identification. They are the clear residue from the cloudy waters of life's interactivities.

What people seem to remember in vignettes are those who enhanced or depreciated them and the circumstances surrounding these events. If we apply this to religious education, we might ask exactly how much people remember of their religious instruction. Do they remember specific lessons? Do they recall the force of logical presentations? Or do they, rather, remember the teacher who gave a gift or administered a punishment? The interactional moments are the impressing moments in life.

A fundamental self-awareness is developed out of a dialogue between what we might call the "within" of the person, that is, one's self-understanding as one has internalized it up to this moment, and the "without," the new experiences that impinge upon one's consciousness. The person is not defined finally by others but by the interplay between the self and the other. Another can contribute to the modification of a person's awareness, and this can occur even through the mass media, but the nuclear dynamic always involves one particular other at one particular moment.

So, in religious education, the dynamic is between people who interact with each other. One reveals one's faith life-style, which includes its cognitive, emotional, intuitional character; the other shares of this what appeals to him or her in keeping with his or her self-conceptualization at that time. The faith-sharer is not an inveterate or involuntary buyer. In his or her selectivity resides his or her freedom. The "faith-model" is a sharer in his or her own right, going away enhanced in a manner appropriate to his or her self-awareness at that moment. It helps people themselves when they teach others. Faith-sharing is a two-way street.

If what we have proposed in this essay has some validity for the reader perhaps we can suggest some practical conclusions that might be helpful for those engaged in religious education.

First, since human interactional activity begins at birth and ends only at death, the faith-sharing process goes on throughout the lifetime of the person. Religious education cannot possibly be just for children. People at every age in their lives need the help of faith-sharers. As their insights and their problems change, so do their faith needs. A comprehensive religious education program introduces faith-sharers to each other at all age levels.

Second, anyone planning a program of religious education has one essential task: to engage the services of loving and committed people. This is the first organization task; it is not setting up a curriculum or making a book list.

Third, since faith-sharing is bound up with the communication between persons, those who presume to share their faith with others must be prepared to share themselves with others. Faith cannot be shared by simply "telling." A teacher or preacher who has the temerity to engage in "religious education" must establish personal relationships with his or her sharers. He or she cannot be present to them only in the pulpit or the classroom. This is too cognitive and too one-dimensional an appearance.

Fourth, since faith-sharing involves far more than mind-sharing, the communication cannot be simply discursive and logical. The mode of expression cannot be simply cerebral. Worship is faith-sharing and a blight to worship among many religious bodies in the United States today is its verbal, literary character. Religious leaders address their congregations, read to them, even read prayers. Participants are provided with leaflets and books to follow services. This "literary intervention" actually retards communication and it retards faith-sharing. It only adds to the celebrative impoverishment now suffered by many Americans.

Fifth, since faith-sharing is also person-sharing, it is capable of cutting away at one of the most pernicious cancers in modern life: isolation. Families are isolated from each other and generations within society are isolated from each other. Religious education demands a rebirth of human communication. We hear much about "building community" these days. Looking at it in a more personal way, we might say that "building community" is really introducing caring faith-sharers to each other. Authentic human communication is a grace; it is the heartbeat of the faith life.

REFINING MODELS

Gabriel Moran
Charles Melchert
Michael Warren

8.
The Teaching of American Religion

Gabriel Moran

Gabriel Moran examines the relatively new interest in "American" religion and affirms its value after making significant distinctions between America and the United States, and teaching and preaching. He then encourages religious educators to cultivate a sense of history and of place among themselves as well as among their students.

The thesis of this article is that the teaching of religion in the United States of America ought to be centered on the teaching of American religion. There are three reasons for this proposal: 1) American religion is a meeting place of Jewish, Catholic, Protestant and other religions 2) American religion is the actual religion of most students in classrooms of the United States 3) American religion cries out for the discriminating work of a teacher.

There is obviously a need for me to clarify what I mean by the term "American religion." Less obvious but just as important is a clarification of the verb "to teach." My advocacy of the teaching of American religion will no doubt seem misguided if the word teaching is neglected. The third reason given above, that American religion is especially in need of teaching, can almost be reversed. That is, teaching and the teaching of religion are especially challenged and clarified by the phenomenon of American religion.

It would be especially dangerous, for example, if preaching and teaching were assumed to be synonymous. We are not in need of the preaching of American religion; we have had more than enough of that. At the beginning of his book, *Fellow Teachers*, Philip Rieff writes: "Preaching is not teaching, except in a church."[1] I cannot believe that Rieff is serious about the qualifying clause constituting a valid exception. On the other hand, if Rieff is stating that only the church misunderstands preaching to be teaching he is being unfair to the church. The misidentification of preaching and teaching runs well beyond the boundaries of church. Before pursuing the distinctive meaning of teaching I must first describe American religion.

The very term "American religion" may be a new one to some people but the topic is much discussed among historians, sociologists and theologians. Current discussion is usually dated from a 1967 essay by Robert Bellah.[2] The effect of that article was surprising because Bellah said nothing that was startlingly new; most of it had been said before by generations of historians. Timing, however, was a key to the essay's significance. The end of the 1960s apparently began a transitional period in the history of the United States and its religion. The topic of American religion is finally ripe for a discussion which will go well into the third century of the country's existence.

I have not used in my title another word that is customary in this discussion, namely, civil. I am avoiding reference to American civil religion for two reasons: 1) The phrase civil religion usually carries a pejorative connotation. The origin of the term is Rousseau's advocacy of replacing traditional religion with a religion of the state. Bellah's essay did not assume this meaning for the term civil religion; Bellah was trying to rehabilitate the term and show its positive side. The task is not impossible but I think the weight of history is against it. 2) The phrase "American civil religion" suggests that American is an instance of some generic concept that applies to all nation states. When Andrew Greeley writes "there will be some sort of civil religious symbols in any modern nation state,"[3] he is correct but somewhat misleading. While there are elements that might be called religious in the essential makeup of the modern state, an extraordinary combination of elements sets off the American experience from other nations. I am not so much interested in the general concept of state or civil religion as in the unique history that produced a new phenomenon: a religion that can be called American.

The outline of that historical development is fairly easy to trace. The United States was founded and then populated by people trying to escape crowding, repression and poverty. (The two important exceptions, the North American native who found the country long before the Europeans and the black African who was forced to come here, will be brought up later as challenges to an American religion.) For the European, "America" meant open land and a place to begin anew. From the charter at Massachusetts Bay down to the latest presidential speech, the language of promised land and chosen people unceasingly colors the national rhetoric. The continuity of biblical language, however, may hide the fact of how dramatically new the American experiment was. The political and religious assumptions that the first settlers brought here proved inadequate. The third and fourth generations found themselves alone in the wilderness and in need of new concepts of religion and political freedom.[4]

The search for freedom included opposition to a state church. The project of founding the United States was pervaded with religious imagery and motivation but it was also intertwined with fear of an "establishment" of religion. This common enemy, the established church, brought about a strange alliance of pietists and rationalists in the eighteenth century.[5] The founding fathers of the country were the immediate and optimistic products of Western Enlightenment. Though skeptical of traditional religion, it was men like Jefferson, Madison and Franklin who insisted on religious freedom. The sectarian pietists for their part had second thoughts after the French Revolution about their alignment with the "infidels." Nonetheless, space had been provided for an evangelical, emotional and individualistic religion that flourished in the nineteenth century.

The religion that is distinctively American still shows the effects of the original coalition: scientific know-how and biblical imagery. Great concern is expressed for the "separation of church and state" but the family, the schools and the government itself are suffused with evangelical piety. The attitudes and imagery grouped under the term American have an unmistakable flavor. "To be an American," said George Santayana, "is of itself almost a moral condition, an education, and a career." If one were to put it most strongly, when someone says, "I am an American" he or she is not so much stating citizenship as giving his or her religion.

The American religion is not separable from European Christianity but it gave special emphasis to some elements within Christianity. By its use of eden, covenant, kingdom and promised land, American religion drew heavily upon the Jewish scriptures. Christian use of the "old testament" always presents a highly ambivalent situation for Jewish religion: an apparent acceptance of Judaism but a neglect of the contemporary Jew and a subtle undercutting of the Jewish scriptures.

Not surprisingly, one of the severest criticisms of American religion comes from a Jewish writer, Will Herberg. The attack which he made in the 1950s in his book *Protestant, Catholic, Jew* remains essentially the same in the 1970s. Herberg finishes a recent essay by writing: "To see America's civil religion as somehow standing above or beyond the biblical religions of Judaism and Christianity, and Islam too, as somehow including them and finding a place for them in its over-arching unity, is idolatry."[6] While one may sympathize with much of Herberg's criticism and share some of his fears, the use of the word idolatry in the above sentence is clearly inaccurate and works to weaken his case. Worshiping the country would be idolatry. That the previous forms of Judaism, Protestantism, Catholicism and Islam have been drastically altered by an American umbrella may be dangerous or destructive but it is not idolatrous.

A word like Christianity is a high abstraction which is not very descriptive of actual religious life. Herberg thought it scandalous that Catholic school children in this country thought of themselves as Americans who were Roman Catholics rather than Roman Catholics who happened to be American.[7] Perhaps the school children were being realistic and knew that the religion of Brooklyn, New Orleans or Santa Fe has a distinctive character not covered by the term Roman Catholic. The conception of American religion as a "fourth faith" or a vague religiosity is indeed dangerous. American as the name for the interaction of religious groups and the emergence of ecumenical themes could represent a positive development.

In summary, religion in the United States was allied with certain admirable attitudes. Richard Hofstadter states the case at its best: "The American attitude represented a republican and egalitarian protest against monarchy and aristocracy and the callous exploitation of the people; it represented a rationalistic protest against the passivity and pessimism of the Old World; it revealed a dynamic, vital, and originative mentality."[8] At the same time, the very attitudes which have been the American glory can easily corrupt into destructive forces: enthusiasm for the future leading to neglect of the past, technological skill leading to exploitation of resources, defense of individual rights leading to destruction of social bonds. Perhaps most dangerous/admirable of all is the American impulse to help other countries. Rooted in the missionary spirit of the Christian church, the desire to help other people, even when they don't wish to be helped, is vulnerable to fits of self-righteousness and the exercise of violence.

The dark side of American religion especially emerged in the late 1960s. Many of us who had been brought up as patriotic chauvinists discovered the demonic element in our religion. Harvey Cox glorified the pragmatic, technical and rational attitudes of America in *The Secular City*. Cox's book seemed to herald a new era but within a few years it seemed instead to be the last burst of a dying era. Cox has recently said: "In the 1960s God didn't die but Uncle Sam did." That statement captures the flavor of some of the disillusionment that overtook the American attitude in the late 1960s. The problem of an American religion, however, is not solved by a move from chauvinism to cynicism. What is needed is an educational approach to the problem by people who know what it means "to teach."

I wish now to clarify the meaning of "to teach" when confronted by American religion. I use the verb "to teach" in a positive sense. In the past decade there has been disparagement of teaching, even in educational circles. To say that learning is more important than teaching is true but irrelevant; the choice is not between those two. To say that we should no longer have teachers but facilitators of learning clarifies nothing. There is clearly a need to see that teaching is only a small part of education but it remains a crucial issue to understand exactly what teaching means.

One can first contrast teaching to indoctrination. The religious overtone of the word indoctrination is not accidental. Religions in general and Christianity in particular have strong tendencies toward indoctrination. An elaborate verbal system is pressed upon the hearers and teaching is misunderstood as telling the truth. John Wilson cites as the paradigm case of indoctrination: "teaching Christianity by threat of torture or damnation."[9] I think it would be clearer to say that the attempt to impose Christianity by threat of torture or damnation is not teaching at all. I would emphasize that threat is a sign of indoctrination but so is the word Christianity, a word pointing to a verbal system. I suspect that one cannot teach Christianity at all, though one can teach religion, including Christian forms of religion.

What can appropriately be called teaching requires that there be a learner who is not under physical or psychological coercion. The learner wishes to know how to do something and "knowing how" is always a mental/physical activity. A teacher's first act is to accept the given conditions of learner and environment. The teacher's second act is to begin making distinctions within the accepted situation. Any complicated piece of learning has to be broken down into segments that are learnable while the whole is not lost from view. Teaching is not approval or condemnation or telling people what to think. To teach is to distinguish, which makes possible a better assimilation of truth known and acted upon.

The principles of the preceding paragraph can be exemplified in a teacher's approach to American religion. What teaching does *not* mean here is a denunciation of American religion. As the dark side of American religion surfaced in the late 1960s, many Christian preachers were more than ready to launch jeremiads against America and its religion. The posture is both disingenuous and ineffective. American religion is intertwined with the Christian church so that one cannot oppose American religion with Christianity. No teacher or church in this country can pretend to stand outside the problem and issue proclamations of disapproval. The disingenuousness of denouncing is directly related to the ineffectiveness of such a stand. The denouncer may feel better but the country, the religion and the people remain untouched.

There are four concerns I would suggest that the teaching of American religion entails. The first makes possible the other three. Although it may seem trivial to some people the first point is the indispensable one for a teacher.

(1) A teacher of religion would clearly distinguish between the United States and America. The United States is the name of a country; America is the name of a mythical place. At its best, America has meant a hope and an ideal; at its worst, America has been the name of an idol and an ideology. I do not advocate doing away with the idea of America but it is time to get straight in our minds whether we are talking about an existing country or a hoped-for ideal. If I am referring to the country I ought to say what I mean, namely, the United States.

The two objections in linguistic cases of this kind are that the change is unimportant and that it is clumsy. The first objection is totally false; the second objection is true but highly significant. The absence of nouns in the English language that refer to women as well as men is no accident; whoever owns the words owns the world. The absence of an adjective for the people between the Canadian and Mexican borders is no accident either; whoever owns the word American owns the western hemisphere if not the whole world. Thus, there are Latin Americans, Canadian Americans and *the* Americans. I am conscious of the convolutions sometimes necessary for my distinction but I see no way to bring about educational change without the distinction.

In a few decades it will be considered outrageously insensitive to say "America" when one means "the United States," just as today one does not say "white people and negroes" when one means "white and black people," or one does not say "men" when one means "men and women." If the distinction is not made then we will oscillate between glorifying America and lashing at "America" without ever examining the actual ambiguous condition of the United States. A sociologist writing in Canada began a recent essay with the sentence: "We should avoid the obsession with America."[10] The advice is good but, lacking the distinction advocated here, the author is incapable of following his own advice. His article manifests an obsession with the enveloping myth of America. The necessary distinction, which surely ought to be recognized in Canada, is the difference between the country south of Canada and a myth named America.

An example that runs parallel to this use of America is the Christian church's use of the term Christ. Early in the church's history the name Jesus was overshadowed by the word Christ. The church came to talk of Christ as if that were the name of someone instead of Christ being a function and an ideal.

There is obviously great difficulty in making a distinction that has been blurred for almost two thousand years. It is not a question of the Christian church relinquishing its conviction that Jesus is a fulfillment or expression of the Christ ideal. But it makes a difference whether one refers to Jesus Christ or Jesus, the Christ. Perhaps as a start a hyphen could be introduced: Jesus-Christ. The linguistic change may again seem trivial but there is no way for the church to engage in ecumenical dialogue without it. Conversation with Jews might finally become possible. Furthermore, the Christian church could begin understanding its relation to the cosmos in light of a Christ ideal still to be realized.

While most people are busy with other things, a teacher's job is to insist on distinctions like Jesus and Christ or United States and America. A careful distinction does not destroy our traditions though it does chasten them. It shows special respect for our closest neighbor and it opens the possibility of worldwide cooperation. The long-range effects of an important linguistic change are beyond anyone's imagination.

(2) *Pluralism.* Once it is clear that the teacher is examining the religion called American in the place called the United States, the diversity and richness of the material become apparent. The very act of making distinctions is an acknowledgement that pluralism is a value not to be neglected. American religion avoids idolatry to the extent that ethnic, racial and social diversity are preserved. If the immigrant were totally absorbed into a great melting pot, then the immigrant's religion would be lost to be replaced only by some homogenized and dangerous glorification of America. If, in contrast, the newcomer's old ways are preserved and added to the diversity of these United States, a fruitful tension develops between Catholic and American or Jewish and American.

The topic of ethnic diversity has received considerable attention in recent years. The concern is deserved but should be placed in the context of all kinds of diversity that are desirable in a country whose name expresses unity and diversity. In Walt Whitman's 1855 preface to *Leaves of Grass* he wrote: "The United States themselves are essentially the greatest poem." The most remarkable thing about that sentence is the plural verb. During the past century it would have seemed blasphemous to use a plural verb after the noun United States.

This last point refers to the need of geographical diversity and to the ambiguous results of the United States's civil war. Herbert Richardson has noted that the only thing people seem to agree upon in discussing American religion is that Abraham Lincoln is the high priest. Richardson takes issue with that assumption and suggests that if diversity is what saves American religion, Abraham Lincoln unwittingly presided over the corruption of that religion.[11] The union was saved but at considerable expense of diversity. After Lincoln, the United States disappear and America reigns. Typical of that period is this statement of Henry Ward Beecher: "The South has been proved and has been found wanting. . . . This continent is to be from this time forth governed by Northern men, with Northern ideas and with a Northern gospel."[12] Note that the speaker lays claim not to this country but to this continent and ends with announcement of a northern *gospel*.

An American religion will be the ideology of empire if it is a northern gospel to which all people must conform. A restraint of empire is accomplished by facing up to the diversity within the country. A special challenge for American religion is the religious life of black people. The spirit, language and art of black religion must eventually be confronted by every white person in the United States. The ultimate test of American religion is the religion of the North American native. The religions of both blacks and natives are important influences in the two points that follow.

(3) *History.* It is not just teachers of history who have to speak for the past. Every teacher digs below the surface of present life to show the integral relation of past actuality and future possibility. The United States' passion for a better future has been tied to a reckless and destructive ignorance of the past. The National Commission on the Causes and Prevention of Violence pinpointed the religious origins of this attitude. "Americans have been given to a kind of historical amnesia that masks much of their turbulent past. Probably all nations share this tendency to sweeten memories of their past through collective repression, but Americans have probably magnified the process of selective recollection owing to our historic vision of ourselves as a latter day chosen people, a new Jerusalem."

By confronting what white people have done to black people and red people in the United States, American religion would be purified of a danger that comes from pretended innocence. America may be a good and simple place but the United States is an ambiguous and complicated country. America has no past because it is a mythical place out of time. John Locke's famous words are accurate: "In the beginning all the world was America." That statement may not seem dangerous but there is another side to the myth. The paradise myth that refers to the beginning of time is regularly coupled with a return to origins at the end of time. Thus, the second part of Locke's statement would be: "In the end all the world will be America." Much of United States foreign policy becomes intelligible with this myth. It hardly needs adding that a country which confuses itself with the kingdom of God can be a dangerous force whatever its intentions.

(4) *Place.* The idea of place is intimately related to history and to the diversity of peoples. Place is not space. Place is where people sink their roots and it becomes more their place as they deposit their past in it. A sense of place is essential to a religious life. To the extent that religion loses a sense of place religion becomes an ideology of the mind seeking God in abstractions rather than being a sense of the divine issuing from encounter of human body and universe. An inherent weakness of the Christian religion has been its rush toward premature universalism without incorporating tribe and turf. The traditions of black and red peoples in the United States offer a necessary and powerful corrective to a religion of abstract generalities.

It is customarily said that "Americans" have little sense of place. If one is out to conquer space (the continent, the planet, the moon) one cannot dally with the particularities of place; one has to keep moving. When the complexities of life get too great one can always move out west or at least to the suburbs. The terrible crisis now affecting the American dream is the dawning realization that the United States is a finite place with problems that cannot be solved by moving out of town.

I referred above to the saying that Americans have no sense of place. That may be true but the immigrant settlers of the United States often had a strong sense of place. Many of the Italian, Swedish, Irish or Chinese settlers loved the place they came to. People cultivated the great plains of the midwest and took pride in their urban neighborhood.

I suggest that a major part of religious education in the U.S. should be cultivation of love of one's own place and respect for the place of others. No one chooses where to be born and most people remain very limited in their possibilities of choosing where to live. Yet each person has to find God in the particular physical setting of his or her own life. For the country as a whole, love of place is the only remedy for our mounting ecological problems. No exclusively technical solutions will work; the earth, water, mountains, trees, animals, villages and cities must be lovingly cared for.

The political-religious experiment begun on these shores is not over yet but the distinctions suggested here are urgently needed if the experiment is not to end with a whimper of death or a bang of worldwide catastrophe. It may be that the era of the Americans is coming to an end, but someone will still have to love the people and the land between the Canadian and Mexican borders.

Notes

1. Philip Rieff, *Fellow Teachers* (New York, Harper and Row), 1973, p. 2.

2. Robert Bellah, "Civil Religion in America," in *Daedalus*, Winter, 1967.

3. Andrew Greeley, "The Civil Religion of Ethnic Americans," in *Religious Education*, 70 (Sept./Oct., 1975), p. 500.

4. See Perry Miller, *Errand into the Wilderness* (New York, Harper Torch, 1964), pp. 1-15.

5. See Sidney Mead, *The Lively Experiment* (New York, Harper and Row, 1963), pp. 41-43.

6. Will Herberg, "America's Civil Religion: What It Is and Whence It Came," in *American Civil Religion*, ed. Russel Richey and Donald Jones (New York, Harper, 1974), p. 87.

7. Will Herberg, "Religion and Culture in Present-Day America," in *Roman Catholicism and the American Way of Life*, ed. T.T. McAvoy (Notre Dame, University of Notre Dame, 1959).

8. Richard Hofstadter, *Anti-Intellectualism in America* (New York, Viking, 1963), p. 238.

9. Quoted in Lawrence Byrnes, *Religion and Public Education* (New York, Harper and Row, 1975), p. 76.

10. John O'Neil, "On Body Politics," in *Family, Marriage and the Struggle of the Sexes*, ed. Hans Peter Dreitzel (New York, Macmillan, 1972), p. 251.

11. "Civil Religion in Theological Perspective," in Richey and Jones, *op. cit.*, pp. 161-184.

12. Quoted in Mead, *op. cit.*, pp. 143-144.

9.
The Future of Religious Education: Commitment in Religion and Education

Charles Melchert

By a careful analysis of the difficulties encountered in our use of the term "religious education," Charles Melchert locates the source of much of the tension in our notion of commitment. He suggests the value of a fuller and more complex understanding of the role of commitment in the educational process. After sketching four dimensions to that role, Melchert argues that distinguishing these dimensions enables us to use the tension more constructively and creatively.

It is now commonplace to observe that the language we use both reveals and conceals our meanings. If we are not critically conscious of our language we can deceive ourselves and thus distort our own future. So let us briefly take a look at the wording of this phrase, "the future of religious education."

First, "the future." I am neither a prognosticator nor a futurologist. I shall not attempt to describe what "might happen." Rather I shall suggest that our future is what we and others make it, and the more critically conscious we are of the present, the more hopeful is our future—all other things being equal, which they never are. I intend here to approach the future by helping stimulate an increased critical consciousness of our present words and actions. I am under no illusion that such action guarantees a better future, but surely the Vietnam debacle ought to have taught us that a systematic misconstrual of the problem is dangerous. It is such a misconstrual I am concerned with here.

Second, the term "religious education." Using that term can easily seduce us into thinking almost solely of the church's own internal instruction or socialization, usually with children, and generally in Sunday schools, CCD classes or parochial schools. I think this is too narrow a confine for a Christian and for the future as well.

Third, use of the term "religious education" leads many to think this is a different kind of education. Usually it is thought that this education is different not because of its religious content or context but because it has a different intent, namely, to help people become more religious. Interestingly, we do not make the same assumption with other similar terms. For example, we do not assume that the purpose of sex education is to help make people more sexy or sexual, or that music education is to make people more musical, or that English education is to make them more English. Similarly, we recognize that there are no such things as "religious mathematics," or "religious biology," or a "religious research process." What force does this adjective "Christian" have then? I suggest it is intended to designate what in other times we would have called catechesis, "Christian nurture," spiritual formation, or evangelization, or nowadays, "intentional religious socialization." These are legitimate and important concerns of a church community. But why call them education?

Let me suggest three possible reasons, each of which has an important bearing upon our future. First, by adding the term "religious" to education, we "baptize" the term and are able to trade on the positive connotations associated with that term in the present social climate. Simultaneously, we are able to avoid using the terms "evangelize" or "catechism" which have increasingly taken on negative connotations of late. We fool neither others nor ourselves by this ploy. If it is evangelism or catechesis we want, let's call it that.

Second, we may be calling attention to our intention to take the educational aspect of our task far more seriously than we have in the past. It becomes a way of affirming that education is something of genuine value in its own right. This could be a projection for the future if we are willing to take seriously the lessons of our own history of previous attempts of this sort.

Third, speaking of "religious education" helps us avoid a significant tension that has often been felt between education and religion. I cannot take the time to fully justify this usage here, but I would propose that education has as its purpose helping others to know and understand in the pursuit of truth and wisdom.[1] When that happens, church people have often complained that the effect of such education is that people sometimes lose their "faith" or believe less intensely in what they have been taught. For that reason they need a school or a type of education which will not destroy, but which will build up their faith. That complaint is often true, and we must face it rather than deny it, or pretend that "they don't really understand." On the other side of the ledger, educators have often noted that the pursuit of religious commitment, i.e. evangelism, or the nurture of a faith presumed to be present in the learners, i.e. catechesis, has had the effect of curtailing the search for truth and understanding. This, too, is often true. Is this tension inevitable? Is it intrinsic to the natures of education and religion? I will contend that as these domains have been understood in the past, the tension is erased only by subordinating one to the other, or by changing one to fit the other.

Perhaps one way of examining the possible future of religious education is by not presuming too close a connection from the start. Let us begin by looking at education in its own right, and not simply as an instrument for catechesis or evangelism. This way we can look at education both in schools and in churches, and seek to explore its links with religion.

More specifically, let us pursue the tensions mentioned above. I shall suggest that one root of these tensions is commitment. I shall contend, somewhat arrogantly, no doubt, that no author, to date, has done justice to the functions of commitment in education, in religion, and in their relation with each other. More positively I shall suggest that a fuller and more complex understanding of the role of commitment in the educational process and in religion could enable a much stronger future for education in religion both within the church community and within the schools.

First, let us turn to education within the church community. Throughout the history of the church it was obvious to all that "religious education" was to help make Christians. It was only with Dewey and George Albert Coe, early in the twentieth century, that doubts began to be raised. Yet even those doubts were pushed aside in the rush to neo-orthodoxy, and today most parents and teachers alike know that faith and moral character are what they want from "religious education."

If we turn to the writers of the last twenty years, we find that they approach education in the church from one of two basic frameworks. Either they start from the social sciences, as do C. Ellis Nelson, James Michael Lee, Father Godin, John Westerhoff, Robert Lynn, David Steward, Ronald Goldman, and others, or else they approach education in the church from theology, as do all the evangelicals, as well as R.C. Miller, D.C. Wyckoff, Iris Cully, Sara Little, Gabriel Moran, Gerard Sloyan, Albert McBride, Berard Marthaler, and others. But the debate between these two approaches is essentially one over means, for those on both sides assume that the major purpose of education in the church for Protestants is, to quote the succinct phrasing of John Westerhoff, "the transmission and support of a particular faith and life style . . . described by the adjective Christian."[2] For

Catholics, Rummery sums up a similar assumption as he describes the shifting meanings of catechesis, from its original meaning in the early church as a "second-stage process" of instruction of adults who have accepted faith and baptism, to its later identification with the question-and-answer method and content of catechism, to its present-day usage in schools where it is simply presumed that all are believers. Rummery and others have shown that the basic error here is in "taking as the starting point with children, what was really the end point of an adult investigation." Catechesis presumes a personal faith commitment that is unrealistic to assume for children in schools.[3] In other words, the purpose is evangelistic or catechetical, in that it has a predetermined conclusion or starting point in mind, and then proceeds either to the inculcation of a faith, or spiritual formation as a Christian.

Let us look more closely at this assumption. When the argument is explicitly formulated, it goes something like this: the nature of the church is thus and such; obviously one part or activity of the church (education) cannot be contrary to the nature and purpose of the church; therefore, we need to shape the church's education to serve the basic purpose of the church. That sounds quite plausible. But no one has asked whether education can or ought to do what is expected of it here. Is it possible that education has characteristics or effects which may inhibit the desired goal, commitment to Christ? Or is it possible that if the educational process is coerced into such a use that it is destroyed or damaged in the process? Recall that Lynn and Wright conclude that every time the churches have tried to make the Sunday school, that renowned creator of evangelical piety, into a serious educational enterprise, it failed.[4]

The educational process has its own intrinsic intentionality and integrity. It does not seek justification beyond itself. To create an educational goal is not to seek something to aim at which stands outside the educational process, but is rather to clarify and concretize activities within the educational process. Thus most of the so-called objectives for "Christian education" are not in reality educational objectives, but are rather theological statements about the place and function of education in the church. To treat education thus instrumentally, however, has some fairly obvious side effects which must be noted. We can see the destructive nature of these effects both in public schooling and in church schooling. When people argue that education is for something other than for its own sake, e.g. to get a better job, or more money, or as a means to church membership or faith, the attainment of that goal signals the end of the educational process. It is no longer needed. On the other hand, if education is a process of helping another gain understanding in the pursuit of truth and wisdom, then by its very nature, it is unending.

But church people ask, rightly, if the process is unending, when can one take a stand on anything? When does one affirm a commitment? Again we see the nature of the tension.

Before looking at how a fuller understanding of commitment might affect the evangelistic or catechesis intent of education within the church, let me say a few words about education outside the church.

One of the more impressive things about the church of the 1960s was its insistence upon the corporate social and ethical responsibility of the churches. Social ethicists affirmed the church's participation in the political domain, the corporate world, bureaucratic and governmental agencies, judicial bodies, indeed, in any institution that shapes our society. Except one. The school. It seems the church's primary concern with the schools has been how to get more religion into them, or the last vestiges of religion out of them.

I would contend that the future demands that we pay significantly more attention to our public and parochial schools, and particularly, to the quality of life and to the quality of the educational processes within them. Christians need to do this in part for their own interests, for the attitudes to education which children, young people and adults bring with them to church are "picked up" from their experiences in public and parochial schools, as well as from their home and neighborhood environments. Second, these schools, in which participation is compulsory, have embedded in their very structures and daily routines certain assumptions about the nature of the human being, and Christians will want to examine those assumptions.

I would suggest that a Christian's concern for social justice will also motivate a deeper involvement with our public and parochial schools, especially since the widely reported "mutilation of spirits"[5] by our schools is so widely supported by family life, business and corporate structures, government bureaucracies and the media.[6]

In the language of Freire, what is the effect of the school upon its occupants? Does it liberate or domesticate them? [7] Most curricular materials and most teachers presume, and thus teach children to presume, that someone other than the learner must always decide what they must learn, why learn it, when to learn it, when to stop learning it, how to learn it, how to report that it is learned, etc. When I get the schools' graduates at the university, presumably their best, most of them no longer trust their own curiosity and the adolescent's immature passion for truth is reduced to getting the grades "so I can get the credits to get the certificate for college admission so I can get the grades so I can get the diplomas so I can get the job so I can get the things I see on TV to use when I retire."

What happens to human freedom when a young person is told he or she is free to choose his or her own courses, but it soon becomes clear he or she is free to choose only from among the courses others have already chosen to offer?

What happens to the human spirit and the religious sensibility when every subject (sometimes even including religion) is approached from a technical or scientific perspective? So that even poetry and literature become not a matter of glimpsing the vision of human feeling being expressed, but of isometric examination of iambic pentameter? Or when in literature the subtle sarcasm that reveals the absurdity of so much of the human condition is reduced to an analysis of the historical-cultural setting of the author and a psychoanalysis of the author's dependence on his mother and hatred of his father, ad nauseam?

Where in our public and parochial institutions is there a concern for the education not of an object to be filled up with courses and content and knowledge and competencies, but the education of a *subject*, one who is creating a human being and participating in the shaping of history? Only when education is seen in such a light will we begin to understand Whitehead's affirmation of the duty and reverence which make education essentially religious.[8]

In other words, to be more explicit, I am saying that Christians need to be involved in the schools not only to help free the prisons we call "blackboard jungles," but also to exercise our critical faculties in those schools which *are* working. We must ask, for what are they working? Is it possible that Christians, who have learned to be based in their traditions and institutions without being bound by them for the future, can offer a critique of schools as educational agencies which neither blesses traditional forms for their own sake, nor retreats to the cloying romanticism of so many reformers?

When we turn to explicit religion in these schools, we find that denominational schools fit the catechesis intent of the church's education and that public schools adopt exactly the same understanding of commitment and conclude, "We can't touch that." Even in places where religion is offered as a subject in the public schools, we find writers consistently affirming (in North America) that commitment cannot be the goal (Engel, Piediscalzi, Warshaw, Michaelson, the McKay Report of Ontario, et al.). But what is left of religion if commitment is ruled out-of-bounds? And equally important, can one become fully educated without being committed? I will contend, no; that the absence of commitment inhibits not only religion but also education.

Now I must have stooped from poetry to paradox or nonsense. First I say that the evangelist's or catechist's stress on commitment leads to the destruction of education, and then I say that education in religion cannot proceed without commitment. Surely both can't be so?

Part of the difficulty here is that evangelists and catechists and school educators have adopted a too simplistic notion of commitment. They all conceive commitment as essentially two-dimensional. The critical factors are the *object* of the commitment: "To what or to whom are you committed?" and the *intensity* of the commitment: "How committed are you?" These are perhaps appropriately the focal concerns of the evangelist and the catechist, but they severely inhibit the educator if that is all he or she can see in commitment.

Some recent work in the social sciences has led me to believe that there are at least four dimensions to commitment, and that educators, on the one hand, and evangelists and catechists, on the other, while both concerned with commitment, have different focuses of attention.

First, there is the *object* of personal dedication. "I believe in Jesus Christ." "I am committed to a high moral standard." Educators as well as evangelists and catechists are interested in the object of commitment; the evangelist to call one to be committed to that object, the catechist to nurture one's commitment to that object, the educator to examine critically the adequacy of that particular object and the beliefs the person holds concerning it. The educator wants to test, Wilson has shown, whether or not this particular object is worthy of my investment, and whether my beliefs about that object are grounded and sound.[9] This difference indicates one basic distinction between the educator and the others. The educator has a different object of commitment. Whereas the religionist will urge commitment to beliefs or to divine beings, the educator is committed to seeing that a religionist's beliefs are reasonable or that they are reasonably held. This does not necessarily demand that the beliefs or commitments be demonstrably true, but it does entail that there be good reasons (given the circumstances of the one with the commitment) for being committed, that the commitment is not blindly or ignorantly held.[10]

Second, there is the *intensity* of the commitment. This is primarily a concern for the evangelist and the catechist. "How deeply do you believe?" The educator only becomes involved with intensity of belief when it is determined that a particular object of commitment (for example, the worship of the automobile) is not worthy of that commitment. The intensity of belief in that case may become a barrier to other understandings. But even then, the educator's interest is more in the object than the intensity.

Third, there is what Michael Johnson calls the behavioral or *constraint* dimension.[11] "He can't back out now, he's committed himself." There is an expectation that one's previous actions or commitments have served to willingly or unwillingly coerce one to continue this line of action. These constraints may be social, as when one youngster says to another, "If you don't do it, you're chicken!" Or they may be organizational, as in the familiar churchman's strategy, "If you want to keep your members, get them involved in the committees and organizations of the church." For our immediate purposes this dimension is only of indirect significance, for both the educator and the evangelist will be concerned with this dimension to the extent that it becomes a substitute, nonetheless effective, for personal dedication.

The fourth dimension of commitment is what Perry calls the *"style"* of commitment.[12] It has to do not with to whom, nor with how intensely, but with various balances in the "how" of one's commitment. Let me illustrate.

How does committing myself to this affect my range of interests; can they be broadened, or will they be narrowed? How do I balance the private and personal aspects of that to which I commit myself? Can I make a permanent commitment and still be flexible, or as one student put it, "Sometimes you have to go into something with the feeling that you'll be in it forever even when you know you probably won't be." There is the relation of action and contemplation, as one reports, "I've come to learn when to say to myself 'well, now, enough of this mulling and doubting, let's do something.' " There is the tension between control and openness. It is felt you have to have a plan, but also that you have to learn when to let go of the plan. Then there is a need to balance one's immediate involvement with detachment or perspective. "You have to have detachment, or you get lost . . . and yet if you stay detached you never learn from total involvement, you never live."[13]

In these areas of concern a person feels keenly the tension between the need for commitment and the need to weigh carefully the options and seek the truth. The evangelist and the catechist are right; we must choose, we must commit ourselves to some object or person or we cannot act. The educator is also right; we must carefully consider the alternatives and the grounds for choosing, and be willing to reconsider, at least occasionally. The style of one's commitment is how one copes with these tensions, and that style is fundamentally important to the future of one's own education, and thus also to the educational effects one will have on others. If I never decide, I am immobilized; I cannot have faith, and thus I limit my educational horizon. If I decide there is absolutely only one option, I put an end to education as well. Thus I will contend that this dimension of commitment is the focal concern of the educator, whether he or she functions within or outside of the church.

Perry's research has shown that educationally there is a fundamental reorientation (he even calls it a conversion in some places) which must occur in the learner's conception of knowledge. A person begins thinking of knowledge as being absolute; it is either right or wrong, and the learner's task is to accumulate the right parts and throw away the wrong parts. Then gradually a recognition emerges that there may be more than one right answer to most of the important questions, and that one must choose among them, although absolute certainty is never again to be had.

This research is effectively a critique of both relativism and absolutism epistemologically, for Perry shows that the most mature position is one in which an absolute must be chosen, but it is chosen within an acknowledged relativism. Such a progression demands both maturity and moral courage, for Perry reports that students who stopped or regressed in their movement consistently reported a sense of having failed. Whether they stopped with absolutism or dualism of rights and wrongs, or with a thoroughgoing relativism, they reported varying degrees of despair, defiance, guilt and even nostalgia for the days when learning was easier and things were either right or wrong. They even reported guilt arising from a feeling of having avoided assuming their own personal responsibility.[14]

Obviously this all implies that the educator's concern with this dimension of commitment will be with older young people and adults, more than with children. Interestingly, Perry reports that his subjects felt that their identity was shaped less by the objects of their commitment, than by their own particular style of commitment to it.

Perry notes that the educator's own style of operation with learners is fundamental to helping students through this basic reorientation.[15] The teacher must expect that the student will give serious consideration to more than one understanding of the issue at hand, and that there may well be more than one acceptable conclusion. (This is an approach the evangelist or catechist has often not been able or willing to take.) It also means that the teacher must attend to the style and modes of thinking, and not just to the rightness and wrongness of the answers.[16] The students also reported another very important factor which helped them through this reorientation: the willingness of their teachers to support them in their gropings, explorations and syntheses. Teachers need to occasionally share their own "growing edge," their own groping and styles of commitment, not as an answer or the "way you should also resolve it," but as a way of creating a more profound sense of partnership in a mutual learning endeavor, a shared search for truth and wisdom.[17]

It is true that the educational and the evangelistic and catechesis functions complement each other as they relate to commitment. When an evangelist calls for commitment or when a catechist seeks to build a deeper faith, he or she must presume some degree of knowledge and understanding about the object of that commitment. When an educator seeks to examine commitments and help to enable a more mature style of commitment, he or she must presume at least a minimal intensity of commitment to someone or something. Yet the tension persists, for while the evangelist and catechist urge wholeheartedness and singlemindedness, the educator urges understanding alternatives and openmindedness.

I would argue that these emphases must be held together, for only when they are joined can each stimulate the other and keep each other honest. When they are divorced or separated, as they often are in churches and schools, we begin to see familiar distortions of education and religion. When people are repeatedly called to the same commitments without also being helped to expand or deepen their understandings, their commitments become stale and harden into dogmatism. When an understanding is expected but there is no opportunity for or expectation of taking a stand or expressing a commitment, students rightfully cry "meaninglessness." When neither commitments nor understanding are expressed in actions, both are divorced from the root source of their vitality, their life, and the whole endeavor sinks into irrelevance.

This more complex relation of education and religion in commitment does not erase the tension, but awareness of these dimensions and their relationships may enable us in the future to use this tension more constructively and creatively in the schools and churches for the benefit of all. It is a future that is likely to be even more lively than the present, and will demand all the resources we can muster. But it is such a future for which we are responsible. As Soren Kierkegaard so aptly put it,

There always lurks . . . in a man, (and I am sure, in a woman, too) at the same time indolent and anxious, a wish to lay hold of something so really fixed that it can exclude all dialectics; but this desire is an expression of cowardice, and is deceitful toward the divine.[18]

Notes

1. Part of this explication of the meaning of "education" can be found in my article, "Does the Church Really Want Religious Education?" *Religious Education*, Vol. LXIX, No. 1 (Jan.-Feb., 1974), pp. 12-22.

2. John H. Westerhoff and Gwen Kennedy Neville, *Generation to Generation*. Philadelphia: United Church Press, 1974, p. 82.

3. Richard Rummery, "Catechesis and Religious Education," in *New Movements in Religious Education*, N. Smart and D. Horder, eds. London: Temple Smith, 1975, pp. 149-161.

4. Robert W. Lynn and Elliott Wright, *The Big Little School*. New York: Harper and Row, 1971.

5. Charles E. Silberman, *Crisis in the Classroom*. New York: Random House, 1970.

6. This follows the observation that schools reflect their society rather than change it. For example, see Thomas F. Green, "Schools and Communities: A Look Forward," *Harvard Educational Review*, Vol. 39, No. 2, 1969, pp. 221-252.

7. Freire, "The Adult Literacy Process as Cultural Action for Freedom," *Harvard Educational Review*, Vol. 40, No. 3, 1970, pp. 452-477.

8. Alfred North Whitehead, *The Aims of Education*. New York: Macmillan, 1929, p. 26.

9. John Wilson, *Education in Religion and Emotions*. London: Heinemann, 1971.

10. *Ibid.* Chapter 4 is currently the best explanation of this complex matter.

11. Michael P. Johnson, "Commitment: A Conceptual Structure and Empirical Application," *The Sociological Quarterly*, 14 (Summer, 1973), pp. 395-406.

12. William G. Perry, Jr., *Forms of Intellectual and Ethical Development in the College Years*. New York: Holt, Rinehart and Winston, 1968, pp. 136-37, 145-49, 153-76.

13. *Ibid.*, pp. 38-39.

14. *Ibid.*, pp. 177-198.

15. *Ibid.*, p. 167.

16. *Ibid.*, pp. 210.

17. *Ibid.*, pp. 211-213.

18. Soren Kierkegaard, *Concluding Unscientific Postscript*. Princeton: Princeton University Press, 1941.

10.
A Framework for Catholic Education: Opportunities for the Future

Michael Warren

At least some of the difficulties in religious education can be traced to a confusion with regard to many of its fundamental terms. Michael Warren discovers the difficulties that flow from the identification of schooling with education or the use of catechesis and religious education as synonyms. He sees value in the fact that the pastoral letter To Teach As Jesus Did *proposes ministry rather than education as the horizon for catechesis. He discusses these values in some detail.*

The purpose of this essay is to clarify what we mean when we use the terms "education," "Catholic education," "religious education," and "catechesis." The writer presumes, and would hope to show, that there has been some confusion regarding these words, especially as they have been and are being used by American Catholics. The clarification of this terminology could have concrete, practical implications for what goes on in some of our parishes and even for what some of us do with our lives.

One place to begin our clarification of these terms is with the re-examination of the history of American education that has been going on for the past ten years, thanks, partly at least, to the historical research of Dr. Lawrence Cremin of Columbia University.[1] Cremin, who himself has undertaken an exhaustive history of American education,[2] has done considerable research on other, earlier histories of education in the United States. While conducting his research he discovered that the histories of American education have tended to be histories of American schools, that is, histories of but a single stratum of education.

Cremin's book exploring this problem, published in 1965, is entitled *The Wonderful World of Ellwood Patterson Cubberley*.[3] Ellwood Cubberley, professor of education at Stanford from 1898 until the 1930s, published in 1919 a work that for almost forty years was viewed as one of the monumental and definitive histories of American education. Cubberley's classic was entitled *Public Education in the United States*.[4]

Although Cubberley's work was to influence more than two generations of American educators, it was not actually a history of public education; it was rather a history of public schooling in the United States. By tending to identify education and schooling, Cubberley's history unfortunately put education into a frame of reference that could not take into serious consideration the major problems that have faced education since 1920.[5] Even as Cubberley was busy preparing his book for publication, events were taking place that would eventually demand that education be viewed in the broadest possible way, rather than in the narrow categories of schooling.

> At the very time he (Cubberley) wrote, a revolution was in the making, in the rise of mass media of communication and in the organization of a growing number of private, quasi-public, and public agencies committed to education but not organized as schools. The revolution has since occasioned a complete contemporary education, one that clearly suggests the need for a more inclusive account of our educational history.[6]

Cremin points out that whatever the centrality of the public school in American educational history, it must be seen as one component of a variety of other educational agencies that have functioned throughout our history and which have helped shape American thought, character and sensibility over the years. In addition to schools, educational history must also be aware of the educational influence of "families, churches, libraries, museums, publishers, benevolent societies, youth groups, agricultural fairs, radio networks, military organizations, and research institutes."[7] An adequate history of education would have to explore the role of newspapers in the eighteenth century, of social settlements in the nineteenth and of mass television in the twentieth. Within the context of such varied educational influences as these, one might better understand the shifting influence of schools and colleges.

Although Cremin wrote *The Wonderful World of Ellwood Patterson Cubberley* for students of American educational historiography, his thesis about the need to view education in a much wider scale than that of schooling can be important to all of us concerned about the matter of education, including Catholic education.

One might expect the events of the last several years, including the selling of the president by the advertising marketeers and the great Watergate noncredit television course in civics and problems of democracy, to make us powerfully aware of the educative forces that influence us daily, long after we have terminated our formal schooling.

One might expect in the wake of Cremin's little book that some historian would examine the histories of American Catholic education to see if the Cubberlian bias existed in these histories too. Such a historian appears to be Vincent Lannie, professor of education at Notre Dame.[8] Not surprisingly, Lannie has discovered our very own Ellwood P. Cubberley among our historians of Catholic education. His name is Reverend James A. Burns. Burns received an M.A. from the Department of Education at Catholic University in 1907, after having written his thesis on "Catholic Education in the United States."[9]

During the six years following his degree at Catholic University, Burns produced two works dealing with the Catholic school system. The first was entitled *The Catholic School System in the United States: Its Principles, Origin and Establishment;*[10] the second, *The Growth and Development of the Catholic School System in the United States.*"[11] Burns explained the reason for his focus on the schools thus:

> A direct relation existed between the development of the Church and the development of Catholic schools. . . . The main factors in the Church's development—immigration and migration, the hierarchy, parish and diocesan organization, the religious Orders, the Councils—have constituted also the main factors in the growth of the schools. And the influences that were at work to retard the Church's progress have had a correspondingly hampering effect upon the schools. The relation between Church and school has been, in fact, so close that it is impossible to disassociate the history of the one from the other. The parish school has been from the very beginning an agency of the Church.[12]

In other words, one can trace the development of the American Catholic Church in an examination of the development of the Catholic school system in America. In viewing matters this way, Burns was a man of his times. According to Lannie, his main ideas about the progress of the church and of Catholic schools can be also found in the bulk of Catholic educational histories written in the nineteenth and early in the first decade of the twentieth centuries. In addition,

Burns's error was not entirely without logic. The largest part of the church's commitment to education in his day was bound up in schools.

Since Burns and Cubberley were both influenced by the type of educational history written before their time and with which they were familiar, it is not surprising that Lannie finds a parallel between their histories on every major point, except that Burns "baptized" Cubberley's secular victories for schools into Catholic triumphs.[13]

> Whereas Cubberley saw the rise of the public school as inextricably tied to the progress of America, Burns saw the rise of the Catholic school as inextricably tied to the progress of the Church in America. . . . Just as Cubberley's public school seed evolved from colonial times and engaged in a series of major battles before it became an integral part of American society, so Burns' Catholic school system existed "in embryo" in colonial times, fought a host of battles against Protestantism and secularism during the nineteenth century and became an integral part of Catholic life in the opening decade of the twentieth century.[14]

If Cubberley's approach to educational history influenced the perspective of his successors for decades, one might expect and indeed does find Burns's preoccupation with Catholic schools as a dominant theme of Catholic educational historiography for the next fifty years. In fact one finds what might be called the Burns bias at the heart of the most recent general history of Catholic education. Written by Dr. Harold Buetow of Catholic University and entitled *Of Singular Benefit: The Story of U.S. Catholic Education*, this history appeared in 1970.[15]

Although at the outset of his work, Buetow defines education from an encouragingly broad point of view, in short order the term is used as a synonym of schooling. Thus on the second page of his introduction, he writes:

> Education . . . is very frequently confused with such other terms as "teaching," "instruction," "training," "discipline," "schooling," and "formation." Etymologically, "education" comes from two cognate Latin words, "educere" and "educare", meaning to lead forth or draw out. A real definition in modern times adds nothing to Pythagoras, who spoke of education as that which enables a person to become what he is. . . . Other disciplines refer to it also as acculturation and socialization.[16]

However, later in the same introduction he refers to Roman Catholic education in the restrictive sense of schooling, a use that characterizes the whole of his book.

> All of this brings us to the question of why we wrote this book. First, the subject is both relevant and important—not only because it shares in the advantages of history in general and in the history of education, but inherently. True scholarship recognizes that there has always been more than one pattern of education in this country, and at the present time the largest sector of American private education is the Roman Catholic. This establishment—tens of thousands of schools, hundreds of thousands of religious and lay teachers and staff, and many billions of dollars—is responsible for educating about one out of nine children in the United States, a sizeable proportion of the future of our country.[17]

In general, although Buetow, like his predecessor Burns, purports to discuss Catholic education, he focuses his attention almost exclusively upon schooling. Vincent Lannie judges that in so doing, this recent historian of American Catholic education missed an opportunity to break new historical ground in understanding the total educational experience of the American Catholic Church.[18]

Of course, the concern here in reporting of Cremin/Cubberley and Lannie/Burns is not of itself a concern for historiography, as important as that matter may be. The writer's concern is the practical results these ways of viewing our history have for our pastoral efforts within the Catholic Church. We have just seen that from a secular point of view, education is much broader than schooling. To ignore this long-neglected fact is to forget the impressive contribution to human life made by countless ingenious systems, programs, and procedures by which men have communicated and influenced one another. The American library system, American newspapers, ethnic-oriented societies of various sorts, and political rallies have all contributed important, if unexamined, contributions to the fabric of American life. To pretend that schooling has been the sole source of education does a disservice to the facts.

We have also just seen that Catholic education is a much broader reality than Catholic schools. One can make the assertion boldly, without any implication of a slight to the impressive and, yes, monumental contribution of Catholic schools. In any history of the Catholic Church in this country, the Catholic schools must have a place of honor. The fact remains however that they have not done the whole job. Even among Catholic children not more than 50% have been enrolled in Catholic schools at any time in our history.[19] The genius of the Catholic Church in the United States is that it buttressed the impact of the schools with a variety of other educational initiatives. In a fine summary of the question, Lannie puts the matter thus:

> . . . Roman Catholicism had long operated under the doctrine that it is the sole agency of salvation. The laity needed instruction in the sacramental system of grace and guidance in the Church's assessment of cultural values. Catholics thus had to be socialized to accept the Church's rendition of the earthly city in order to gain entry into the heavenly kingdom.
>
> American Catholicism escalated the Church's commitment to this task. Interpreting American culture as antithetical to Catholic values, the immigrant hierarchy of the nineteenth century seemed overwhelmed by its religious and cultural responsibility. The growing number of Catholic immigrants and their ignorance of the faith confronted a fledgling Church with a seemingly impossible task. Thus, all available means had to be enlisted in the work of socialization: sermons to instruct those who could find seats in overcrowded churches; periodic religious revivals to reach beyond the Sunday congregations; catechism and Sunday school classes to prepare the young for active participation in the sacramental system; a network of sodalities dividing the parish by age, sex, marital status and providing moral instruction and social intercourse for specific "stations in life," a system of educational and social agencies including parochial schools, private academies and colleges, asylums and protectories and hospital and prison apostolates. The written word was not forgotten. Priests and laymen edited diocesan newspapers and religious periodicals; and Catholic publishing houses printed European and American devotional, catechetical and fictional works under episcopal imprimatur.[20]

This statement of Lannie gives some inkling of the ground that would have to be covered to survey adequately the true scope of Catholic education. As usual, where truth is concerned the whole story is much more impressive than a part of the story, even when that part is the impressive story of Catholic schools.

Using the above controversy about schooling and education as background, the remainder of this paper will seek to clarify the way we think about catechesis, about Catholic education, and about religious education. The need for this clarification became more important to the writer as he came to realize how thoroughly the American bias about schooling has influenced the way we have tended to think about catechesis.[21] Since the clarification of these terms and of the relationship among them is something that must evolve through serious study and discussion, and, if necessary, through a restructuring of pastoral agencies at the diocesan and national levels, this essay represents an attempt to move the discussion along.

If we can accept the guidance offered by the *General Catechetical Directory* promulgated in Rome in 1971,[22] catechesis is an aspect of the pastoral activity of the church. Although the *Directory* would never deny the fact that catechesis is educational, yet it chooses to view catechesis, not within the framework of education but within that of ministry. Thus catechesis is one of the forms of the ministry of the word in the church.[23] Other forms of the ministry of the word are those of missionary preaching or evangelization, liturgical proclamation, and the systematic investigation of the truths of faith called theology.[24]

Thus catechesis is set within the category of ministry as one of the forms of the ministry of the word in the church. Education, always a possible horizon within which to view catechesis, is not the horizon selected by the *Directory*. By choosing the category of ministry, the *General Catechetical Directory* offers the possibility of close links between catechesis and other ministries in the church. Other horizons could certainly have been adopted by the *Directory*, but it is now a fact of historical significance that the perspective actually selected and maintained throughout is that of ministry.

If the *Directory* views catechesis as ministry rather than as education, then it also knows none of the American preoccupation with schooling. The following is the most succinct description of catechesis offered by the *Directory:*

> Within the scope of pastoral activity, catechesis is the term to be used for that form of ecclesial action which leads both communities and individual members of the faithful to maturity of faith.[25]

Here the *Directory* emphasizes catechesis as an "ecclesial action." Thus, if the *Directory* ties catechesis to any human structure, it is the structure of community, not that of schooling. The document continues:

Within the aid of catechesis, communities of Christians acquire for themselves a more profound living knowledge of God and of His plan for salvation, which has its center in Christ, the incarnate Word of God. They build themselves up by striving to make their faith mature and enlightened, and to share this mature faith with men who desire to possess it.[26]

Far from limiting catechesis, the *Directory* takes pains to show that the forms of catechesis are varied, indeed unlimited.

Because of varied circumstances and multiple needs, catechetical activity necessarily takes various forms. . . . In a word, catechetical activity can take on forms and structures that are quite varied, that is to say, it can be systematic or occasional, for individuals or for communities, organized or spontaneous, and so on.[27]

The *Directory* is suggesting that the forms of catechetical activity are limited only by the human imaginations of those who seek to help their fellows grow in the faith that binds us together in Christian community.

Admittedly, there is little that is startling in either of these two insights of the *Directory*, i.e. 1) catechesis has unlimited forms and 2) that catechesis is pastoral activity seen in the context of ministry rather than education. Yet the implications of both these insights are influencing the lives of all of us engaged in the educational apostolate of the church and will continue to influence us in the future. However, because we are Americans with the American bias toward Catholic schooling, and American Catholics with a Catholic bias towards Catholic schooling, we expect to see ourselves and others resist these implications. There are available concrete examples to illustrate how each of these insights about catechesis has influenced the American church in its recent and current history.

The following example illustrates the American bias toward schooling and its effect on our approach to catechesis. In doing research for a doctoral dissertation on the influence of the French catechist, Pierre Babin, on American catechetics over a ten-year period, the writer had to translate from the original French many of the catechetical writings of Babin. The writer set out to compare his literal translations with the popular translations that were widely sold in the United States.[28] He discovered that at a certain point in his career, Babin began to exclude carefully from his writings all words related to schooling. Thus Babin never referred to the young as "students." He chose instead to call them "young people" or "the young." He carefully referred to those who did the catechizing, not as "teachers," but simply as "catechists" or as "adults." Further, catechetical sessions were not called "classes" but "catechetical sessions" or "meetings." What Babin was doing was carefully using language that would allow for the myriad forms of catechesis. He realized that in many catechetical settings, young people are not students at all. After all, even during their years of schooling, young people are students for little more than five hours a day. In some situations, catechists are functioning not as teachers but more as guides or facilitators or group leaders. The insight is an important one that anticipated the broad catechetical categories of the *General Catechetical Directory*.

However, in almost every case, and most especially in the translations of his famous little books, *Options* and *Methods*,[29] the American translator dismissed Babin's carefully chosen language and recast his thought almost entirely in the categories of schooling. In their Englished forms, *Options* and *Methods* are clearly about teaching religion in Catholic schools, rather than about setting up situations where young and older Christians can meet and begin to share and thereby grow in faith.[30]

At this point someone will perceptively point out that the American translator was writing out of an American situation where catechesis has been carried on mostly in classrooms and in situations of formal instruction, where the categories of teacher and student are appropriate. To a point one could agree with that observation. However, in recent years the situation in the United States has shifted rapidly. Fewer and fewer of our teenagers are in Catholic schools. On the other hand, more and more of those who must be catechized in out-of-school programs are resisting catechesis done on a schooling model.

In a survey of all the dioceses of the United States over a two-year period, the writer found that the most successful catechetical programs for young people not in Catholic schools are those characterized by informality and much group interaction. Thus the single most successful catechetical program now in use for young people appears to be the youth retreat. Now, while these retreats do offer authentic oral instruction in basic truths of faith, they avoid anything like what we would understand as classroom instruction. Few written materials are used. Adults function in a role of advisor, friend, witness-to-faith, and fellow journeyer-to-faith. Another way of describing this development would be to say that catechesis of teens is succeeding better when done on a model of andragogy, of adult learning, than when done on a school model, which is the model of pedagogy, of child learning.

To illustrate the effect of viewing catechesis within ministry rather than within education, I would like to examine briefly the pastoral of the American Bishops, *To Teach as Jesus Did*.[31] *To Teach as Jesus Did* is an attempt, a somewhat successful one,[32] to call all of Catholic education back to its true nature as a work of ministry within the church. The document insists that Catholic education is not simply a matter of good instruction in religious and secular matters. Catholic education is to be marked by the signs of the church itself, that is, to be marked by dimensions of faith community and service to one's fellow humans.[33]

In effect, *TTJD* is saying that if education is broader than schooling, Catholic education has a scope that is broader than secular education. It must have its own characteristics as a ministry of the church. Paragraph 14 of *TTJD* describes Catholic education as an educational ministry in the following words:

> The educational mission of the Church is an integrated ministry embracing three interlocking dimensions: the message revealed by God (didache) which the Church proclaims; fellowship in the life of the Holy Spirit (koinonia); service to the Christian community and the entire human community (diakonia). While these three essential elements can be separated for the sake of analysis, they are joined in the one educational ministry. Each educational program or institution under Church sponsorship is obliged to contribute in its own way to the realization of the threefold purpose within the total educational ministry. Other conceptual frameworks can also be employed to present and analyze the Church's educational mission, but this one has several advantages; it corresponds to a long tradition and also meets exceptionally well the educational needs and aspirations of men and women in our times.[34]

This paragraph makes clear that Catholic education, at least as it is conceived of in official church documents of recent years, falls within a framework of ministry.

There are several important implications of these recent efforts to take seriously the full scope of education, especially Catholic education.

First, those who are engaged in catechesis or in Catholic education would do well to recognize that they are engaged in a ministry.

But who ever denied that, someone will ask? Probably few have ever denied it in theory. However, we can more clearly affirm Catholic education as a ministry and then align our practice more systematically with that insight. Doing so would demand collaboration between those who engage in educational ministry within schools and those who do so outside of schools. Doing so would also open those in catechetical ministries to greater collaboration with other ministries in the church. It is less and less viable for any one aspect of the church's ministry to be cut off from or to be out of touch with others, especially in the matter of financial resources and utilization of facilities. When diocesan priorities have to be set, an intelligent overview of all the ministries of the church and their interrelations must provide the basis for decision-making. Further, at the individual level rather than the diocesan level, many have seen what happens when some members of religious orders realize that in their deepest core they were not called solely to education but rather to ministry. Is it true that as these members get older they tend to become more ministry conscious than education conscious? The variety of ministries now being filled by religious and lay men and women seems to be a healthy result of a correct framework for their activities.

Secondly, those seriously interested in Catholic education can serve it best by recognizing what a broad concept it actually is. If schools up till now have been the dominant structure for Catholic education, we must clearly recognize that they are but a single dimension of the educational ministry of the church. Ironically, it is the schools themselves that will benefit by this recognition.[35] It is possible that we have been expecting the schools to do too much and so have been frustrating those devoted to this important aspect of the church's ministry. When the history of Catholic education is more accurately written, we will see that from the beginning our efforts in some way have been to serve the needs of the entire community. A wit once remarked that in the Catholic Church to have your educational needs taken seriously you have to be under seventeen and preferably under thirteen. Such a statement can be made only if we take education in the narrow sense, that is, if we equate it with schooling. Those of us who have engaged in educational ministry to adults have long recognized the acute needs adults have for making Christian sense out of life.

Thirdly, it would seem wise to begin being more judicious in the way we use the term "religious education." As the conjunction of two words, "religious" and "education," these words have nothing necessarily to do with assisting fellow Christians in the development of faith. "Religious education" is a very broad term that could cover anything from teaching about religion in public schools to a course on religious sociology given by an atheist professor in a university. A course about Mohammed's thought in a Moslem school must be classified under "religious education." It is a broad umbrella term under which one can fit any activity that combines education and religion.

To equate catechesis and religious education is, if not erroneous, at least misleading. "Religious education" has a broad denotation. Cathechesis is more basic and fundamental, of richer history and more pregnant in meaning. It relates specifically to conversion therapy and kerygma, particularly for those being first born in Christ as well as those being constantly born anew by an ongoing process of conversion therapy. Catechesis includes such concepts as conversion, Christian initiation, the church as the faith community, shared responsibility for mission, expressed concern for the gospel, worship as the faith response of the Christian community, etc. Catechesis is much more than religious instruction, it is a process of growth in faith; a means of learning to live as a Christian by being in, among, and with Christians.[36]

If we should use "religious education" more carefully and less often, we should use the word "catechesis" whenever we are talking about an effort to help people grow in faith. What would happen in many of our Catholic schools, for instance, if those in the religion program thought of themselves not as religion teachers but as catechists, that is, as nourishers of faith? For one thing, they might be more willing to experiment with quasi-instructional methods of fostering the faith development of young people. On the other hand, catechetical ministry to adults might make more progress if catechists steadfastly refused to approach it from the perspective of schooling. There are still further implications, which all of us must now begin seriously to explore.

One of these implications has to do with the nature of education. What is education anyway?[37] What are its parameters? Is there a difference between education and educational influences? Must education be deliberative or can it be so informal as to be almost accidental? Another way of phrasing these same questions: What is the relation between socialization, i.e., all those processes a society uses to pass on its meaning to its members, and education? These are questions society itself is asking as background to an attempt to provide all persons with opportunities for lifelong learning. Answers to these questions will probably evolve over the coming years, thanks to the efforts of an international cadre of educators working to broaden our concept of education.

Within the church, we have a similar large question that will demand a new look at what education is and what its relationship should be to the church and the church's ministry. Any serious attempt to address this larger question will involve broad collaboration among a vast number of agencies that until now have been working in isolation from one another. For example, to identify properly the task of adult education and adult catechesis within the church there must come together many agencies which we have not yet grouped under "adult education" or "adult catechesis." Yet these agencies form a network of sophisticated programs devoted to the growth of adults. Consider for example the following: Christian Family Movement, The Marriage Encounter, the Cursillo Movement, parish councils, Liturgical Commissions, Christian Life Communities, and the Legion of Mary. Such groups have had an important role in the church's ministry to the adult, and they should be in touch somehow with those in a diocese formally charged with adult education or adult catechesis.

In any new look at the role of education in the ministry of the church, those associated with schools will be needed for their insights and collaboration. After all they have the facilities, the equipment, and above all, the know-how. The school people will enrich and be enriched by collaboration with those who approach the church's ministry from other angles. Again, these answers cannot be blueprinted or diagramed beforehand. They will have to evolve gradually from the right questions. This essay has been one attempt to suggest some of these questions.

Notes

1. For useful background on the scope of recent educational revisionism, see, Marvin Lazerson, "Revisionism and American Educational History," *Harvard Educational Review*, 43 (1973), 269-283.

2. Cremin's chronological studies of various periods in the history of American education are not yet complete. See, Lawrence A. Cremin, *American Educational History: The Colonial Experience, 1607-1783* (New York: Harper and Row, 1970).

3. Lawrence A. Cremin, *The Wonderful World of Ellwood Patterson Cubberley* (New York: Teacher's College Press, 1965).

4. Ellwood P. Cubberley, *Public Education in the United States* (Boston: Houghton Mifflin Co., 1919).

5. See, Cremin, *Wonderful World*, pp. 46-48.

6. *Ibid.*, pp. 46-57.

7. *Ibid.*, p. 48.

8. Vincent P. Lannie, "Church and School Triumphant: The Sources of American Catholic Historiography." Talk given at a meeting of the History of Education Society, Chicago, October 24-27, 1973. See also, Vincent Lannie, "The Teaching of Values in Public, Sunday and Catholic Schools: An Historical Perspective," *Religious Education*, 70:2 (March-April, 1975), 115-137.

9. See, Lannie, "Sources," p. 2, note 4, for an account of the problem of Burns's doctorate.

10. Rev. J.A. Burns, CSC, *The Catholic School System in the United States: Its Principles, Origins, and Establishment* (New York: Benziger Brothers, 1908).

11. Rev. J.A. Burns, CSC, *The Growth and Development of the Catholic School System in the United States* (New York: Benziger Brothers, 1912).

12. Burns, *Catholic School System: Principles*, pp. 14-15.

13. See, Lannie, "Sources," pp. 29-42.

14. *Ibid.*, pp. 10-11.

15. Harold A. Buetow, *Of Singular Benefit: The Story of Catholic Education in the United States* (New York: The Macmillan Co., 1970).

16. *Ibid.*, p. xii.

17. *Ibid.*, p. xv.

18. Lannie, "Sources," p. 23.

19. See, Vincent Lannie, "Catholic Educational Historiography in the Twentieth Century." Unpublished address given before the History of Education Society, Atlanta, November 1974, pp. 27 and 31.

20. *Ibid.*, pp. 26-27.

21. An examination of catechetical liturature of other countries shows that this bias is not exclusively American. The writer's hunch is that where a nation has a well-developed Catholic school system or allows for religious instruction in state schools, catechesis tends to be cast in the categories of schooling. Such countries include England, Ireland, Australia, and to a lesser extent, Germany; France and Italy seem, especially in recent years, to have resisted viewing catechesis within the perspective of schooling. On the other hand, catechists in so-called missionary countries and third-world countries see catechesis as a pastoral function with its own principles and procedures, one reason why valuable catechetical theory is emerging in these countries. See, Joseph Colomb, *Le Service de l'Evangile* (Paris: Declee et Cie, 1968), Vol. I and II; R.M. Rummery, *Catechesis and Religious Education in a Pluralist Society* (Sydney: E.J. Dwyer, 1975); Joseph Pathrapankal, ed., *Service and Salvation: Nagpur Theological Conference on Evangelization* (Bangalore: Theological Publications in India, 1973).

22. Congregation for the Clergy, *General Catechetical Directory* (Washington: United States Catholic Conference, 1971).

23. See, *GCD*, Part I, Chapter II, "Catechesis in the Pastoral Mission of the Church," pp. 19-28.

24. *Ibid.*, par. 17.

25. *Ibid.*, par. 21.

26. *Ibid.*

27. *Ibid.*, par. 19.

28. See, Michael Warren, *The Approach of Pierre Babin to Adolescent Catechesis and Its Influence on American Catholic Catechetical Literature, 1963-1972* (Washington: Catholic University of America, 1974). Unpublished doctoral dissertation.

29. Pierre Babin, *Options*, translated and adapted by John Murphy (New York: Herder and Herder, 1967); Pierre Babin, *Methods*, translated and adapted by John Murphy (New York: Herder and Herder, 1969).

30. See, Warren, *Babin*, especially pp. 156-204.

31. National Conference of Catholic Bishops, *To Teach as Jesus Did: A*

Pastoral Message on Catholic Education (Washington: U.S. Catholic Conference, 1973).

32. The writer wishes to note here in passing his conviction that *To Teach as Jesus Did (TTJD)* has several serious deficiencies, most of which arise from the lack of a clearly delineated perspective on either ministry or education. These must be examined at length in another place. The value of *TTJD* is as an *attempt* to broaden the scope of education to include a clear note of ministry. The weaknesses of the document are understandable in the light of its somewhat "mongrel" origins. See, William E. McManus, "To Teach as Jesus Did: A Chronicle," *The Living Light,* 10:2 (Summer, 1973), 278-283; and, Mark Heath, "*To Teach as Jesus Did:* A Critique," *The Living Light,* 10:2 (Summer, 1973), 284-295.

33. See, *Ibid.*, pars. 5-32.

34. *Ibid.*, par. 14.

35. See, Harvey Steele Commager, "The School as Surrogate Conscience," *Saturday Review,* January 11, 1975, 54-57. Commager decries what happens when informal educational arrangements are bypassed in favor of more formal educational institutions. He claims that such a shift puts unrealistic demands on schools.

36. See, Robert Hovda, "A Time for Every Purpose Under Heaven," *Living Worship,* 10:6 (June, 1974), 1-4.

37. In a superb article, Dwayne Huebner, Professor of Education at Teachers College, Columbia University, has set forth the distinctiveness that educational efforts in the church should have. Although others such as Gabriel Moran have carefully elaborated similar ideas, Huebner's article has a special cogency. He warns church educators of the dangers of aping the worst aspects of secular education gone mad. On the other hand, Huebner insists that true education develops the religious side of personality, especially by prizing reflectiveness. See, Dwayne Huebner, "Education in the Church," *Andover-Newton Quarterly,* 12:3 (January, 1972), 122-129.

DEEPENING MODELS

Bernard Cooke
Charles Healey

11.
Living Liturgy:
Life as Liturgy

Bernard Cooke

*Bernard Cooke suggests that only when our lives are human,
Christian, worshipful, sacramental and vital will our liturgies be
qualified by depth. He offers criteria for authentic life and liturgy, and discusses at some length the steps one should take to
implement the proposed ideal.*

In religious education circles, there is rather general agreement
that religious instruction should prepare for meaningful worship.
There is also quite general agreement that genuine liturgical experience is the most critical component of, and the culminating stage in,
true religious education. One has heard statements such as these so
often in recent years that they have become truisms; but as all too
often happens with truisms, their repetition does not mean increased
understanding nor increased commitment.

It is obvious a priori that religious instruction should lead logically to more intelligent and personal religious practice; what is far from
clear is what constitutes genuinely meaningful liturgy, truly personal
corporate worship. This means that we are not very certain what it is
that our religious instruction should be leading to, nor certain of the
manner in which religious education should find its fulfillment in liturgy.

When do we have an act of corporate worship that deserves the
name "living liturgy"? Is it a matter of lusty singing, of high excite-
ment, of shared enthusiasms, of carefully ordered ceremonies, of famil-
ial atmosphere, of awe-filled reverence? It seems that our first order
of business must be some attempt to answer this question, sketching
out tentatively the lines of an ideal liturgy. Though each liturgical celebration cannot be a full realization of such an ideal—and for some
time to come we will have the educational responsibility of helping
people benefit as far as they can from sadly inadequate liturgy—our
religious instruction should describe and prepare for ideal liturgy, in-

dicate how it can come into being, and provide the elements of understanding (biblical, theological, etc.) and attitude out of which such a true liturgy can emerge. In talking about "living liturgy," the word "life" is to be taken seriously and specifically. Liturgy is meant to be an act of living, an instance of that consciousness and affectivity and freedom which are properly the life of humans, a privileged instance because it involves men and women on the highest level of personal consciousness—that which is brought into being by human confrontation with the divine.

Authentic liturgy, then, *must engage the consciousness of those who participate in it*. This is something more than saying that people should understand what it is they are doing, that people should be aware of the basic structure and nature of the liturgical action, that they should understand the meaning of the various texts and prayers employed in a given liturgy—though these are certainly to be desired. Authentic liturgy should catch up and absorb people's attention—not by way of entertainment, but by way of challenge and illumination and discovery. Liturgy should be a situation of *awakening*, of intensified insight, of tension and even of conflict as prejudices and deceptions and rationalizations are challenged by the presence of Christ.

To say that liturgy is not meant to be entertainment is not to say that it is meant to be dull or oppressively serious. People should enjoy themselves in liturgy; after all, it is intended to be genuinely human celebration. But liturgy is not intended to be superficial or frothy enjoyment; it is intended to be a deep-reaching enjoyment of humanness, an enjoyment that is basically lighthearted because it does not bear the burden of artificiality, an enjoyment that can endure alongside mature realization of the sorrows and problems of human life.

Because it is the proclamation of the gospel, the liturgy is intended to present a constant challenge to Christians. To those who can hear what it says, the liturgical action provides tantalizing glimpses of that wisdom, that "answer to life," which interested humans have always sought. To those who can bear to face the radical dimensions of its challenge, the gospel opens up exciting vistas of insight and hope which are perennially "new." What the gospel says are the things humans want to hear, the things that would most absorb their attention—could they but believe that it was all true, and face up to the responsibilities it entails.

Clearly, the liturgical action can never be such an experience of insight and joyous discovery until people become aware of what is happening in the liturgy, until those who do liturgy are aware of what it is that they are doing. This, obviously, is where religious education (at all levels) is meant to make a major and indispensable contribution. Knowledge of what is to be done will not guarantee its being done; but without such knowledge it is certain that it will never be done.

When we say that liturgy must engage people's consciousness, we are talking about real men and women—not about some abstraction, "people." This means that living liturgy must deal with persons where they are, taking into account the actual understandings and questions and attitudes and life-styles of those who are gathered for any particular liturgical celebration. The proclamation of the gospel, if it is to be effective, can never be neutral and safely general; it is always meant to be a word about the present situation in which humans find themselves, a word which makes it impossible to hide from the demands and potential of that present.

Difficult though the task admittedly is, *liturgy must come to grips with whatever it is that really matters to those celebrating the liturgy.* It must bring out into the open their deepest questions, human and religious; it must confirm or challenge the manner in which they identify themselves as humans and as Christians; it must give them realistic hope in the face of the obstacles which do seem to doom them to lives of mediocrity and insignificance; it must guide and support them in confronting with mature responsibility those basic life decisions which most profoundly shape the personality of each of us. Obviously, this means that *liturgy must be celebrated according to the culture forms proper to a given group,* those culture forms that bear the images and insights and values and eschatologies that are the deepest wellsprings out of which societies live and act. The movement to use of vernacular languages was an important step in this direction, but it was only a beginning; it provided an indispensable instrument, but the organic interpenetration of Christian liturgy and human cultures is a much further-reaching enterprise. For one thing, the "adaptation" of liturgy to culture (really, a very inept way of expressing what is involved) is not just a matter of taking into consideration the differences we associate with national cultures: within any national or linguistic grouping there are innumerable subcultures, and these also must be incorporated into any liturgy that intends to affect people as people.

All this may sound a bit erudite and unrealistic. Just the opposite: what we are saying is that men and women will only hear what is addressed to *them.* Now, they may not listen to it even then, because the gospel may be a challenge they do not want to hear; but they will certainly not listen to it as gospel if it seems to have no direct contact with what they know their daily lives to be. Men and women's secularity is Christian in proportion as they live by faith; this is what liturgy is meant to celebrate.

To turn to another basic characteristic of genuine liturgy: *it must be the action of a community.* Again, there is a surface realization of this in just about every sacramental act—though it is a bit hard to see it in private masses celebrated without any attendant congregation, or in anointings performed hurriedly in some hospital room. Sunday congregations do represent a level of community, though it is not clear what kind of community they are, what they have in common. It might help in understanding where exactly we are in our "liturgical renewal" if we asked and answered that question. Our purpose, however, is not that of directing appraisal or criticism to what has been or is now being done, but instead to determine what kind of community should exist in liturgy.

In this matter certain statements are axiomatic: liturgical actions are meant to be professions of faith; the external enactment of the liturgy is meant to be a true expression of the attitudes of all those in attendance; those gathered at liturgy are there precisely because of their Christian faith, i.e., that faith is the very thing they presumably have in common; those gathered for liturgy have not come to do simultaneously and in one spot the individual actions that they could just as well have done in separation from one another. All these add up to the simple principle: the liturgy is meant to be a *corporate* action, one in which men and women really share, one in which they not only cooperate but also participate in a common experience. It is the sharing in this experience that makes them a community of believers. The fact that we can state this ideal so simply does not mean that it is simple to attain the ideal. As a matter of fact, it is very difficult for Christians even to understand the description of liturgy we have just given: unless one has had some experience of truly *corporate* religious activity, it is well-nigh impossible to know what such would be.

What makes the realization of this ideal so imperative is the fact that the very life of Christianity depends upon it. Christian faith must be nurtured within community, just as it must originate in community; because for each Christian the faith of his fellow believers acts as support and criterion for the reality and accuracy of his own belief. Christianity becomes a true community, one capable of sacramentalizing ultimate human community in the kingdom of God, in proportion as there is genuine community in faith. And there will be such genuine community in faith in proportion as liturgical celebrations become truly corporate actions.

Finally, *truly living liturgy will be an integral part of people's lives*, indeed a most important part, one which will have focal impact on the rest of life. Genuine liturgy will be this because of its very essence it is a decisive individual and corporate response to the demands of people's actual life situations. It would be a mistake to understand this aspect of liturgy as something added to worship, as "practical applications" of the liturgy. Instead, the basic human decisions that underlie the various activities in which men and women are engaged are the decisions made in liturgy, the response to the challenge of God's word. What Christians decide in their liturgy is to live fully as humans, to live according to the set of values revealed in Jesus' death and resurrection, to live with concern for their fellow humans, to live with hope and optimism. Their decision is not a reluctant one, for the liturgy celebrates this decision; and consequently the decision is really appropriated by the men and women who make it, which means that it then finds honest implementation in their lives.

Liturgy is simultaneously a hearing of the word of God and a response to this word; truly open listening to the gospel is already the most important step in response. Liturgical response to the word cannot, however, be in any way separated from the response of a Christian's total life; liturgy is the formal and public commitment to a particular way of life, a commitment that can only be true when it finds realistic implementation in actual living. Liturgical ceremonies are idle words if they are not the straightforward pledge by a community to live more fully according to the gospel.

What Is Needed?

Really, there is very little need to defend the understanding of living liturgy that we have just outlined; what is desperately needed is that we begin a serious effort to bring such liturgy into being. Despite certain official changes that have opened up the possibilities of decent liturgy, the general state of Christian liturgy is close to desperate. The majority of men and women who continue to participate regularly in Sunday services are for the most part subjected to a ritual that is poorly understood by them, in which they have little active role, and to which they give only an impersonalized, "religious" attention. But realistically what can we do to move toward a truly living liturgy?

1. First of all, there must be a *correct understanding* of liturgy. Basic and accurate theological information about the nature of liturgical action is absolutely necessary; without it, people do not even have well-informed knowledge that anything is now amiss with liturgy. How can they know what it is of which they are being deprived?

All they have is a vague dissatisfaction or boredom.

It is only common sense that men and women must know what it is they are doing in order to do it intelligently and effectively. If they are to enter humanly into the performance of liturgical worship, Christians must know what is meant by "worship," "liturgy," "sacrifice," "prayer" and like terms that are constantly used, but whose meaning is poorly or incorrectly grasped. Sheer ignorance would be bad enough; incorrect understandings are much harder to handle, since people think that they understand. Element after element of eucharistic liturgy (and of other sacramental liturgies as well) is misunderstood: in what sense Christ is present, how "grace" and sanctification develop through liturgy, what is the proper role of the celebrant, what is the nature of Christ's sacrifice, how any given liturgy is linked with Jesus' death and resurrection, etc., etc.

Sophisticated theological reasoning is not a prerequisite for authentic celebration of liturgy; theologically correct understanding of Christian faith is. For too long we have exploited a poorly understood doctrine of *ex opere operato* efficacy in sacraments and joined this with a view of Christian sanctity in which sincerity could substitute for truth. As long as people showed up for the Sunday service regularly with the intent of doing "the will of God," they fulfilled the commandment "Keep holy the Sabbath" (transferred, of course, to Sunday) and "gained the graces" to keep the other nine commandments. This is what they were told and this is why they came—and still come. Only one thing can reverse this evisceration of Christian worship: tell Christians what liturgy really is and the genuine reasons for celebrating it.

2. Secondly, we must provide opportunity for Christians to *experience some genuine liturgy*. Without such experience, it is almost impossible to acquaint them with correct understandings; it is a bit like trying to give a course in art appreciation to persons who have never seen color. Admittedly, we are faced with what seems to be a vicious circle: people need to be educated about liturgy in order to celebrate it authentically, but they can't be so educated unless they have the experience of authentic liturgy. The difficulty is not, however, insoluble. Only a few experiences of living liturgy are needed to make people realize what might be; in some instances, one such experience is enough. Once such a real liturgy is experienced, the inadequacy of routine liturgy is only too painfully apparent, and people can begin to see what might be if they just had the opportunity to learn what true Christian worship was and then to implement this new understanding. In all honesty, though, it must be admitted that it is not

always easy to motivate persons to desire such a new liturgical experience: many see no reason for any change, or they do not wish to face any changes; they simply wish to leave things the way they are. How this problem can be met is a matter of proper strategy for each individual situation; but the key to successful strategy will be to concentrate on providing good experience of liturgy rather than criticizing the inadequacies which now exist.

3. Thirdly, and most fundamentally, Christian men and women must progressively *discover the sacramentality of their basic life experience and learn to celebrate it*; this is the foundation of all Christian liturgy. Because this principle is so important, and because we have for so long failed to take it into consideration in our sacramental theology and our liturgical practice, it might be good to discuss it at some length.

Human life in order to be truly human must have meaning. Even suffering and sorrow can be bearable, if men and women can only see some significance, some purpose in it. On the contrary, unless some meaning attaches to it, a life of comfort and pleasure quickly settles into boredom and restlessness. Men and women are intelligent beings; their psychological structures are such that they undertake activities in order to achieve some goals; but there can be no goals worth seeking if everything in human existence is meaningless. Strangely, in our age when there could be so much to excite people, when the mind boggles at the possibilities opening up to the human race, there is widespread disillusionment about the human experience, even despair. As seldom before in human history, mankind needs hope—and the reason is that men and women have ceased to find any clear and ultimate meaning for themselves or for anything that they do.

On principle, Christian sacramental liturgies are meant to cope with this problem, though it will take us some time before we see more clearly how this should happen. When we talk about "sacraments," we are talking about actions that are special precisely because of their meaning; by definition, a sacrament is that which has some effect on humans because of its meaning. Succinctly put, Christian theology would say that "sacraments cause by signifying"—another one of those profoundly true statements which, though constantly repeated over the centuries, has scarcely begun to be understood.

What sacramental liturgies are meant to do is to build upon the meaning of those key experiences that are common to all humans and that most profoundly color the entire significance of our lives: birth and death, pain and sorrow and joy, risk and success or failure, love and fear and guilt and expectation. As we actually go through such experiences, some of them alone and some along with others who are friends or enemies or associates or passing acquaintances, the subtle consciousness of what the experience means (or does not mean) interprets for each of us the meaning of ourselves and of our existing on this earth. Experience of a deep friendship, for example, will convey an awareness of being important for someone, of having a worth that another appreciates, of being able to contribute to another's happiness, of being trusted with another's interests and questions and dreams; in short, it will break any sense of utter isolation, because it is the experience of community with another person.

All too often, humans do not have the kind of experiences that would feed their sense of self-worth or that would reflect some authentic meaning to their life. As a result, men and women grow into insecurity, boredom, lethargy, and mediocrity; or they plunge into a quest for something outside themselves (wealth, power, social prestige, camaraderie) which hopefully may represent some kind of achievement and shield them from the meaninglessness of their individual personhood. Such fundamental tragedy is all too common; it is the theme of our literary tragedy, which highlights it by casting it in a somewhat heroic mold, but it is also the theme of millions of lives whose humdrum meaninglessness has nothing of the heroic about it. To express it all in religious terms, there is a widespread need for humans to be saved from meaninglessness, from insignificance; unless this be done, "salvation" can have no reality for them. Christianity claims that the meaning of human existence that is revealed in the life and death and resurrection of Jesus of Nazareth is such a saving force; not only does it provide meaning for those lives which patently are "insignificant," it injects into all human experience a depth of meaning that it could not otherwise have. The promise of unending life of human fulfillment, a promise already realized in Jesus' own situation and already being communicated to those who do not refuse his gift of such life, provides for all human happenings a frame of reference in which they find an ultimate evaluation. Since all human experiences somehow enter into the shaping of a person, and since no person (in the Christian perspective) is without importance, there is no intrinsically meaningless experience. But such statements of what has happened in Jesus' Passover are too abstract—what is revealed in Jesus is that *God cares what happens to men and women;* that is what makes everything meaningful. It is that caring, that divine love, which is not only the promise but the causative principle of human personal realization.

If such a force is to operate in human lives, it must somehow be appropriated in human consciousness: we cannot be encouraged and enriched by someone else's love if we have no awareness whatsoever of that love. So, for the meaning revealed in the death and resurrection of Jesus to be transformative of human experience, it must be injected into that experience. Men and women must learn increasingly the new and fuller depth of significance that attaches to human lives—and most focally to those key experiences whose significance permeates the entire fabric of human experience. Christian liturgy exists to provide just such a coalescence of meanings: the experienced meaning of birth and death and fear and love and all the other "peak experiences" and the evangelically proclaimed meaning of Jesus' own life-death-new life experience. For each Christian, his or her own life experiences give realistic insight into Jesus' experience; Jesus' experience provides unique understanding by which today's Christian can discover some ultimate meaning for today's happenings.

If one examines theologically the Christian sacramental system, the traditional "seven sacraments" (however different Christian churches grant more or less sacramentality to each of them), it becomes increasingly clear that they are what they are precisely because there is a certain fundamental range of basic and universal human experience (such as birth and death). By transforming these basic experiences, the sacramental liturgies are meant to touch and change all human consciousness. Christian sacraments build upon—and can only exist because of—the sacramentality of those human experiences that are most ordinary and universal.

One of the thorniest problems facing liturgical revitalization comes, however, precisely from what we have just discussed: many humans have little if anything of what can be called "human experience"; they are so deprived by their circumstances, so caught up in the desperate struggle to survive, or so mired in a routine participation in "the system," that it would be cruelly ironic to talk about "peak experiences" to them. Without too much exaggeration it would be true to say that things simply happen to such people; they do not experience them. Some experiences, of course, are so drastic that they seem inescapable—such as the death of a parent or child—but for many persons these happenings are so baffling that they handle them by refusing to experience them.

Some understanding of life, some appreciation of what it means to be human, some sensitivity to the human condition, are prerequisites of a truly human experience. These can come only by education—which need not be formal schooling. A person must be initiated into some knowledge of what life and love and freedom and risk and responsibility and sorrow and joy can and should be. Obviously, this is a task that reaches far beyond the scope of religious education, though religious education has an indispensable role to play. As a matter of fact, as things now are, it may often happen that religious educators will have to supply much of this broader humanization in order to then go on to their own proper task. No man or woman who fails to understand what it means to be human can understand what it means to be a Christianized human.

Authentic Christian liturgy demands, moreover, a definite attitude toward life's peak experiences. Liturgy is a *celebration* of life, it is a corporate expression of genuine thankfulness for things as they are. This does not imply any naive or unrealistic ignoring of life's challenges and problems and pains; it does imply a mature and straightforward acceptance of the present moment in human history, with its limitations and potential. Christian liturgy says that those celebrating it have faced themselves, have honestly accepted themselves as good but far from perfect, are grateful for what they are though eager to live yet more fully. Because it is also a celebration of community, Christian liturgy implies that those gathered together on any given occasion are grateful for one another and accept one another as brothers and sisters—despite whatever differences there might be in social status.

People cannot effectively celebrate life's key experiences if such celebration is confined to the moments of public liturgical worship. Life's more important experiences (and the lesser ones, too) must be celebrated as they happen: sharing time together with a close friend is itself a celebration of being human, the birth of a child is a moment of keen celebration, watching at the bedside of a dying loved one is a different mode of celebrating our humanity but still for a Christian an occasion of genuine celebration. When we learn to celebrate our human experience as it unfolds for us from birth through death into new life, then we will be able to share such celebration with one another when we assemble to profess our Christian belief that life is to be celebrated because Christ's death and resurrection have given it meaning.

Christian life and Christian liturgy exist in continuity with one another because the "Christ meaning" proclaimed and celebrated in liturgy carries over into our life experience, but also because the "Christ meaning" proclaimed and celebrated in life's experiences carries into and gives meaning to the liturgy. In the liturgy the meaning of the risen Christ and the meaning of the assembled Christians illumine and deepen one another. This is so, because the liturgical action

—even that of the eucharistic celebration—is not Christianity's act of worship; it is the liturgical moment in Christianity's act of worship.

Which brings us to our last and perhaps most basic remark about the sacramentality of Christian life: *gratefully responsible acceptance of life*, expressed in working to realize life's potential, is the *fundamental and indispensable act of Christian worship*. Only if Christians deal with life this way is their faith proclamation of God as their Father an honest statement. What we have just said may sound like rhetorical excess until one stops to examine it: *worship* is the acknowledgement of the true God, acknowledgement that he is what he has revealed himself to be, acknowledgement that his word about his relationship to men and women is a true word; the God of Christianity has revealed himself in Jesus as one who in love has given to all men the gift of personal life, so that in living that life as genuinely as possible in awareness and love and freedom and joy they can reach unending life; and the joyous acceptance of self and the world is the acknowledgement of this God, it is worship.

The catechetical conclusions of our reflection are obvious:

1. religious educators must convey the understanding of how our life experience is *human*, is *Christian*, is *worship*, is *sacramental*;

2. they must explain the role of sacramental liturgies in formally injecting Christ-meaning into human experience;

3. they must then share, according to varying opportunities, in creating liturgical celebrations in which the meaning of Christ and the meaning of Christians can interpenetrate one another. Hopefully, liturgy will then come to life and life will become continuing liturgy.

12.
The Spirituality of the Religious Educator

Charles J. Healey, S.J.

Religious educators often find that attempts to deepen their spiritual lives are frustrated by a decrease in the supportive structures that formerly energized their efforts. Charles Healey speaks to this difficulty by outlining a faith perspective for work and by exploring the elements that nourish a spirit of hope and the factors that sustain a person in wholeness.

Introduction

We live in a period in which many persons are seriously and sincerely seeking to discover or rediscover the sources of strength and vitality that enable them to be productive and loving persons in the service of God and their neighbor. The present-day interest in spirituality in general and prayer in particular attest to these widespread hopes and desires. This seems to be particularly true in the case of the religious educator, given the challenges, responsibilities, and demands that can be part of the important ministry of religious education. What provides and sustains a spirit of hope, purpose, and perseverance? What nourishes the faith-filled vision that is so necessary for this ministry? There is nothing new in these questions but they do seem to take on an added urgency today with the particular demands of our times and the challenges and difficulties of today's apostolate in religious education.

There has been much advancement and progress in the various areas of professional growth for the religious educator. Persons in general are bringing to their work a higher degree of training and competency through graduate education, various workshops and forms of professional growth. Many important insights have been utilized and assimilated from psychological theories of development, personal growth and maturity, as well as leadership training and communication skills and techniques. Still, this does not seem to be enough and many are seeking some deeper interior resources to nourish and sustain their demanding apostolic endeavors. Call it what you want—a yearning, a restlessness, a searching, a strong desire for a deeper interior life. Perhaps it is part of that longing that St. Augustine speaks of in his words: "Our hearts were made for you, O Lord, and they will not rest until they rest in you." But at any rate the searching and the desire for a rich interior life and a life of union with God is certainly in evidence in the lives of many.

There are, of course, no easy answers and no ready-made programs to provide instant solutions. We know that we are involved in and caught up in a process that seems to be always beginning while at the same time always continuing. Yet it does seem to take on an added sense of urgency today with the absence of so many of the familar structures and guidelines that may have been part of our lives previously. It certainly is an emerging issue for the religious educator and one that does merit our thoughtful concern and reflection. What provides and sustains a spirit of hope, purpose, perseverance and direction in the work of the religious educator? What nourishes the faith-filled vision that is so important and necessary? This essay will seek to respond to some of these issues by offering some reflections on the various sources of support, challenge and nourishment that will hopefully meet some of the present-day needs and desires. They are offered as reflections and potential seeds of thought that may add to the ongoing process of rediscovery and remaking effective in our lives the necessary sources of nourishment for our lives of faith, hope and love.

For the sake of some order and clarity we might focus our reflections, first around those aspects that sustain a faith-filled perspective in the lives and work of religious educators; secondly, upon the elements that nourish a spirit of hope in light of the constant pull toward discouragement; and thirdly, the factors that can be helpful in sustaining someone as a loving person, motivated by a spirit of service, concern, and compassion in his or her ministry.

1. A Faith-Filled Perspective

The entire work of the religious educator has to be situated in the context of faith, for above all we are engaged in a ministry of faith. Through our lives and our work, we are caught up in the unfolding of God's divine plan and the mystery of God's love. God can and does work through us; we are his instruments. So much of our ministry is helping others to penetrate the mystery of God's love in their lives just as we seek to penetrate this mystery in our own lives. And yet it is so easy to forget this or at least limit the actual awareness and effectiveness of it in our daily living. We can get so caught up in *our* work, *our* cares, *our* successes, and failures and disappointments. At times and even frequently, the faith dimension of our ministry recedes to the background.

What has to be brought to the fore, then, is a readiness and a responsiveness to the power of God working in us, and that openness to the Spirit that is expressed in the words of the psalmist: "Here am I, Lord, I come to do your will." I suppose it comes down to the consciousness and appreciation of a loving God working in our lives. It is that spirit characterized by the prayer long associated with Francis of Assisi: "Lord, make me an instrument of Thy peace; Where there is hatred, let me sow love; Where there is doubt, faith; Where there is despair, hope; Where there is darkness, light; and where there is sadness, joy."

This, again, is so easy to speak about but the question naturally arises: What nourishes this dimension of faith in our lives? First of all, we might begin with the strong *desire* itself that is present on the part of many to seek and find God continually in their lives and deepen their awareness of his presence and reality. There is the visible desire of many to deepen their own union with God and to establish or reestablish what they consider the essentials and priorities in their lives and to make any required decisions in a context of faith and prayer. This desire for some may be expressed and articulated very clearly, while for others it may be a vague awakening and searching. For some it may be intense and persistent, while for others it may be passing and slight. Whatever form it does take, it is God's grace working within us. This desire is so important for it is the starting point for and the foundation of so much other activity. Thus it should be constantly attended to and nourished, for it can fade away as gently as it came or it can be the source of a deepening and ongoing awareness and sensitivity to the power and presence of God.

A second source for nourishing the whole faith dimension in our lives is through a deepening growth in the awareness and conviction of God's personal love for us. It is the deep awareness of God's personal love that heals, frees, strengthens and encourages one to respond generously. When a person is conscious of God's love in spite of one's sins, limitations, and failures, he or she can focus on the Lord in a spirit of great trust and confidence. An ability to relax and be confident in God's love is a tremendous help to growth. Among other things it can lead to a freeing spirit of gratitude, a gratitude that can expand persons and their outlook tremendously and arouse the deep desire for God alone and the carrying out of His will. It can lead to a trust and confidence that we can be instruments of God's peace, hope, and love and that God can do great things through us if we are united to him in a spirit of deep faith.

Thirdly, a faith-filled perspective is greatly enhanced by keeping alive within us a sense of awe and a sense of wonder at God's continual marvels that unfold before our eyes. Unfortunately it is so easy to take things for granted and we can become oblivious so easily to the many traces of God's presence in the world and in our lives. Even though the world is full of God's glory, the perception of this glory often becomes a rare occurrence as a sense of wonder is dimmed by indifference and routine. Keeping alive a sense of wonder is a favorite theme of Abraham Heschel for whom "the beginning of our happiness lies in the understanding that life without wonder is not worth living. What we lack is not a will to believe but a will to wonder."[1] In a similar vein, Thomas Merton speaks of the seeds of God's presence, the seeds of contemplation that are so much a part of our lives.[2] Most of these seeds perish and are lost because so often we are not prepared to receive them or we are not sensitive to their presence. In a very true sense, it is only the faith-filled person, the contemplating person who is acutely sensitive to these seeds of God in his or her life. The goal is to seek and find God in all things and to be contemplatives in the midst of action.

Importance of Prayer

In the context of the above, we might recall the close connection between a faith-filled perspective and a spirit of prayer. Prayer is being used here in its broadest sense, that is, the continual response of persons who are convinced that they belong to God and seek to grow in union with him. It is an abiding attitude which seeks to deepen and nourish the awareness of God and his love and the actual workings of his love in our lives. Prayer helps us to grow in our awareness of God's presence and his unique call to each of us. It invites God more fully into our lives and gives him the opportunity to speak to us while at the same time allowing us to adopt a more listening and responsive attitude to his gentle initiative and movements both within us and around us. It helps us to become more sensitive to the many ways God does speak to us and it enables us to grow as seekers after the Lord and his presence. It helps to keep us aware of whatever limits our freedom to respond generously to God and his service, and also aware of the constant need we do have of his help and grace. Prayer involves a stance of true humility and simplicity before God.

The religious educator is faced today with many decisions of a varying nature and as a result some process of discernment is called for in many cases. Since there is the evident desire of many to make any required decisions in a context of faith and prayer, we might recall some of the basic ideas connected with any discerning process. Discernment focuses on the ongoing attempts to clarify and ascertain God's will in our lives and seeks to specify what actions and decisions are required in the life of one who wishes to follow Christ totally. The process presupposes an intense desire, hunger, and willingness to seek God's will and to embrace it generously once one has come to a reasonable certitude regarding it. Discernment in prayer, then, is an ongoing process that seeks to find God and his will in our lives; it involves a constant seeking of God and an awareness of his presence in our lives. Through discernment one seeks to hear God's continuous call, to recognize it as clearly as possible in order to follow it as faithfully and generously as possible. It seeks to answer the question: How can I best love and serve God in the present circumstances of my life? It is an ongoing process because our lives, our experiences, our work, our relationship with God are an ongoing process.

What has to be kept in mind above all is that the whole context of any discerning process is prayer and our patient, persevering and generous efforts to grow in our awareness of the reality of God and his presence in our lives. The context of discernment is a very normal, full and serious seeking after God.[3]

Mention should also be made in this context of the central role Christ should play in our lives. It is no exaggeration to say that every Christian religious educator is called to signify Christ's presence in the world. This can only be done, of course, to the extent that one does reflect the mind of Christ and the fruits of his Spirit, namely, mercy, kindness, humility, meekness and patience. One can only be a true witness to Christ if Christ is known personally and intimately. Prayer itself is a necessary means for deepening our relationship with Christ and it is through prayer that we seek to know him more intimately, so as to love him more ardently and follow him more closely in our daily lives. We will be effective in our following of Christ and our bearing witness to his message to the extent that we are united to him, united to him as the branch is united to the vine, so that his power, his life, and his love can work through us dynamically and effectively.

Finally, it is so important to see all the concrete experiences of our lives—our joys, hopes, sufferings, failures, etc.—as our living out and participating in the death-resurrection of Christ, in the paschal mystery.[4] We seek to say more fully with St. Paul: "I live, now not I, but Christ lives in me"; and "All I care for is to know Christ, to experience the power of His resurrection, and to share in His sufferings, in growing conformity with His death, if only I may finally arrive at the resurrection from the dead" (*Philippians* 3:10-11).

2. *The Sustaining of Hope*

Discouragement is a constant danger for everyone, no matter what type of work he or she might be engaged in, for it is so much a part of the human situation. However, it often is a special difficulty and obstacle for those engaged in religious education. This seems to be true for many reasons. There are the many demands and challenges of the work, the difficulties inherent in working on so many different levels and with so many types of persons, the seeming lack of results and the apparent failures, personal doubts and difficulties—all of these and the many others which need no detailing can take their toll and slowly wear thin one's enthusiasm, perseverance, patience and hope. Thus the sustaining of a spirit of hope for the religious educator cannot be overstressed.

It is interesting to note that a mark of a magnanimous and generous person is the capacity and ability to sustain a spirit of hope amid constant disappointments and hardships. When we look more closely at the lives of those whose apostolic efforts were seemingly crowned with much success, we find that disappointments and frustrations were never absent. The apostle Paul comes readily to mind. He certainly had his share of disappointments and trials and failures; and yet he was constantly sustained in his apostolic labors by a deep sense of hope, a hope based not only on his own power but the saving power of the Christ he loved and served.

But given the importance of hope, the question still remains for us: What does help to maintain a vital and vibrant sense of hope within the religious educator? First of all, I think we must constantly strive to keep before our minds the mystery of the work we are involved in. We are caught up in God's ways which so often do not correspond to our ways. For example, we often do not know when we touch someone significantly or when we are truly effective in our efforts. What really is success or failure in the long run? Often we can only plant and leave the harvesting to a time or place or manner we may never know.[5] Often we can only do our best and leave the rest to God, trusting in his infinite love and goodness and confident that in his mysterious and loving way he will take care of things.

Secondly, it is important that we be able to draw consolation and strength from the seemingly small events that constantly occur in our ministry and are truly glimpses of God's working mysteriously in our lives. It might be leading someone to greater faith, or hope, or to an awareness of God's love. It might be bringing a measure of peace or joy or consolation where there was only turmoil, or sadness, or grief. Maintaining a sense of wonder and awe at the way God works in people's lives and how he uses us as his instruments can be a continuous source of nourishment for our own spirit of hope and a source of consolation in the Lord. God's love does hover over our work and our efforts and we can find him in all things; but we can lose a sensitivity to that dimension and that presence so easily, particularly if we are caught up in our own worries and concerns.

Perhaps it comes down to saying that we must trust God and trust in his providential love, convinced that we are in his hands and that he does make all things aright in his own way and in his own time. It can be helpful to look back on our own lives, for the realization that he has been with us and has brought us to this point of our lives with much to be grateful for, can nourish and strengthen us in the present and lead to the facing of the future with greater confidence and trust.

But above all, it is important to realize that God is with us and that we are not alone, and that there is great meaning and significance to our work and efforts. We have within ourselves the resources and strength to respond fully and effectively and to be ministers of peace and hope for others, as we seek to reassure them, too, of God's loving care and activity in their lives and their own strengths and resources to cope fully and effectively.

3. A Loving, Productive Person

The psychologist, Gordon Allport, has an interesting observation in one of his essays regarding the importance of the person in the learning situation. Recognizing that social learning is a very subtle process, he states that often what is actually taught turns out in the long run to be less important than the manner of teaching.[6] He is referring to the influence parents have upon their children and the power of their good example, but his remarks have wide application. We can see this in our own experience in the case of persons who have been significant influences for us. Often we remember the persons because of their goodness and sincerity and example long after we have forgotten what they have actually said or taught. All of this highlights the importance and significance of the person in any type of religious education.

The religious educator is basically an apostolic person engaged in a ministry of education and service. The work and ministry of the religious educator should be marked by that same spirit of service to others that characterized Christ's own ministry who came "not to be served but to serve." The goal is a person of concern and compassion who loves unselfishly, actively, and effectively. Not only is there an acceptance, respect, and genuine appreciation of those he or she touches or is touched by, but there is also a sense of wonder and awe at the mystery of God's love unfolding in their lives. This is the goal and the ideal but it certainly does not come about in any automatic fashion. Once again we are left with the question: What helps to sustain someone as a loving and productive person?

Among the many factors that could be developed in response to this question, I would like to focus here on one aspect. It is the aspect of interior freedom, for it is such an important basis for any person who seeks to love and serve in a generous way. The freedom I am referring to is the freedom that allows a person to give to God and his will the central place in one's life; it is a freedom and detachment from all other things that would prevent or hinder one's striving to focus on God. It is an attitude characterized by a profound conviction that the most important thing in life is to love God and to serve him in a spirit of simplicity and joy.

Freedom in this sense implies a sense of harmony and order in one's life. It implies a sense of integration and peace and wholeness that is opposed to any interior turmoil, conflict, or fragmentation. It presupposes a certain level of maturity and a relative freedom from the fears, anxieties, and hostilities that can be so paralyzing. An ability to face reality, adapt to change, control anxieties, the capacity to love and give of oneself—these and all the other characteristics of maturity greatly influence the extent of a person's sense of freedom.

There is one particular aspect of our lives that can severely limit this spirit of freedom; it is the hold or grip the work itself can maintain over a person. It often happens in the case of a religious educator that the work with all its demands and seemingly unending aspects can exercise a tyrannizing influence over the person. One can easily be caught up in a "merry-go-round" type of activity that can be all-consuming. This attitude not only limits a person's freedom and flexibility but in the long run leaves one far less effective and productive. It can leave a person with a sense of either being overwhelmed or at least fragmented and pulled in many directions. One must either control the work itself or be controlled by it. Thus it is so necessary to set limits, establish priorities, give time and attention to one's legitimate personal needs. Any type of a "messiah complex" or "martyr complex" can leave a person far from being free and far from the peace and serenity and wholeness that is so important if one is to function as a loving and productive person.

In order to maintain this spirit of freedom, it is important to keep before our eyes the larger view of things and the total perspective. This is another way of stating the need to view our work and everything connected with it as objectively as possible. The big things should remain big things but the little things should remain little. In practice this often is not as easy as it sounds. Getting the needed distance from our work from time to time can be an excellent aid to maintaining this. There must be moments to relax and be refreshed, time to be with friends, opportunities to be nourished physically, spiritually and emotionally. There is need for a certain amount of time to be alone periodically and regularly; not in any sense of isolating oneself from one's work and withdrawing from reality, but for the purpose of returning inwardly refreshed, at one with oneself, and open and alive to the work itself. There is a unique rhythm in our lives to which we must be attuned as we seek to regulate and harmonize all our activities.

In this connection, too, we might briefly mention the function of spiritual direction and its value for the religious educator. It can be very helpful if there is someone to whom the religious educator can go periodically (and it doesn't have to be very frequent) to discuss what really is important in a spirit of openness, simplicity, and sincerity. What is most to be desired is the capable assistance of someone who knows and understands us in an atmosphere of acceptance and trust. A director can assist us in being sensitive and faithful to the promptings of the Holy Spirit and in providing the encouragement and reassurance we all need at times. A director can provide a fuller contact with the larger faith community, help us objectify our experiences, and help us to maintain and increase the freedom and proper perspective we need to function as well as possible. In a word, a director can assist us to grow in a spirit of faith, hope, and love before God and our neighbor.

Recently, I heard a lecturer mention in some context or other that "pioneering demands discipline." This struck me as a perceptive statement and one that was open to varied applications. It would seem to apply here in the sense that religious educators today are often pioneers in many ways. They frequently may be assuming new positions which call for the creation and implementation of many new programs. Many of the familiar structures that are found in other ministries may not be present and the work may bring one into uncharted waters. With the absence of familiar structures and supports, greater responsibility is placed upon the individual, thus requiring a greater degree of inner control and discipline. The goal, again, is a sense of order and harmony in our lives, but attaining this does require a certain amount of discipline and abnegation in our lives and the realization that we are in constant need of healing and purification.

Finally, we constantly have to remind ourselves, too, that the life of the Spirit has to be worked at, not in any Pelagian sense, but one that rises out of a realistic awareness of ourselves and our need to rise above the routine, the monotony, and the heaviness that can settle upon us so subtly but so effectively. Needs and difficulties vary from time to time and from person to person. But for everyone it does take patient and persevering effort and sacrifice on our part to maintain the spirit of freedom so necessary to give God and his will the central place it deserves in our lives and to be open and flexible in our attitude before him. The cost of discipleship has to be a constant reality in our lives and we must be able and ready to "say *no* to ourselves in the name of a higher *yes.*"[7]

Conclusion

Our attention has been focused on such questions as what nourishes the faith-filled vision that is so necessary for the ministry of religious education, and what sustains the religious educator as a hopeful, loving, and productive person. There is nothing new in these questions, but we are continuously facing them anew. For so much of our Christian lives of faith, hope, and love involves us in a process of rediscovery and awakening, particularly to those aspects and elements that speak to our present-day needs and experiences. We are involved in a continual process of renewal and conversion, as we seek to come alive again and again to the gospel message in our own lives and bring it more effectively to life in the lives of others. We are called to a life of holiness, to a full sharing in the life of him who is holy. When everything is said and done, isn't this what really counts?

Notes
1. cf. Abraham J. Heschel, *God in Search of Man* (New York: Harper Torchbooks, 1960), p. 46.
2. cf. Thomas Merton, *New Seeds of Contemplation* (New York: New Directions, 1961), p. 14.
3. cf. the present writer's "Prayer, the Context of Discernment," *Review for Religious* (March, 1974), pp. 265-270.
4. This theme is developed in *The Spiritual Renewal of the American Priesthood*, edited by Ernest E. Larkin and Gerard T. Broccolo (Washington,

D.C.: U.S. Catholic Conference, 1973), where we read on p. 3, "Christian spirituality consists in the living out in experience, throughout the whole course of our lives, of the death-resurrection of Christ that we have been caught up into by baptism. It consists in living out in our day and in our lives the passage from sin and darkness to the light and warmth of God's gracious love."

5. The words of Reinhold Niebuhr come to mind here: "Nothing that is worth doing can be achieved in our lifetime; therefore we must be saved by hope." cf. *The Irony of American History* (New York: Charles Scribner's Sons, 1952).

6. cf. Gordon Allport, *The Individual and His Religion* (New York: Macmillan Publishing Company), p. 35.

7. cf. Abraham J. Heschel, *Man is Not Alone* (New York: Harper Torchbooks, 1966), p. 189.

EVALUATING MODELS

Richard P. McBrien
Pheme Perkins
Anthony J. Ipsaro
James W. Fowler

13.
Ethics: A Systematic Exploration

Richard P. McBrien

Richard P. McBrien surveys various ethical positions and offers criteria for evaluating their worth and relevance to religious educators.

This essay addresses three problems related to ethics and ethical reasoning: the problem of defining ethics; the problem of grounding ethical principles; and the problem of connecting ethical thinking with religion and theology. Controversy continues to surround each of these questions, and this article does not pretend to resolve centuries-old debates. It proposes only a way of viewing these issues in a more coherent and systematic manner.

I. *Defining Ethics*

"What ethics or moral philosophy is, and at best ought to be, has always been variously conceived by philosophers," Kai Nielsen suggests. "There is no uncontroversial Archimedean point from which ethics can be characterized, for the nature and proper office of ethics is itself a hotly disputed philosophical problem."[1] The same kind of observation could be made of several other important intellectual disciplines, not excluding theology. But lack of agreement can never justify lack of effort. Too often practitioners of various disciplines simply ignore the challenge of definition entirely. They address themselves in detail to one or another problem associated with a given field, and may even establish for themselves an extraordinarily substantial reputation in the process, but their written work rarely, if ever, confronts the fundamental issues in their scientific area. In Christian theology, for example, the fundamental issues have to do with revelation (i.e., the availability and knowability of God), the meaning and use of religious language, the interrelationship between faith and doctrine, and so forth. The situation here is beginning to improve.[2]

Ethicists seem as reluctant as their brothers and sisters in other academic disciplines to construct and defend straightforward definitions of their enterprise. Exceptions in any field are always gratefully received.[3] One of those in ethics is the text, *Approaches to Morality: Readings in Ethics from Classical Philosophy to Existentialism*, edited by Jesse Mann and Gerald Kreyche. Ethics herein is defined as "that practical philosophical study that seeks to find some principle of order for those human actions for which we are freely responsible and over which we have rational control."[4] In the simplest terms, ethics has to do with the free shaping of human behavior. As a separate discipline, ethics is a reflective examination of *how* we freely shape our behavior according to one or another set of criteria (descriptive ethics), and of *why* we *ought* to do so (normative ethics).

Ethics, whether descriptive or normative, is further subdivided into theological, professional, and philosophical. *Theological* ethics has to do (descriptively and/or normatively) with a general pattern or "way of life," as in Buddhist ethics or Christian ethics—about which more will be said in section III of this essay. *Professional* ethics has to do (whether descriptively or normatively) with sets of rules of conduct or "moral codes." And *philosophical* ethics has to do (descriptively or normatively) with an inquiry *about* ways of life and rules of conduct. Doctors and lawyers, for example, are immediately concerned with the second, professional ethics, but their concern cannot be divorced finally from the philosophical and, in some cases, from the theological. While every professional person brings to the study of ethical codes his or her experience of having made ethical decisions in connection with the supplying of professional services, what is required beyond this experience (or the memory thereof) is analysis at the philosophical level in order to provide some rational consistency to such actions. Action without such reflection may lead to unwarranted action or to action less appropriate than it could have been.

There are two subsidiary questions related to this general problem of definition: Are "ethics" and "morality" one and the same? What is social ethics?

Regarding the first: most commentators seem to agree that "ethics" and "morality" have the same meaning. The terms are employed interchangeably in most of the literature. But there is no unanimity either of theory or of practice. Indeed, "moral philosophy" rather than "morality" is the generally agreed-upon synonym for "ethics." Paul Lehmann is one author who does insist upon a distinction between ethics and morality. Morality, he suggests, applies to behavior according to custom, while ethics applies to behavior according

to reason, i.e., reflection upon the foundations and principles of behavior.[5] Because questions of a distinction between ethics and morality
cannot finally be resolved, it is important that we be clear about our
use of either or both term(s). I should argue for the view that "ethics"
has a much broader meaning than "morality," and therefore the two
terms ought not to be used interchangeably. "Morality" is coextensive
with *theological* ethics, but not with professional or philosophical
ethics.

Regarding the second subsidiary question: since ethics is, in a
sense, always social, a better adjective would be "societal." What we
really mean by "social ethics" is the evaluation of societal organization
and public policy in the shaping of the human community. Social
ethics is concerned with moral rightness and goodness in the construction of society. "Social ethics is, thus, the expression of ultimate commitments in the shaping of man's future, embodying a view of man
and his fulfillment in concrete recommendations for public policy."[6]

II. *Grounding Ethical Principles*

Neither is there any universally agreed-upon basis for grounding
all ethical principles and judgments. On the contrary, there are many
different starting points for the derivation of such principles and
judgments, the multiplicity of which history disconcertingly reveals.[7]

From the very beginning, the fundamental issue has been joined:
whether the formulation of ethical judgments be a critical process or
one not subject to rational analysis. It was Socrates' view that only by
the use of reason can we arrive at a set of ethical principles that can
reconcile self-interest with the common good and can apply to all people at all times—a view fashioned over against a prevailing notion in
fifth century B.C. Greek society that rules and norms of conduct are
based solely on religious and social traditions.

The same radical conflict between critical and uncritical reasoning
has also been present from the beginning in Christian theology as
well: various forms of positivism compete against various forms of
what Paul Tillich has called "the method of correlation."[8] The theological positivist holds that theology has its origin in one or another
isolated source, whether Sacred Scripture, the writings of the Fathers
of the Church, the doctrinal pronouncements of popes and ecumenical
councils, or combinations of these. For the positivist, theology is "the
study of the biblical message," or "the study of the teachings of the
church." The positivist never accounts for the *process;* he reflects
only on its various *products.* But it is the process, not the product,
that has to be defined if we are to come to some fundamental under-

standing of the nature and task of theology. The theologian who follows a "method of correlation," on the other hand, insists that the "message" (Sacred Scripture, writings of the Fathers, ecclesiastical documents, etc.) cannot be understood except in relation to, and indeed as an integral part of, the "situation" of human experience and human history. The texts of the tradition are proposed as answers to the perennial questions regarding human meaning and purpose, and these perennial questions, in turn, generate textual answers. The task of the theologian is to show the correspondence, or correlation, between the texts ("message") and human experience and history ("situation").[9]

So, too, from the very beginning have ethicists been divided along positivist and correlative lines. Post-Socratic developments should be read in the light of this basic tension between these two approaches.

Some have argued that ethics is grounded on self-evident axioms derived from ideal Forms, from which we can deduce subordinate principles almost mathematically (Plato and the seventeenth century Cambridge Platonists). For Aristotle whatever promotes personal happiness is good; whatever does not, is bad. Here the virtues dominate; in Hobbes, the passions are supreme.

The Epicureans appealed to personal pleasure as the primary warrant of ethical judgment. Augustine and the Christian tradition generally appealed to divine authority and our obligation of obedience to it. Ethics is the pursuit of the good, and God is the supreme good.

Aquinas, who integrated Aristotle with Augustine, insisted on the interplay between faith and reason, or, in the First Vatican Council's expression, "reason illuminated by faith." This balanced Thomistic approach is at the heart of much of the natural law tradition and is at work in such recent ecclesiastical documents as the social encyclicals of Pope John XXIII (e.g., *Pacem in Terris*), and the Second Vatican Council's Pastoral Constitution on the Church in the Modern World (*Gaudium et spes*), especially article 46 where it speaks of the necessity of relating the gospel with human experience.

Hobbes identified the passion of self-preservation as the basis of all law; Spinoza, metaphysical axioms or rules of nature, deterministically understood; Descartes and Leibniz, innate ideas. Utilitarianism, one of the most enduringly influential schools of ethical reasoning, insists that what is pleasant and useful is good (Locke, the French Encyclopedists, Hume, Bentham, Mill, Dewey, and James). Francis Hutcheson and Bishop Butler appealed to the benevolent affections which are natural and universal. Thomas Reid and Richard Price grounded everything upon common sense. Rousseau and Montesquieu spoke of certain social constructions, and Kant—another of the major forces in contemporary ethical reasoning—grounded ethical thinking in the perception of a duty that is universalizable: "Act only on that maxim which you can will to be a universal law." Such duty, he argued, is higher than pleasure or utility. It is the intention, not the consequence, of human action which determines its moral worth.

For Hegel ethics is rooted in custom and law which are part of a rational system of social and political institutions, which is itself possible only in the modern age of the national state, Christian conscience, and constitutional law. For Marx whatever is conducive to historical progress is good. Ethics is a matter of revolutionary praxis. For Schopenhauer the good is grounded in the universal will. Kierkegaard, on the other hand, pushed the various uncritical approaches to their ultimate, and perhaps their logical, conclusion: there are no objective grounds at all for ethical judgment. One makes a total commitment of faith attained by a leap. Nietzsche appealed to the creative self-assertion of the artist and genius; Sidgwick to self-evident principles perceived intuitively.

In the twentieth century intuitionism's disciples began to flourish. One cannot define what is good; either one is directly aware of it or not (G. E. Moore). Since we cannot give reasons for our obligations, we should not even try (H. A. Prichard). What are thoughtful and educated people thinking? (W. D. Ross). Empirical grounding is unnecessary and, in any case, impossible (F. Brentano). Ethics is about values. Our experience teaches us about them (N. Hartmann). When these values are in conflict, we must pursue the higher ones (M. Scheler).

A second twentieth century approach points to experience as the ground of moral knowledge (Dewey). One cannot separate theory from practice, and neither can an intrinsic good be separated from the consequences of an action (as Kant had suggested). Value judgments, for Dewey, are predictions about the capacity or incapacity of actions, objects, or events to satisfy desires, needs, and interests. As such they are confirmable or not. To say of something that it is valuable, desirable, or good is to say that it is something which would be desired or approved after reflection upon its relevant causes and consequences. (But, of course, it does not prove that X is desirable or ought to be desired.)

A third twentieth century approach is a cluster of so-called emotive theories. Moral statements express attitudes toward an action or state of affairs. Whatever in fact determines our attitudes is, by that very fact, a good reason for moral judgment (I. A. Richards, Bertrand Russell, A. J. Ayer, Charles Stevenson).

A fourth modern approach is existentialist. The world is absurd. All ethical standards are arbitrary (Camus). Principles are moral if they are universalizable, but there is no way of justifying them. Scarcity alone is the root of all conflict (Sartre). Philosophical ethics is to be rejected in principle (Heidegger).

A fifth twentieth century approach emerges from linguistic philosophy. Moral judgments are prescriptive. They function like the imperative mood, but they are different from simple imperative statements in that they are universalizable, i.e., they commit the speaker to making a similar judgment about anything which is either exactly like the subject of the original judgment or like it in relevant respects (R. M. Hare).

A sixth approach has been designated somewhat benignly as the "good reasons" theory. Moral judgment must be universalizable and it must be possible to give factual reasons in support of such judgments (Toulmin, Aiken, Nielsen, Rawls). This position reverses classic utilitarianism: a moral principle is justified if, consistently acted upon, it will most likely lead to the least amount of suffering all around. The "good reasons" proponents insist that their approach has two basic advantages over standard utilitarianism and other views: (1) it is easier to determine what makes us suffer than to say what makes us happy; and (2) this theory relieves us of the task of defining the good. The function of morality is the adjudication of conflicting interests and the harmonizing of desires in order to reconcile them with our fellows—in such a way that everyone can have as much as possible of whatever it is that, on reflection, he wants. (The egalitarian implication of this view has been vigorously opposed by R. Nozick.)

The preceding historical survey has been deliberately and unashamedly schematic. It was not intended as an analysis, even a superficial one, of various schools of ethical thought. Its purpose is to provide the reader—especially the overwhelming majority who are not academically involved in the field of ethics—with some general sense of the diversity and multiplicity of solutions that have, in fact, been offered as answers to the question, how is ethical judgment grounded? The schema also provides some readily discernible context against and within which my own position can be sketched out.

Which of the various approaches are to be preferred? That question is best answered by first identifying those approaches which are least attractive from the standpoint of one who prizes rationality and freedom as the distinctive marks of human existence.

First, I should reject every uncritical acceptance of ethical norms on the basis of custom and/or religious tradition. I should set aside, secondly, Kierkegaard's "leap of faith." Thirdly, the deceptively attractive norm of "common sense." Fourthly, all theories of intuition, without denying that there is always some measure of it in ethical judgments. Fifthly, all emotive theories, but with the same qualification. And sixthly, various selfish norms, e.g., personal pleasure, self-preservation, etc.

Over against these unacceptable (because uncritical and/or irrational) warrants, I should suggest the following general criteria:

First, ethical principles and judgments must proceed from reason (Socrates) that is truly attentive to experience (Dewey) and is, at the same time, open to the insights of all sources of knowledge and generators of experience, including religion which has made ethics an object of special concern (Aquinas, John XXIII, Vatican II). Religion and experience need not be opposed, since theology can itself be defined as the symbolization of experience. One should recall, furthermore, that there are critical religions and uncritical religions. The former do not consistently interpret their constitutional literature (e.g., Bible, Koran, etc.) in a fundamentalistic way, nor is their concept of revelation necessarily or inevitably positivistic and sectarian.

Secondly, whatever is good, right, and/or fit should somehow promote personal and/or the common welfare, i.e., it should, positively, maximize freedom and should, negatively, restrict oppression. It should promote growth rather than regression, life and the fulfillment of human potential rather than suffering and death.

The determination of the good, the right, and/or the fit presupposes a process of reasoning that is attentive to experience and open to all sources of knowledge and generators of experience, including religion.

III. Connecting Ethical Thinking with Religion and Theology

The relationship between ethical thinking and religion is not easily determined, but there are two extreme solutions which can be rejected at once. First, there is the right-wing insistence that all ethics is theological, and even Christian (Barth), or at the very least that philosophical ethics is insufficient (Lehmann).[10] (I should not want to argue that ethical principles, or morality, require religion.[11]) And secondly, there is the left-wing (secularist) prejudice that the religious or theological dimension is always irrelevant, adding nothing at all to ethical thinking. I should also want to dissociate myself from Max Weber's view that Christian ethics, as opposed to his "ethics of responsibility," is an "all or nothing" ethics of ultimate ends, and, therefore, of no real use in the larger socio-political order.

I should agree with Charles Curran that "what the Christian knows with an explicit Christian dimension is and can be known by all others. The difference lies in the fact that for the Christian his ethics is thematically and explicitly Christian."[12] Religious conviction, however, does *qualify* moral judgment because it qualifies the person making the judgment and the group within which he makes moral judgments.

Thus, James Gustafson insists that we need not be apologetic about the distinctiveness of Christian ethics, or of any other kind of ethics for that matter. The word "ethics" always needs a qualifying adjective, just as the word "theology" needs one. "Packed into the qualification," he writes, "is historic particularity and/or affective particularity (in the sense that there are loyalties to values or ways of life that will never be rationally persuasive to 'all rational human beings')."

"We are not going to get ethics unqualified," Gustafson concludes, "until we get rational minds unqualified by affectivity, or persons unqualified by particular histories, or knowledge of a moral order unqualified by historical and embodied experience."[13]

What does the "Christian" qualification contribute to the totality of ethical thinking and decision-making? "Christian ethics must continually recall the reality of sin and the call to conversion on the part of all individuals and societies," Curran writes. "A proper understanding of the paschal mystery in the life of the Christian will show forth the need for the ethical realities of self-sacrificing love, suffering, and hope in the Christian life."[14]

Accordingly, the distinction between philosophical and theological ethics should not be drawn simply on the basis that the former proceeds from reason and the latter from revelation. Both proceed from reason in touch with experience, but the theological method qualifies the reflective process by consciously and sympathetically introducing norms and values which are part of a religious symbol system or tradition, and accounts these as potentially helpful and illuminating to the task of so-called dispassionate or objective reasoning.

Notes

1. "Ethics, Problems of," *Encyclopedia of Philosophy*, D. Edwards, ed., vol. III (New York: Macmillan, 1967), p. 117.

2. See, for example, David Tracy, *Blessed Rage for Order: The New Pluralism in Theology* (New York: Seabury Press, 1975); Edward Schille-

beeckx, *The Understanding of Faith: Interpretation and Criticism* (New York: Seabury Press, 1975); Langdon Gilkey, *Naming the Whirlwind: the Renewal of God-Language* (Indianapolis: Bobbs-Merrill, 1969); and others.

3. For example, John Macquarrie, *Principles of Christian Theology* (New York: Scribners, 1966), p. 1.

4. (New York: Harcourt, Brace and World, 1966), p. 1.

5. See his *Ethics in a Christian Context* (New York: Harper & Row, 1963), pp. 24-5.

6. Gibson Winter, "Introduction," *Social Ethics: Issues in Ethics and Society*, G. Winter, ed. (New York: Harper & Row, 1968), p. 17. See also Paul Deats, "The Quest for a Social Ethic," in *Toward the Discipline of Social Ethics*, P. Deats, ed. (Boston University Press, 1972).

7. The rapid and highly compressed survey that follows is based on Kai Nielsen's article, "Ethics, History of," *op. cit.*, vol. III.

8. For a brief discussion of the positivist-versus-correlative methods in theology, see my *Church: the Continuing Quest* (New York: Newman Press, 1970), chapter 1.

9. Tillich's own description is contained in the first volume of his *Systematic Theology* (New York: Harper & Row, 1968). David Tracy's *Blessed Rage for Order* is an updated version of it. Tracy refers to his own method as "revisionist."

10. *Op. cit.*, pp. 268-84.

11. See, for example, P. H. Nowell-Smith, "Religion and Morality," in *Encyclopedia of Philosophy*, vol. VII, pp. 150-8.

12. "Is There a Catholic and/or Christian Ethic?" in *Proceedings of the Catholic Theological Society of America*, vol. 29 (Waterloo, Ontario: Council on the Study of Religion Press, 1974), p. 145.

13. "Response to Professor Curran," *Proceedings . . .*, p. 159. See also his *Can Ethics Be Christian?* (Chicago: University of Chicago Press, 1975).

14. *Op cit.*, p. 147.

14.
Interpreting Parables:
The Bible and the Humanities

Pheme Perkins

Story telling as a theological activity is a phenomenon which has recently engaged the imagination of religious educators. An analogous situation prevails among biblical scholars where some of the most interesting insights into Scripture have emerged from the study of the parables. Pheme Perkins critically examines those areas in the humanities which have made the most significant contributions to this ongoing study: most notably, existential philosophy, literary criticism, structural anthropology, linguistics and psychology. She then suggests to religious educators those approaches which will best promote the continuing relevance of the Bible among their students.

Introduction

In the past century input from several disciplines has contributed to the great expansion of biblical studies. Developments in historiography were applied to the Bible as scholars sought to obtain from the biblical records an accurate picture of the origins and development of the Jewish and Christian religions. Such a task could never have been conceived without the dramatic increase in our knowledge of biblical times that has resulted from the continuing work of archaeologists. We know much more about the language, culture and history within which the biblical works were written. The most general impact of our increased linguistic knowledge has been in the variety of new translations of the Bible. The positive side to this historical study has been an increasing ability to understand the message of the Bible within the context of its own time. We are better able to visualize the impact that the biblical authors had on those who first heard them and the problems that they were facing.

On the negative side, this intense concentration on what the Bible meant has led to uncertainty as to what the Bible could mean in our culture, which is so radically different from that in which it was written. The radical, theological pluralism (see Tracy, 1975) of our time leaves biblical scholars without a theological consensus on revelation to which they might appeal. Instead, there is a move toward other areas of the humanities as sources for an answer to the continued relevance of the Bible: most notably, existential philosophy, literary criticism, structural anthropology, linguistics and psychology. Those biblical scholars who maintain a strong traditional or neo-orthodox theological position usually do not see the need for such moves beyond the historical-critical study of the Bible. On the other hand, those who engage in such studies may have a variety of reasons for doing so, not least of which is the necessity to justify study of the Bible within the humanities program of the secular university or the public school system, contexts in which a theologically articulated doctrine of revelation is inadmissible.

These developments are clearly illustrated in contemporary studies of the parables of Jesus. The first part of this chapter will describe five methods being used to interpret parables: historical-critical; existential; literary-critical; structural, and psychological. The second and third parts use these methods to interpret the parable of the Wicked Tenants and that of the Prodigal Son. These comparisons display the strengths and weaknesses of each method. It should be noted at the outset that these approaches are not necessarily mutually exclusive, since they view the text from different viewpoints and are asking quite different questions.

Methods of Parable Analysis

1. *Historical-Critical:* This method is aimed at answering the question: what did a parable mean in the context of Jesus' ministry? It involves four procedures: study of the historical background; source criticism; form criticism; and redaction criticism. Most historical-critical study of the parables has aimed at discovering the teaching of Jesus (see Perrin, 1967). Study of the historical background to the parables seeks to explain the customs alluded to in the stories. Knowledge of the legal situation in Palestine (see Derrett, 1970) is crucial to both the parables we will discuss. In the case of the prodigal son, for example, we need to know what laws governed inheritance in order to understand how Jesus' audience would have reacted to the son's request.

Although almost forty years elapsed between the death of Jesus and the writing of the first gospel, the evangelists seem to have had other written sources for their work (see Lk. 1:1). At the beginning of the century, comparison of Mark and Luke and Matthew showed that the gospel of Mark seemed to have been used by the other two. In addition, they share a large number of sayings and teachings of Jesus—for example, the Lord's Prayer and the Beatitudes, not found in Mark. So, scholars supposed that there once must have existed a collecton of the teachings of Jesus—which they designate Q—used by the two evangelists. In 1945, a Coptic translation of a collection of sayings of Jesus, the Gospel of Thomas (GThs), was found in Egypt. This collection cannot have been Q, since it does not contain all of the material required (see Montefiore, 1962). But it does give alternate versions of some sayings and parables, including the Wicked Tenants, and incorporates others not found in the canonical gospels. On the whole, the material in GThs seems to be later than that in the canonical gospels. This means that GThs does not contribute much to our knowledge of Jesus, but it does show that collections like Q did exist in the early church. Finally, scholars ask about the material peculiar to each evangelist, like the prodigal son in Luke: could the evangelist have had some written source for that material as well? The method for detecting such earlier sources is to study the language of each gospel writer carefully. Where a section shows a large number of divergences from the usual language patterns and vocabulary of a writer, scholars suggest that he is copying an earlier source.

Since Jesus did not write anything himself, there was some period in which his sayings and deeds were transmitted orally. The forms in which the teachings of Jesus are put—sayings, parables, short controversy stories, etc.—are suited to such transmission. However, folklore studies have suggested to biblical scholars that material passed on orally from one person to another would be likely to undergo certain changes which could adapt the story to the normal story-telling patterns of the culture. Form-critical analysis, then, seeks to describe the patterns in which the teachings of Jesus were transmitted and to suggest types of modifications that may have occurred in a story or saying as it was passed on from person to person. By such analysis, form critics hope to recover the earliest version of a parable or saying and thus come as close as possible to the story Jesus told.

At the same time as scholars were concerned with recovering the original form and meaning of Jesus' teaching and the oral and written sources available to the evangelists, they were gaining new insight into the gospels as individual wholes. The very substantial differences between the gospels were seen to be not the results of careless editing or differences in sources, but the result of a conscious attempt by each evangelist to articulate in narrative form a theologically distinctive view of Jesus. The evangelist is not just the recorder of traditions; he provides them with an interpretation through his editing of particular material and his overall placing of them within the narrative. Redaction criticism is the study of each evangelist as author and theologian. We may ask of a given parable not only what did it mean to Jesus' audience but also what did it mean to each evangelist (see Carlston, *Parables*, 1975).

So far, the major emphasis in historical-critical study of the parables has been in the area of Jesus' meaning rather than in that of the evangelists' interpretation. This study is largely based on the work of C.H. Dodd and J. Jeremias. Subsequent historical-critical study of the parables has largely been a series of refinements on or footnotes to their work.

2. *Existential Analysis:* One answer to the question of the continued relevance of the Bible, which historical criticism had shown to be very much a book of its time, was found in the existential analysis of human beings and their mode of "being-in-the-world" (see Funk, 1966: 1-122). Jesus is seen to have presented an understanding of authentic existence in the world through his preaching of the "in-breaking" of God's rule. His sayings and parables are challenges to the audience to share that understanding of existence; to share the faith of Jesus. As cultural and historical situations change, that challenge will have to be reformulated in different words and symbols so that it can be heard and answered in a new context. The shift from Jesus' preaching about the kingdom to the Pauline kerygma of the cross and resurrection may be seen as such a transformation (Robinson, J.M., 1962). The philosopher Paul Ricoeur observes that existential interpretation is demanded by the very language Jesus uses in his sayings and parables. They claim to reveal the religious dimension in common human experience (Ricoeur: 127f.).

However, there is an additional postulate shared by most biblical scholars who use existential interpretation: the understanding of existence preached by Jesus is the only guide to authentic "being-in-the-world." Different views are less adequate or authentic. Undoubtedly, such a claim may be derived from Jesus' own preaching, especially his use of eschatological language. When this postulate informs a given existential interpretation of the Bible, that interpretation is no longer strictly philosophical but is theological.

3. *Literary Analysis:* In recent years, a variety of books and articles have applied methods of literary criticism to the Bible. Many result from Bible as literature courses in secondary schools and colleges. Biblical scholars often turn to such methods of anlaysis for different reasons. First, historical-critical analysis has tended to neglect

the narrative character of much of the Bible (see Frei, 1974). Yet recital and narrative are basic modes of biblical language. Both biblical scholars and theologians seek to recover the richness and possibility of narrative as a mode of theological reflection (see Wilder, 1971; TeSelle, 1975; Crossan, 1975). Secondly, the parables themselves are often introduced with the claim that they are images or metaphors, "the kingdom of God is like . . ." However, the parable as metaphor is more complex than those usually discussed in works of literary criticism, since the kingdom of God is being compared to the whole story, "what happens"; the plot is metaphor (see Ricoeur: 92-100).

Since this type of analysis of the parables as aesthetic creations is quite recent, there is no agreed-upon description of Jesus' use of these parable metaphors. However, certain themes recur in the various analyses. The parables begin with commonplace, familiar occurrences but provide a surprising twist in the plot, which runs counter to the expectation of the hearers (Crossan, 1975: 55-60; TeSelle: 69-72; Funk, 1975: 64-72, 102). A certain extravagance in the story demands that the reader view the ordinary as suddenly extraordinary (Ricoeur; 115-19) or that he question his own basic preconceptions about reality (TeSelle: 70-72).

Dan Via (Via, 1966) suggests classifying the parables by plot. A parable is tragic if the protagonist moves from better to worse; comic if from worse to better (see also Ricoeur: 37ff). He observes that the parables are usually focused on a crisis or decision which the protagonists negotiate successfully or unsuccessfully. Thus, the parables of Jesus focus on confrontation and decision. TeSelle (75-80) points out that this focus is essential to the function of the parables: to reorient the willing of the hearers, not only their knowing. This type of literary analysis is closely tied to the existentialist stress in crisis and decision, as Via points out.

4. *Structural Analysis:* Structuralism is one of the widespread intellectual movements of our time (see Lane, 1970). Like its counterparts in other fields, the application of structuralism to literature derives from its use in linguistics (Scholes, 1974). A genuinely structuralist analysis does not deal with the details of an individual work—unlike the literary criticism—nor does it consider the individual author, i.e. Jesus as teller or composer of parables. Rather, it claims to discover an invariant set of functions, relationships or processes not subject to the conscious control of author or hearer. These invariants govern all particular instances of the phenomenon being studied. The meaning of a phenomenon is in its structure. This claim directly contradicts the aesthetic critic, who assumes that an author uses a con-

sciously chosen and articulated literary form to convey meaning to readers, who in turn understand the meaning of a work on the basis of their conscious perception of its genre (Wittig: 172; Ricoeur: 71). Much of what is called "structural analysis" by biblical scholars is really this latter type of genre analysis. Their interest in the specificity of Jesus' message and use of language has largely prevented acceptance of the universalist, ahistorical claims of structural analysis. Structural analysis cannot logically be connected with either the historical or the existential approaches (Ricoeur: 45-64).

Nevertheless, there have been several attempts to apply the narrative analysis developed by A. J. Greimas to biblical materials, including the parables. Greimas argues that certain basic functions are actualized in every narrative. These "actants" may be arranged in a diagram representing six pairs:

ADDRESSER ————→ OBJECT ————→ ADDRESSEE
HELPER ————→ SUBJECT ————→ ADVERSARY

In a specific story, the actant roles need not be semanticized by characters; objects, emotions or attitudes may be used. More than one character may play a given role or a character may fill more than one slot.

Further, the narrative sequence follows an unvarying order represented by a sequence of syntagms, which may be interrupted by subsequences. The narrative may end at any point at which a syntagm is not completed.

I. *Contractual Syntagm:*

Contractual Utterance (CU) 1: The subject accepts or rejects the task (contract) set before him, which is to form the basis of the plot. Often the introduction alludes to previous failures to perform the same contract.

CU 2: If the subject accepts, a helper must then be provided.

II. *Disjunctional Syntagm:* The subject must leave his normal environment and relationships if he is to carry out the contract.

III. *Performance Syntagm:*

PU 1: The subject is confronted by the Addressee's need for the Object.

PU 2: The subject must subdue the Adversary.

PU 3: The subject must deliver the object to the addressee.

IV. *Disjunctional Syntagm:* The subject returns to the environment and relationships that he left at the opening of the narrative.

A particular story may have the subject fail at any point in the sequence and may be complicated by a variety of subplots.

Several ambiguities arise in applying the schema. Sometimes it is not clear how to determine the subject. Is it the main actor? The person from whose viewpoint the story is told? The subject of the majority of the sentences? The "subject" may vary within a story if subsequences are part of the larger whole. Nor is it clear which level of analysis is required. Some authors provide an actant diagram as well as a syntagmic analysis for every statement of narrative action. Others—who use the procedure adopted here—discuss only the story as a whole and its overall progress. Further ambiguities arise when not all of the slots in the actant diagram are semanticized.

Thus, ambiguities in the interpretation of a narrative may result from the unclarity in one or more of the actant categories, which makes one clear reading of the story impossible. Further, it may not be clear—as is the case in some of Via's "tragic" parables—at which point the narrative sequence fails. Finally, since each evangelist has set the parables of Jesus in a specific context, we may find that the evangelist has used his context to decide certain ambiguous points. Regardless of the universality of the structuralist claims, the attempt to apply such a well-defined, formal scheme to a narrative does highlight ambiguities and nuances in the plot which might escape a less disciplined reading.

5. *Psychological Analysis:* Although there have been psychological interpretations of literature and even of the Bible around for some time, competent biblical scholars have only just turned their attention in that direction. Such analysis is similar to structuralism in that the narrative is seen as the product of unconscious, universal processes and conveys meaning because these same psychic structures are present in the hearers (Wittig: 172). The two psychological analyses of a parable—one Freudian and one Jungian—are both of the prodigal son. Both find the meaning of that parable in the psychological dynamics of reconciling conflicting elements within the personality. Lacking further analysis, one would suppose that this particular pattern of interpretation could only be applied to those parables that fall into Via's "comic" category. One may also raise the question—approached by the structuralists from a different perspective (Ricoeur: 100f)—as to whether the method allows for analysis of a single parable. Few analysts would diagnose a patient on the basis of a single dream. At the very least the parables should be treated in groups, if not as a whole.

In one way or another, the last four methods of interpretation contrast with the historical in their claim to provide access to the present, universally valid meaning of the parables. Existential and literary analysis may build on the results of historical criticism insofar as the latter illuminates the competing modes of self-understanding or literary expression contemporary with biblical authors. But the last two claim to be radically ahistorical: neither the deep structure of narrative nor the inner dynamics of the psyche are subject to historical conditioning. Having sketched the methods of analysis being pursued, we may now turn to specific examples.

THE WICKED TENANTS (Mk. 12:1-9 parr.)

1. *Historical-critical:* Versions of this parable occur in all three synoptics and GThs. None of the versions are identical, so a major question for the critic is what was the form of the parable that lies behind these variants.

(a) *Historical Background:* The type of contract entered into by the owner and the tenants is well represented among papyri finds in Egypt. In some instances, the particular duties of the tenants in caring for the vineyard, harvesting and storing the crop are spelled out in detail. It is not unusual for the landlord to live in a different city or village from that in which his vineyard and tenants are located. Sometimes the tenants are to be paid for their work out of the produce of the vineyard. In other contracts, their wages include money as well as produce. The tenants may also guarantee the owner a certain profit on the vineyard, which they must pay regardless of the agricultural circumstances in a given year. Thus the owner has a guaranteed return on his investment. Such contracts include assurances that everything will be done at the proper time, that the landlord may send his agents to check on the tenants, and that the rent will be paid when due. Economic conditions were similar in Palestine, and the audience must have understood Jesus to be referring to a similar agreement.

Though many ingenious solutions have been tried (for example Jeremias: 74ff.) no one has been able to show that the tenants' claim that they would inherit the vineyard at the death of the son has any legal basis. Barring new evidence, it seems reasonable to assume that the claim is intended to be outrageous—not a reflection of reality—and that Jesus' audience would have understood it as such.

(b) *Source Analysis:* In addition to the synoptic versions, the following is found in the Gospel of Thomas:

A good man had a vineyard. He let it to workers so that they might work it and he receive its fruit from them. He sent his servant for the workers to give him the fruit of the vineyard. They seized his servant. They beat him—a little longer and they would have killed him. The servant returned. He told his master. His master said, "Perhaps they did not recognize him." He sent another servant. The workers beat the other one. Then the master sent his son. He said, "Perhaps they will be respectful of my son." Those workers, since they knew him to be the heir of the vineyard, seized him. They killed him.

(GThs 65; translation by the author)

Some scholars (see Crossan, 1973: 91-95) claim that this version is an example of an earlier form of the story than that in the synoptics. It lacks any allegorical allusions, is less exaggerated in its treatment of the servants, and has a more plausible explanation for the master's sending of his son.

However, Montefiore (51; 64f.) observes that GThs is generally less allegorical than its synoptic counterparts and often lacks Old Testament allusions found in the latter. He argues that the versions copied into GThs were probably independent of the synoptics but that that independence does not imply use of traditions closer to the original. One may further argue that GThs avoids the two features of the parable which cause the interpreter difficulty: (1) the explicit claim that the tenants expect to inherit the vineyard; (2) the seeming irrationality of the master in sending his son into such dangerous circumstances. Simplification of difficulties usually occurs as a story is passed on. In this case, the motivation for killing the heir is left out and the story left somewhat truncated. Thus it seems more likely that GThs is a later stage in a story which originally contained the difficulties mentioned.

(c) *Form and Redaction Criticism:* Our discussion of GThs as a possible source for an early version of the story has already appealed to some form-critical judgments on the transmission of stories in rejecting that version. GThs also ends without any allusion to the master's reaction. Most interpreters agree that the original probably ended with the question (Mk. 12:9a)—a device typical of Jesus (Crossan, 1973: 111; Smith: 133). In the parable tradition, allegorical details are often included or expanded to refer the hearer to Jesus or the church. The answer added to the question clearly contrasts the Christians, the new tenants, with the Jews. All three evangelists have interpreted the servants sent by the master as allegorical references to the Old Testament prophets and expanded the details accordingly. Mark even includes John the Baptist. Matthew and Luke make the son's death take place outside the vineyard, a closer parallel to the death of Jesus outside Jerusalem (Crossan, 1973: 86-90). Because folktales usually work on a pattern of three, most assume that originally two groups of servants were sent to the tenants and followed by the son (see Dodd: 100 n. 1, who also observes that "beloved" is characteristic of the third son in folktales).

Without these additions the parable would read as follows:

> A man planted a vineyard, (and set a hedge around it, and dug a pit for the wine press, and built a tower and let it out to tenants,) and went into another country. When the time came he sent a servant to the tenants to get from them some of the fruit of the vineyard. And they took him and beat him, and sent him away empty-handed. Again he sent them another servant, and they beat him and treated him shamefully. He had still one other, a beloved son. Finally he sent him to them, saying, "Perhaps they will respect my son." But those tenants said to one another, "This is the heir. Come, let us kill him and the inheritance will be ours." And they took him and killed him and cast him out of the vineyard. What will the owner of the vineyard do? (RSV)

Some scholars, following Jeremias (70), would exclude the material in parentheses—an allusion to Isaiah, 5:2—from the original. They claim that it was added when the parable was interpreted allegorically to refer to Israel and observe that GThs and Luke lack the allusion. Others (Dodd: 97ff.; Carlston, *Parables:* 185) point out that Luke's parables often show a tendency to de-allegorize, that the comparison of Israel to a vineyard was well known and is fundamental to the impact of the story. (A similar division of opinion is found with other allusions to the O.T. in Jesus' parables.) The allegorical interpretation that reads the parable as contrasting Christians and Jews does not require Israel to be the vineyard, since it makes Israel the first tenants. In Isaiah 5, on the other hand, Israel is a vineyard carefully tended by God. When it fails to produce fruit, it is destroyed. Some object that the implied allegory master=God is inconsistent with the characterization of the owner in the story. Again, on the principle that including the allusion is a more difficult reading and would make it more likely to be dropped, we would retain it.

What, then, did the original story mean? There are almost as many views on this point as interpreters. To a certain extent, an interpretation of one of Jesus' parables depends on a given scholar's overall view of Jesus and his ministry. Crossan's claim (1973: 96) that Jesus deliberately tells a story of a successful and shocking murder rests on the view that Jesus' parable-telling as a whole is structured on reversal, on shattering the hearer's sense of the normal world. While one can hardly deny that the parables present challenges and surprises, Crossan's view owes more to contemporary fascination with religious language as paradox than to first century parallels. Further, the concluding question suggests the eventual doom facing the tenants. Plausible historical interpretations center around two poles: either Jesus is referring to his own ministry, or he is referring to God. Those who see this parable as referring to Jesus suggest either that it intends to vindicate his preaching to the poor and outcast against Pharisaic criticism (Jeremias: 76) or that he is condemning his own generation and hinting at the fate he expects to befall him (Dodd: 102). Both interpretations are found in the settings given the parable by the evangelists.

The difficulty with such views is that Jesus rarely—if ever—talks about himself in his parables. The common introduction claims them as an analogy for what God's rule (= kingdom) is like. On that reading, the focus of the story would not be on the tenants but on the slowness with which the master takes action. The Isaiah quote sets up an analogy—not an allegory, since we have already seen that the detailed correspondence required by allegory is not present—between the master and God. Smith (134) suggests that the audaciousness of the tenants is to be viewed as their false response to the leniency and forbearance of the master. In light of similar legal contracts, we may even suggest that that behavior was provoked by his failure to send agents to check on the tenants' progress prior to the demand for rent. That would suggest that God's rule is as radically forbearing as the master's. But one should not be deceived by that phenomenon into thinking that "anything goes." This interpretation would fit in with such explicit teaching on God's forbearance as that in Matthew 5:43-48. One may further assume that it is the vision of God presented in such parables that both motivates Jesus' preaching to the "religious nobodies" and provokes the hostility that leads to his death.

2. *Existential Interpretation:* Two types of existential interpretation may be applied to the Bible (see Via, 1966: 135-37). A purely existential interpretation, applicable to any type of literature, would exclude all references to God. Using the theological position that holds that all human God-talk is about our "being-in-the-world," one might see this parable as a comment on the human refusal to accept limitations (Via: 136). We always seek to be master, to dominate our world and others no matter how terrible the cost of such action. Via (137) even sees the vineyard setting as suggesting that this mode of human

behavior not only destroys other people but also our relationship to nature.

Theologians propose a second type of existential interpretation, which preserves the God reference in biblical language. The parable is one of "unfaith" (Via: 137). It shows what becomes of our efforts to reject the limitations God has placed upon us. We reach a state of appalling inhumanity. Even worse, we are totally ignorant not only of the absurdity of our actions but also of the destruction that they will ultimately bring upon us.

3. *Literary Analysis:* Unlike the usual tragic or comic plot sketched by Via, this parable is strangely unresolved. The hearer expects doom to come upon the protagonists (Via: 134), but that amorphous "doom to come" is all one has to give shape to one's expectations. One may imagine a "recognition scene" and go away from the story with the "well won't they be surprised" feeling. One imagines this story to eventually follow the tragic denouement. Further ambiguity is introduced by the possibility of seeing the owner as the subject of our story. In that case, the story ends on a tragic "good guys finish last" note with barely enough of a hint at an upturn from the master's perspective to prevent our wholehearted assent to that piece of conventional wisdom.

Those who suggest that Jesus' parables are often satirical or ironic (see Crossan, 1975: 99f.; Funk, 1975: 23, 60-63) raise a further literary question. They suggest that Jesus has intentionally exaggerated, inverted and parodied well-known images from daily life and from Israel's religious tradition as part of his attempt to present a new religious vision. The Isaiah allusion sets up the vision of God that is to be pushed to the extreme (Ricoeur: 115). God is not merely the careful owner of a vineyard, which he destroys when it fails him, but he even refuses to move against it until what he loves most and cannot replace has been destroyed instead. Even then, one has the uneasy feeling that he might delay the threatened vengeance. God has a strange passivity that seems willing to suffer any evil rather than to destroy it.

4. *Structural Analysis:* According to the usual linguistic model, ambiguities in an utterance result from incomplete semanticization of the underlying deep structure. The hearer may construe the sentence according to several patterns. The ambiguities already encountered in interpreting this parable suggest that we will encounter structural ambiguities as well. Two possible actant diagrams may be suggested:

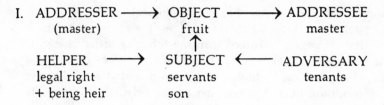

I. ADDRESSER ⟶ OBJECT ⟶ ADDRESSEE
    (master)   fruit   master
                        ↑

    HELPER ⟶ SUBJECT ⟵ ADVERSARY
    legal right   servants   tenants
    + being heir   son

II. (themselves) ⟵ vineyard ⟶ tenants
                     ↑

    strength of ⟶ tenants ⟵ master
    numbers

The ambiguous position of the master in the story can then be seen as the result of the fact that he never takes the position of actantial subject—even though the story may well be about him. The ending leads us to expect a sequel to the story in which the following obtains:

III. (master) ⟶ vineyard ⟶ master
                 ↑

    force of arms ⟶ master ⟵ tenants

Precisely the conclusion reached by the evangelists. But, even here, the story is incomplete. The master has not been able to exercise his legal rights in the normal manner to gain the original object, profit from the vineyard. He must start over again with another group of tenants. Will they be any better than the first group? Only Matthew resolves that ambiguity by stating that the second group will fulfil the terms of the lease.

Thus, Matthew alone explicitly expresses the successful completion of the narrative sequence stipulated in the opening syntagm. Other versions are indefinite. The sequence has aborted three times at the point of confrontation. Neither the master nor the tenants as addressees initially obtain the object involved. We may all unconsciously "fill in" the successful conclusion that Matthew supplies, but formal analysis reveals the ambiguity of the other versions at that point. They, in turn, are less ambiguous than the initial version in that they semanticize more of a further sequence suggested by the concluding question. We are less uncertain as to whether the master will at last take up the role of subject. But with each resolution of the parable's semantic ambiguity, another facet of its interpretation is decided and the wealth of possibilities provided by the original is reduced.

5. *Psychological Analysis:* No psychological analysis of this parable has yet been undertaken by a New Testament scholar. It seems clear that it cannot be forced into the schemes of psychic harmony used for the Prodigal Son. On the surface, one might suggest that the psychodynamics of human aggression and destructiveness would be appropriate here. Via could, perhaps, identify the tenants with the Jungian ego concept (Via, 1975: 225). In the ego's alienation from the self (= master) it becomes inflated beyond its proper limits. Rejecting all messages and warnings presented by the unconscious, the ego continues on its disastrous course to destruction (insanity?) rather than to reconciliation and psychological maturity.

THE PRODIGAL SON (Lk. 15: 11-32)

1. *Historical-Critical Interpretation:* The only version of this parable is in Luke. The interpreter must try to discover the shape of the story as it came to Luke from that version.

(a) *Historical Background:* Legal information clarifies the situation in this parable. A father might distribute his property in advance to avoid conflict between his sons after his death. The eldest son would inherit the family farm. As long as the father remained alive, he would still have the right to run the property. But he could no longer sell it or make it over to someone else without the consent of the eldest son. And, if the eldest son chose to sell the farm, the buyer would not get it until after the father's death. As far as we can tell, it would have been acceptable for a younger son to sell his share of the inheritance and go elsewhere (Jeremias: 128f.). We must presume that his "sin" consists in squandering his property and adopting the occupation of swineherd, one which Jews considered equivalent to becoming a "gentile sinner."

(b) *Source Criticism:* Since we have no other versions of this story, the source question is whether Luke had a source at his disposal for all or only part of the parable or whether the whole is his own composition. Carlston (*JBL*, 1975: 368-83) has carried out a detailed analysis of the language of the parable and compared it with Lucan style. His study shows that both parts of the parable contain a high enough proportion of non-Lucan linguistic features to suggest that he has copied a source, which he revises in much the same way that he does when he uses Mark or Q. The source is responsible for the details of Jewish life and thought that are uncharacteristic of Luke (379).

(c) *Form and Redaction Criticism:* Carlston's analysis would support those scholars who agree with Jeremias that this is a double-edged parable (131) against claims that the original ended with the

younger son's return in verse 24. He points out that those who claim
that Luke added the second part not only have linguistic evidence
against them, but the theological orientation within Luke as well. Luke
is characteristically a moralist, who understands repentance as turning
away from evil conduct. He uses this story because of the element of
repentance in the first part. Had Luke composed the second part, some
moral comment or call for repentance would have been made about
the elder son (Carlston: 386f.). Jeremias (37 f.) makes the further claim
that in parables which have this double form the emphasis is on the
second member of the pair. If such an interpretation is accepted, it
would run contrary to most of our habits in interpreting this parable.

In the following text of the parable those expressions typical of
Luke are in italic (see Carlston: 369-73):

> *And he said,* "There was a man who had two sons; and
> the younger of them said to his father, "Father, give me the
> share of the property that falls to me." And he divided his
> living between them. *Not many days later,* the younger son
> gathered *all* that he had and took his journey into *a far
> country,* and there he squandered his property in loose liv-
> ing. And *when he had spent everything, a great* famine arose
> *in that country* and he began to be in want. So he *went and
> joined himself to* one of the *citizens* of that country, who
> sent him into the fields to feed swine. And he would gladly
> have fed on the pods that the swine ate; and no one gave him
> anything. But *when he came to himself he said,* "How many
> of my father's servants have bread enough and to spare, but
> I perish here with hunger! *I will arise and go* to my father,
> and I will say to him, Father, I have sinned against heaven
> and *before* you. I am no longer worthy to be called your son.
> Treat me as one of your hired servants." And he *arose and
> came* to his father. *But while he was yet at a distance,* his fa-
> ther saw him and had compassion, and ran and *embraced
> him and kissed him.* And the son said to him, "Father, I have
> sinned against heaven and *before* you; I am no longer
> worthy to be called your son." But the father said to his ser-
> vants, "Bring quickly the best robe and put it on him and
> put a ring on his hand and shoes on his feet; and bring the
> fatted calf and kill it, and let us eat and make merry; for this
> my son was dead, and is alive again; was lost and is found."
> And they began to make merry.
>
> Now his elder son was in the field, and as he *came and*

drew near to the house he heard *music and dancing*. And he called one of the servants and *asked what this meant*. And he said to him, "Your brother has come and your father has killed the fatted calf, *because he has received him safe and sound*." But he was angry and refused to go in. His father came out and entreated him, but he answered his father, *"Lo these many years I have served you*. I have never disobeyed your command; yet you never gave me a kid that I might make merry with my friends. But when this son of yours came, who had devoured your living with harlots, you killed for him the fatted calf." And he said to him, "Son, you are always with me, and all that is mine is yours.

"It was fitting to *make merry and be glad* for this your brother was dead, and is alive; he was lost and is found."

The younger son's internal dialogue in deciding to return is also typical of Luke. (He provides a similar dialogue for the master in the Wicked Tenants.) He likes to have the content of an earlier narrative repeated later as the servant and the elder brother do in the second part. The final sentence of the parable, a repetition of what the father has said earlier, may also be Luke's conclusion to the entire chapter. He has organized chapter 15 around the theme of Jesus' table fellowship with sinners as a sign of heavenly rejoicing over the repentant sinner (cp. Scott: 191). Luke's modifications have left the basic structure of the story unchanged.

The twofold structure of the parable has been the major difficulty for interpreters. A satisfactory interpretation must include both halves of the parable. For that reason, most interpreters have accepted the suggestion Luke makes by the context in which he puts the parable: it concerns Jesus' association with sinners. One need not allegorize the story to see it as an example of Jesus' attitude not only toward sinners but also toward the righteous and dutiful son. Carlston has pointed out forcefully that the elder brother is *not* made into a sinner in this story. His claim is in fact asserted (387). Thus, interpretations which turn this parable into a reversal of good/dutiful vs. evil/prodigal (so Crossan, 1973: 74f.) seem to go too far beyond the text. Jesus' images for the kingdom tend more toward inclusivity than toward polar reversal. Or, God can love the sinner without hating the righteous.

2. *Existential Interpretation:* Both sons have the same understanding of existence as governed by law, duty and merit. Both assess their lives, actions and individual worth in terms of what they are owed. They expect others to respond to them within the same frame-

work. But the father does not respond within the context defined by their understanding. When he responds instead with love and acceptance that is not defined positively or negatively by the merit system, that understanding of existence is shown up as limiting, deadening and petty. Human life and personal worth conceived within the framework of law and duty is shown to be less than authentic, enriching and joyful.

A theological reading, which Via notes (172-175) is subsidiary to the parable's focus on the present, would see the possibility of such a new understanding as given in Jesus' vision of God. He shatters the boundaries defined by law, duty and merit when applied to God's forgiveness and makes it possible for the believer to live out of such a new self-understanding in this world with one's brother or sister, the sinner and even one's enemy.

3. *Literary Analysis:* Via argues that the younger son is the protagonist throughout the narrative. He must invoke verse 32 as evidence that the second part fits into that focus (1967: 165-67). Luke's arrangement of chapter 15 would agree with Via's claim that the prodigal's decision to return home is the dramatic turning point of the plot (168). Jeremias (128f.) is probably closer to the truth. He insists that the parable be entitled "the father's love." That perspective would make the scenes between the father and his sons "recognition scenes" in which the plot takes its decisive turn toward the comic resolution which characterizes the story in any reading.

Another mode of analysis, which may be pursued on a literary level or on a structural one, would compare this story with other Old Testament stories of older and younger brothers. Scott (198-201) pursues this theme as an example of a binary opposition mediated by the story in the manner of Claude Levi-Strauss. Gal. 4:1, for example, shows that a first-century author could make conscious use of such stories. Therefore, it would seem more appropriate to understand this motif as an example of Jesus' intentional ironic modification of Old Testament symbols and stories.

Anyone familiar with the Old Testament stories of two brothers would have a certain plot in mind as soon as the story is introduced. It would be tied to the Old Testament stories which make inheritance the issue between the two brothers. On the basis of that pattern, the hearers would expect that the father loves the younger son more than the elder; that the elder brother would have some negative quality of stupidity or resentment—the negative element makes his rejection somewhat more acceptable; that the younger son would be clever and return home successful; and that the younger son would somehow obtain all, or a much greater share than at first, of the inheritance. With this pattern in mind, it is clear that Jesus does not tell the type of story his audience would expect to follow his introduction. Only the slightly churlish behavior of the elder brother is retained from the standard story. The younger brother does not show any ingenuity or cleverness. He loses *all* of his inheritance. Thus, unlike the usual pattern which ends with a status reversal between the elder and younger brother, Jesus' story preserves the status of the elder, while insisting upon the joyful acceptance of the younger brother, who returns a failure, not a success. One might suppose that the elder brother should be glad he has such a stupid younger sibling. On the literary level, then, Jesus has drastically reworked the traditional story pattern so that both brothers may be included in the final "happy ending."

4. *Structural Analysis:* The structural ambiguity in the parable derives from the alternation of subjects (see Scott: 191-96). The Lucan context of the story understands it to be semanticizing the following actantial diagram:

I. God $\longrightarrow$ forgiveness $\longrightarrow$ younger son
$\uparrow$ (sinners)
father $\longrightarrow$ younger son $\longleftarrow$ older son
(Jesus)   (sinners)   legalism
(Pharisees)

The appearance of the father in the helper role makes it possible for the younger son to attain the object, forgiveness.

In line with our literary analysis of two brothers stories, one might suggest the following actantial diagram being worked out in a narrative which likewise attains the desired object:

II. custom $\longrightarrow$ inheritance $\longrightarrow$ eldest son
law
$\uparrow$
(duty) $\longrightarrow$ eldest son $\longleftarrow$ younger brother
father

In the traditional tales, the dutifulness of the eldest son is never sufficient to overcome the cleverness of the favored younger son. Jesus' story implies that the elder brother succeeds not merely out of duty or because his younger brother is less gifted than usual but because the father—unlike the usual pattern—is revealed as his helper too.

Finally, some commentators have tried to see the father as the overall subject of the story (see Scott: 194-96):

III.   ?   ⟶   two sons   ⟶   father
     (father?)
                              ↑
     (his position   ⟶   father   ⟵   sons' perception of
     as father; younger   duty as the basis of
     son's need?)   their relationship to
                                     the father

In this view, the sons, or their attitude, are opponents of the father's project. While casting the father as subject might seem closer to the view that this parable is about "the father's love," the strong literary parallels between this story and others about two brothers suggest that the brothers are the subject of the narrative. On the structural level, we might compare the use of the father in this parable with that in the Wicked Tenants. The father—who may be analogous to God—semanticizes a nonsubject slot. There, as adversary; here, as helper.

The narrative sequence with the elder brother as subject is left uncompleted. The interpretation of the story followed here presumes that the reader completes the story with the elder son's submission to the father. But many interpreters read the elder brother sequence as implying failure: he remains outside.

5. *Psychological Analysis:* Both a Freudian (Tolbert) and a Jungian (Via, 1975) interpretation have been suggested for the parable. Although the terminology and picture of intrapsychic dynamics differ between the two schools of analysis, both interpreters seek a model which culminates in the reconciliation of conflicting psychological drives. All the figures in the parable are treated as entities in the dream life of a single individual. But the narrative structure of the parable leads both interpreters to treat it as though it recounted the entire process of psychological integration. In the Freudian view, the precarious balance struck by the ego (= father) between the unrestrained pleasure principle, or id, which violates all norms (= younger son), and the harsh, judgmental stance of the super-ego (= elder brother) is represented here. In the Jungian interpretation, it is the process of the ego (= both brothers) alienated from the self (= father) becoming reconciled with the self through a process of integrating elements from the shadow (weak, unconscious or evil) side of the personality.

Several methodological questions arise. First, if we are to treat a parable as a reflection of unconscious, intrapsychic processes, can we use one parable to illustrate the whole process? Dreams are also narrative in character, but it requires a whole series of them to illustrate the processes described here. Both Freud and Jung deal in cases when they present such material, and we might expect all the parables to constitute a single case. Secondly, one may ask whether or not the authors have chosen the appropriate level of psychological interpretation. The Freudian and post-Freudian analyses of inner family psychodynamics would seem more appropriate to a story about older and younger brothers—sibling rivalry is quite openly expressed in the stories of this type. Further discussion will be required to resolve the complex methodological questions involved in using psychological theories as a basis for interpreting the parables of Jesus.

CONCLUSION

Because the parables are a type of religious language that seeks to persuade the audience to adopt new vision and action, they involve many dimensions of human experience. The declarative sentence, "The Prodigal Son shows that God's love is boundless," will never capture all the meaning of that parable. Such a sentence does not involve the hearer in the same process of surprise and discovery that the rearrangement of his familiar story patterns does. When he changes the story line, Jesus dares his hearers to imagine that a different type of relationship is possible for those who live out of his vision of God (see Tracy: 131-34).

The use of concrete narrative as analogy for the rule of God suggests that it will never be possible—or indeed, even desirable—to ascribe a single, univocal interpretation to one of the stories. It is in the nature of parable to have more than one meaning (Wittig: 173-80). The interpreter must choose those methods of interpretation suited to the questions he or she brings to the biblical story.

Any literature teacher can testify that students find it difficult to adjust to the idea that most literary works cannot be assigned a single, univocal meaning. The different methods of parable interpretation provide the religious educator with a variety of approaches to biblical material. All audiences are fascinated by historical information about the world Jesus lived in. Psychological interpretation, on the other hand, remains pretty limited to groups with some prior knowledge of the psychoanalytic personality theories being employed. Once introduced to the techniques of existential, literary or structural analysis, students can begin to use them in creating their own interpretations of the Bible, since they do not require the detailed philological and historical knowledge that historical criticism does. If the Bible is to be more to Christians than just another "great book," the religious educator must encourage students to develop their own understandings of biblical narrative. Only then will the parables engage twentieth century readers in the process of liberating, religious vision inaugurated at their first telling.

Works Consulted

Parables in general:

Carlston, C.
1975   *The Parables of the Triple Tradition.* Philadelphia: Fortress Press.

Crossan, J.D.
1973   *In Parables.* New York: Harper & Row.

Derrett, J.D.M.
1970   *Law in the New Testament.* London: S.P.C.K.

Dodd, C.H.
1963 (1947[1])   *The Parables of the Kingdom.* New York: Schribner's.

Gouldner, M.D.
1968   "Characteristics of the Parables in the Several Gospels." *JTS* 19: 51-68.

Jeremias, J.
1963   *The Parables of Jesus.* rev. ed. New York: Scribner's.

Linnemann, E.
1966   *Parables of Jesus.* London: S.P.C.K.

Perrin, N.
1967   *Rediscovering the Teaching of Jesus.* New York: Harper & Row.

Robinson, J.M.
1962   "The Formal Structure of Jesus' Message," W. Klasser & G. Snyder eds. *Current Issues in New Testament Interpretation.* New York: Harper & Row. pp. 91-110.

Smith, C.W.F.
1975   *The Jesus of the Parables.* rev. ed. Philadelphia: Pilgrim Press.

Via, D.O.
1966   *The Parables.* Philadelphia: Fortress Press.

The Prodigal Son
Carlston, C.
1975   "Reminiscence and Redaction in Lk 15:11-32," *JBL* 94: 368-90.

O'Rourke, J.J.
1971/72   "Some notes on Lk XV. 11-32," NTS 18: 431-33.

Sanders, J.T.
1968/69   "Tradition and Redaction in Lk 15: 11-32." NTS 15: 433-38.

Scott, B.
1975   "The Prodigal Son: A Structuralist Interpretation." SBL 1975 Seminar Papers vol 2. Missoula: Society of Biblical Literature. pp. 185-206.

Tolbert, M.
1975   "The Prodigal Son: An Essay in Literary Criticism from a Psychoanalytic Perspective." SBL 1975 Seminar Papers vol 2. pp. 207-18.

Via, D.O.
1975   "The Prodigal Son: A Jungian Reading." SBL 1975 Seminar Papers vol. 2. pp. 219-32.

The Wicked Tenants
Crossan, J.D.
1971   "The Parable of the Wicked Husbandmen." JBL 90: 451-75.

Montefiore, H.
1962   "A Comparison of the Parables of the Gospel According to Thomas and of the Synoptic Gospels." Thomas and the Evangelists. StBT 35. Napierville: Allenson. pp. 40-78.

Robinson, J.A.T.
1974/75   "The Parable of the Wicked Husbandmen: A Test of Synoptic Relationships." NTS 21: 443-62.

Snodgrass, K.P.
1974/75   "The Parable of the Wicked Husbandmen: Is the Gospel of Thomas Version the Original?" NTS 21: 142-44.

Interpretation: Existential, Literary & Structural
Barthes, R. et. al.
1971   Analyse Structurale et Exégèse Biblique. Neuchâtel: Delachaux et Niestlé.

Crespy, G.
1973   "De la structure à l'analyse structurale." ÉtudesTheolRel 48: 11-34.

Crossan, J.D.
1975   *The Dark Interval: Towards a Theology of Story.* Niles, Ill: Argus.

Doty, W.G.
1973   "Linguistics and Biblical Criticism." *JAAR* 41: 114-21.

Frei, H.
1974   *The Eclipse of the Biblical Narrative.* New Haven: Yale Univ. Press.

Funk, R.
1975   *Jesus as Precursor.* Philadelphia: Fortress.
1966   *Language, Hermeneutic, Word of God.* New York: Harper & Row.

Galland, G.
1973   "Introduction à la methode de A.-J. Gremias." *ÉtudesTheolRel* 48: 35-48.

Greimas, A.-J.
1966   *Semantique structurale. Recherche de methode.* Paris: Larousse.
1971   "Narrative Grammar: Units & Levels." *ModLangNotes* 86: 793-806.
1973   "Les actants, les acteurs et les figures," C. Chabrot ed. *Semiotique narrative et textuelle.* Paris: Larousse.

Guttgemanns, E.
1971   *Studia Linguistica Neotestamentica.* Munich: Kaiser.

Hendricks, W.
1973   "Methodology of Narrative Structural Analysis." *Semiotica* 7: 86-102.

Lane, M. ed.
1970   *Introduction to Structuralism.* New York: Basic Books.

Lapointe, R.
1972   "Structuralism et exégèse." *Science et Ésprit* 24: 135-53.

Ricoeur, P.
1975   "Paul Ricoeur on Biblical Hermeneutics." *Semeia* 4: 29-145.

Scholes, R.
1974   *Structuralism in Literature: An Introduction.* New Haven: Yale Univ. Press.

TeSelle, S.
  1975   *Speaking in Parables*. Philadelphia: Fortress.
Tracy, D.
  1975   *Blessed Rage for Order*. New York: Seabury. pp. 119-145.
Wilder, A. N.
  1971(1964)   *Early Christian Rhetoric: The Language of the Gospel*. Cambridge: Harvard Univ. Press.
Wittig, S.
  1975   "A Theory of Polyvalent Reading." *SBL 1975 Seminar Papers* vol. 2. pp. 169-84.

15.
The Congruency Factor: An Essential Element of Effective Religious Education Programs

Anthony J. Ipsaro

Anthony Ipsaro shows that the processes of implementing a religious education program must be congruent with the program's stated goals. He offers some practical strategies to close the gap which often exists between these two elements.

The congruency factor is at once so obvious and yet so elusive. Observing human behavior, we readily take notice of the incongruencies. Oftentimes we find ourselves saying of others: "Why doesn't so-and-so practice what he/she preaches!" The commonness of such incongruencies, or the dichotomy between what is said and done, has led us to simply dismiss this phenomenon as part of the human experience.

Christian tradition, too, has recognized this phenomenon of incongruence; it is called original sin. St. Paul sensed the presence of this dichotomy in his own life; "I cannot understand my own behavior. I fail to carry out the things I want to do, and I find myself doing the very things I hate . . . the will to do what is good is in me, the performance is not, with the result that instead of doing things I want to do, I carry out the sinful things I do not want" (Romans 7:15,18).

We are not at all sure of the origins of this dichotomy, of this incongruence; but we do know how it is passed on. The social scientist, H.C. Kelman, says that children learn this mode of operation from their parents and significant others because the behavioral worlds of the family, the school, and other social settings conform to this dichotomy. Kelman calls this process compliance and identification, which are based on learning through rewards and penalties rather than internalization according to which the individual tries out new behavior and makes it part of his repertoire because it is intrinsically satisfying.[1]

While we know *how* incongruence is passed on, it is important to examine *why* it is knowingly passed on. Basically, the answer is: That's the way things are! Simplistic as this answer appears, it hides a rather sophisticated philosophical view of the person. In attempting to give an explanation of the nature of the person, philosophers have accepted this dichotomized view and built their systems upon it. Unfortunately, such philosophical expositions have tended to reinforce the normality of such human behavior. This general acceptance has resulted in a deep permeation of society and culture almost predetermining people in subtle and unconscious ways. Unless we make efforts to continually surface and reflect upon this phenomenon of incongruence, we will remain its prisoners without even knowing it.

One important way to reflect upon this phenomenon is to examine what our philosophical inheritance says about incongruence and the nature of the person.

Although the problem dates back to Plato, it was Descartes and Kant who drew out the phenomenon and articulated it in a readily acceptable manner. While it is beyond the scope of this essay to give a detailed exposition of the philosophies of Descartes and Kant, it is nevertheless important for our present discussion that a brief and simplified statement be presented.

Descartes must be viewed in an historical context. He lived in the period that witnessed the Inquisition, Galileo, the Thirty Years' War, and Kepler. It was a period not too different from ours, of rapidly advancing scientific discovery. The then existent philosophy, almost totally identified with theology, was moving toward an almost complete breakdown under the weight of scientific discovery. The church and science appeared to be diametrically opposed. Given this state of affairs, Descartes attempted to resolve the issue of the nature of man by considering him in a dichotomized way.

The person, according to Descartes, was composed of psyche and body. The body was viewed by him as a mechanical model, subject to physical laws as any other material object in the universe. It could be measured and analyzed by the perfect science of mathematics. The psyche, on the other hand, was seen by Descartes as an entity which resides in the body. For Descartes, a person uses one's body, but one's body is not oneself. This Cartesian dualism is quite different from the Aristotelian notion that the psyche, far from being a separate entity, is the principle of operation of the body. For Aristotle the idea of man was an integrated one of *forma* (psyche) and *materia* (body).

The Cartesian presentation of dualism was readily accepted for it answered many of the issues prevalent in his culture. If one relied on a scientific and materialistic approach to life, the body became a symbol of concrete reality while the psyche was relegated to uncertainty, abstractness, or obscurity. For the believer in God, the psyche, or soul, became the focal point of all goodness; the body, the center of weakness. It was fitting, then, for the religious person of that age to view the body with distrust and fear, and as sinful. The body was a vehicle for uncertain emotions, strong passions, and unreliable feelings. It was to be forced into submission by the soul. Unfortunately, this submission of the body was to the mind, the rational, and not to the soul, the nonrational. The best way to govern oneself, then, was to rely on the intellect—the cold, impersonal, hard facts approach. The further one was removed from the body—instincts, feelings, emotions: in a word, the nonrational—the "purer" one was. The nonrational was seen as the corruptor of the rational.[2]

Charles A. Curran views this state of affairs:

> As a result, the practical and even human side of things came to be regarded as inferior. Matters concerned with pure intellectualism were considered superior to those concerned with soma. Practical and human concerns having to do with feelings, instincts, and the body were less important than those having to do with the clear, the logical, the conceptual aspects of man. Even the body was important only when it was studied and treated this way. The human engagement was often ignored in the process.[3]

Working off this Cartesian base, Kant introduced his own dichotomy with his idea of "pure reason." The more logical a concept appeared to be, and the more uncorrupted by human contingency, the purer it was. Or, to put it another way, the further a concept or a thought was removed from feelings, emotions, and instincts, the "purer" it was. The purer the concept, the more certain was its existence.

Kant also introduced the concept of "practical reason." "Practical reason" was to deal with everyday situations. Kant mistrusted this lower concept of "practical reason" because it was not clear or pure. To counteract this lack of clarity and purity, Kant presented the concept of a "sense of duty." This sense of duty was known through the voice of conscience. An individual must obey his conscience, an internal practical judge. Obedience for Kant was of paramount importance

—not only obedience to the voice of conscience, but to others. Curran sees people today living out of an ". . . unconscious Kantianism, making law an end in itself and the source of an inner categorical imperative (conscience) binding each man despite his own reasonable protest and feeling."[4]

Dichotomized Personhood and Religious Education

The Cartesian-Kantian separation of personhood is a powerful, ever-present overlay in many areas of our contemporary life. We experience the conflict between the intellect and emotions, the rational and the nonrational, the person and the technological. So subtly has this dichotomy invaded our lives that even when we consciously, or intellectually, reject such a separation of personhood we find it present in many of our attitudes, viewpoints, and behaviors.

The area of religion has not escaped this Cartesian-Kantian separation of personhood. Much of the theorizing, or content, in religious thought and religious education speaks of the holistic view of person, of the unity of body and soul, of the linkage between the sacred and the secular, of the close relationship of the immanent and the transcendent. Nevertheless, the actual behavioral or operational expressions—the context—of these nobly stated convictions have shown a heavy emphasis placed on the intellectual and the rational. The nonrational world, although receiving nodding awareness, has been avoided and even disregarded. This has been unfortunate. The nonrational world—emotions, feelings, dreams, imagination—is an essential element for prayer, mysticism, and the life of faith.

There is safety in the rational approach to religious education; it is logical, definitive and systematic. We know where we stand. We have a sense of surety; we are secure. The nonrational world, descriptive rather than definitive, is sometimes illogical and incapable of being articulated cleanly. Such uncertainty easily causes us to be fearful and mistrustful, and rightfully so. The world of the nonrational has great power. Nevertheless, such fear and mistrust has led individuals not to rely on or trust themselves. And, in a Kantian manner, they have placed absolute reliance on laws, rules, and regulations. For them authority is security which requires blind obedience. In some ways religious education has reinforced such views.

What now appears to be essential for the field of religious education is a movement to study, identify and integrate the nonrational in religious development. New models are urgently needed to assist individuals in learning about, working with, and incorporating the nonrational into their religious development. Until this is done we will continue to promote the process of dichotomizing the individual, in spite of our updated content.

Practical Models for Personal Congruency

This essay thus far has attempted to indicate the need for a greater awareness of the congruency factor. The lack of congruency may exist between the content and the context in religious education. It has been shown that incongruence emanates from the basic dichotomy of the rational and nonrational aspects of the individual. Such a dichotomy has been fostered by certain philosophical systems and by a lack of awareness by society. It has become apparent that a serious and conscious effort must be made to close this gap. Religious education must be a leading agent in pursuing this unification, this congruency, this wholeness.

This process of promoting greater congruency in religious education programs must begin with those individuals who have significant responsibility for setting the climate of the environment. In any organization the tone or climate rests in a major part with the leader. Thus, in religious education programs on the diocesan level, the major tone-setter is the director or supervisor; on the parish level, the coordinator; on the classroom level, the teacher; and so on. Greater congruency in an environment comes about by conscious efforts and by osmosis. Congruency is achieved not only by doing something, but by being someone. An individual who is personally congruent expresses this congruency by every word and action.

If religious educators are concerned with increasing congruency in their programs, and thereby promoting greater effectiveness, it is clear that an examination of one's own level of personal congruency is the place to begin.

How does one go about this process? It is important, first of all, to remember that this phenomenon of incongruence is deeply imbedded in one's psyche, in those around us, and in the total culture. A world in which there is complete congruency will never be. Secondly, because this lack of congruency is so much a part of each of us, the process of working toward greater congruency will be a lifelong pursuit.

Once these two basic assumptions are accepted, it would be helpful to have a model or method. It is important to recognize that a model or method is simply a guideline. It cannot be considered an iron-fast, lockstep procedure that guarantees absolute success if followed. To view a model or method this way is immediately to put one back into the formalistic and mechanistic context of the rational world. The model or method simply offers basic ingredients or components which are to be considered. After these basic elements are discovered, it is important for one to create a model or pattern that is uniquely his or hers.

One of the most helpful models for personal congruency is that of Chris Argyris and Donald A. Schön.[5] The authors label what one *believes* as one's "espoused theory." What results from an examination of one's behavior, or what one *does*, is called one's "theory-in-use." Although sometimes unconscious, one's theory-in-use contains basic assumptions about self, others and situations—in short, one's *real* worldview, rather than one's *theoretical* worldview.

In their research Argyris and Schön found that despite an espoused theory—such as concern for others, peace, etc.—most behavior, or theory-in-use, is competitive, win/lose, rational and diplomatic. This type of behavior promotes an ongoing self-fulfilling prophecy that says the world is a jungle with a dog-eat-dog existence. The authors label this type of behavior as Model I.[6]

Argyris and Schön offer Model II as an alternative.[7] It is not in opposition to Model I, but different from it. Model II is expressed in behavior that is minimally defensive and open to growth. People who follow Model II hold their theories-in-use firmly, but they are equally committed to having them tested, confronted and revised. The authors admit that Model II behavior is more an ideal form of behavior. For the religious educator Model II behavior could be seen as an expression of Christianity.

To assist one to move from a recognized Model I behavior to a Model II, the authors offer a transition program.[8] The transition program features seminars where participants examine their theories-in-use and study the differences or similarities between what they say and what they do.

Argyris and Schön state several fundamental components of their transition program. First, that the individual *is* aware of the inconsistencies in his/her life. Secondly, the need for an "instructor," some other person who is aware of this phenomena in his/her own life and is actively involved in his/her own process of consistency. Besides offering needed support, the role of the instructor is to mirror the individual's behavior patterns so as to indicate the inconsistencies. Thirdly, after projecting the implications of possible new forms of behavior, the individual begins to experiment publicly. Many times these new forms of behavior bring into question old values and create new ones. Finally, the individual seeks to internalize and take responsibility for the new behavior.[9]

Another model or program that may be used in this process for individual congruency is the one offered by Morton Kelsey.[10] Since this model is based in a religious context, perhaps some religious educators may find it more helpful.

Kelsey bases his program on the belief that if an individual is to make contact with the spiritual realm the total individual must give himself to the encounter. For this total immersion, Kelsey offers a twelve-point program which he culled from his years of experience as an Episcopalian priest and as a Jungian analyst. Although a more detailed reading of this program would be essential, a simple statement of Kelsey's twelve-point program will offer the reader an overview of his proposal.

Kelsey's twelve rules are: Act as though you believe in the spiritual realm; undertake the quest with serious purpose; seek companionship and spiritual direction for the journey; turn away from the busy-ness of the outer world in silence and introversion; learn the value of genuine fasting; learn to use the forgotten faculty of the imagination; keep a journal; record your own dreams; be as honest with yourself as you can and get someone else to help you be honest; let your life manifest real love; gird yourself with persistence and courage; and, give generously of your material goods.

It is evident that the Argyris-Schön model and the Kelsey program both subscribe to a strong emphasis on one's individual growth and development. Both employ the findings of depth psychology. In our present discussion of religious development the linkage of depth psychology and the living of the Christian life is self-evident. A human being's affective life, dreams, fantasies, and so on, all move him/her into the realm of the nonrational. This, in turn, can lead one deeper into the realm of mysticism, prayer, and the spiritual life. This view is substantiated by the depth psychologist, James Hillman: "When the ultimate becomes the inner person, and the transcendent the wholly immanent, then the minister must go into the depths of the psyche. Therefore he is obliged to turn to psychology."[11]

John Sanford further reinforces this position in his book *The Kingdom Within* by showing how depth psychology can shed light on our Biblical heritage.[12] The works of Carl Jung hold the position that depth psychology is imbedded in religion. Jung believed that the goal of depth psychology was to release and develop the divine within each individual.[13]

Organizational Congruency

As individuals lack congruency between what they say and do, so do organizations. The basic elements involved in the congruency phenomenon apply both to individuals and to organizations. However, organizations have a built-in complexity as a result of having many individuals work toward one common goal. This complexity requires some explanation and understanding if organizational congruency is to be achieved. This information is especially important for religious educators who are continually involved in organizing programs.

The social scientist, Amitai Etzioni, states that each organization —be it an institution, a program, or a classroom—has *real* and *stated* goals.[14] Stated goals are those which the organization sees as a desired end and which the organization attempts to realize. Many times these stated goals are found in the philosophy or purpose of the organization. The real goals of the organization are those indicated by the structures and processes of implementation: distribution of personnel and material resources, how conflict is handled, decision-making practices, and so on. One may liken the stated goals of an organization to Argyris-Schön's "espoused theory"; the real goals, their "theory-in-use."

Congruency between real and stated goals of an organization is essential for overall effectiveness. Congruency is most difficult when the stated goals of an organization are basically abstract. This point is especially important for a church or a religious education program possessing "the increase among people of the love of God and neighbor" as its purpose.

Such an abstract goal can be made more concrete in terms of objectives. Niebuhr speaks of the objectives of the church as the nurturing of the Christian life and the salvation of souls; the building up of the life of the church; the preaching of the gospel; the dispensation of the sacraments; the strengthening of the life of prayer and worship; the winning of disciples to the Christian cause; the fulfilling of responsibility in society.[15] Even these objectives remain somewhat abstract.

What we begin to see, then, is that the basic goal of the church, and subsequently religious education programs, is in the realm of mystery. Avery Dulles, S.J. states:

> There is something of a consensus today that the innermost reality of the Church—the most important constituent of its being—is the divine self-gift. The Church is a union of communion of men with one another through the grace of Christ. Although this communion manifests itself in sacramental and juridical structures, at the heart of the Church one finds mystery.[16]

Dulles goes on to state that the term mystery, when applied to the church, signifies many things: that the church is not fully intelligible to the finite human mind, and that the reason for this lack of intelligibility is not the poverty but the richness of the church itself. Thus, Dulles sees that because of this mystery, we cannot objectify the church for we are involved in it; we know it through a kind of intersubjectivity.[17]

Because of this element of mystery, it is evident that the stated goals of the church and of its religious education programs will be most difficult to concretize. Such abstractness of goals increases greatly the possibility of incongruence. If one is not sure of precisely how the goal is to be accomplished, how can one be sure that the structures and processes of implementation really succeed? Furthermore, how does one determine the best structures or methods of implementation?

In the realm of real goals, although it is still difficult, one can be more objective. If a religious education program requires every individual to attend every session; if it requires that all the individuals be absolutely quiet during the sessions; if it requires that all information be known exactly; then we can determine that the real goal may be discipline. Wisely does Scripture remind us "by their fruits you shall know them."

A further possibility for the presence of incongruence in an organization rests in the area of evaluation. An organization determines its worth or success by its results. Measuring the results of an organization whose goals are based in mystery presents difficulties. In such a situation these organizations move to more measurable factors. In a religious education program more measurable factors include the number of participants, the testing and grading of knowledge, and the degrees held by the teachers. While these factors are helpful to indicate the possible success or worth of the religious education program, they cannot be all-inclusive. To overemphasize such measurable factors, Etzioni says, tends to encourage an overproduction and an over-concern for these aspects.[18] Less measurable factors, such as the growth and development of the individual's religious attitudes, can become more and more neglected.

This discussion of stated and real goals indicates a major point of obvious correlation between organizational theory and religiously oriented activities. For example, what is said about the goals of any organization can be transposed readily into a consideration of the purpose of the church. Another obvious point of correlation is the nature of leadership in an organization; and so the function of the leader in an organization becomes the role of the minister in a religiously oriented activity.

Beyond these overt relationships between organizational theory and religiously oriented activities are a number of issues which are basic presuppositions. Organizational theory would call these presuppositions one's view of life; religiously oriented organizations, the group's theology. These presuppositions are made evident by the choice of decision-making practices, the methods used to gain compliance of the membership, the manner of communication, the way conflict is dealt with, and so on.

For example, the nature of compliance in organizational theory involves some fundamental assumptions about human nature. Max Weber, the German sociologist, said obedience to commands of the leader should be prompt, automatic and unquestioning.[19] Weber's assumptions about the nature of the human person elicits the belief that an individual was robot-like and mechanical. In terms of a religiously oriented organization, if one's theology concerning the purpose of the church is similar to Dulles's institutional model, compliance of the members would be interpreted as strict obedience. In the institutional model, "the Church is not conceived as a democratic or representative society, but as one in which the fullness of power is concentrated in the hands of a ruling class that perpetuates itself by cooption."[20]

On the other hand, if one's theology of the church is based on the view that the church is a mystical communion, compliance of the members becomes operative when ". . . one can establish rich and satisfying primary relationships—that is, person-to-person relationships founded on mutual understanding and love."[21]

Thus, it is evident that the relationship between organizational theory and religiously oriented organizations is, as Peter Rudge states, ". . . not merely a chance correlation on a few selected topics but rather the expression of similar ways of thinking about life itself. The two are rooted in a common stock of ideas."[22] This fact is extremely important for religiously oriented organizations. Many times the leaders of these organizations dismiss any reference to organizational theories or matters by saying that their organization is excused from such elements because it is of a spiritual nature.

It is vital, then, that all administrators of religiously oriented organizations have some degree of sophistication in the knowledge and understanding of organizational theory.[23] Such basic understandings, coupled with a sensitivity to the existing underlying assumptions or theology, will better enable the administrator of religiously oriented organizations to shape and implement structures and processes that will be more congruent with the purposes and goals. The greater the congruency, the more effective the results promise to be.

A Model for Treating Organizational Incongruency

Earlier in this writing I discussed the existing phenomenon of incongruence in the individual. The models of Argyris-Schön and Kelsey were offered as practical guidelines for the religious educator interested in entering into the process for congruency. In our discussion of organizations it was indicated that they, too, have the strong possibility of being incongruent. A model for treating this organizational incongruence is now in order.[24]

Throughout my years of working with religiously oriented organizations, I have found the model of Process Consultation as described by Edgar Schein to be the most effective. The crux of Schein's approach is that a skilled third party (consultant) works with individuals and groups to help them learn about human and social processes so as to better create environments that assist individual and organizational growth and development.

The process counsultant employs many different skills germane to the fields of psychology, organization and administration. It is not any single thing the consultant does.

> The job of the process consultant is to help the organization to solve its own problems by making it aware of *organizational processes*, and of the mechanics by which they can be changed. The ultimate concern of the process consultant is the organization's capacity to do for itself what he has done for it. Where the standard consultant is more concerned about passing on his knowledge, the process consultant is concerned about passing on his skills and values.[25]

Some particularly important organizational processes for Schein include: communications, the roles and functions of group members, group problem solving and decision making, group norms and group growth, leadership and authority, and intergroup cooperation and competition.[26]

Schein states that one of the major responsibilities of the process consultant can be expressed in the terms of coaching and counseling. "The consultant's role then becomes one of adding alternatives to those already brought up by the client, and helping the client to analyze the cost and benefits of the various alternatives which have been mentioned."[27] Thus, the consultant, when counseling either individuals or groups, continues to maintain the posture that real improvement and change in behavior should be those decided upon by the client. The consultant serves to reflect or mirror accurate feedback, to listen to alternatives and suggest new ones (often through questions designed to expand the client's horizons), and to assist the client in evaluating alternatives for feasibility, relevance and appropriateness.

Schein's model of a process consultant requires, as we have already mentioned, that he/she possess the knowledge and skills from the fields of counseling psychology, organization and administration. For the process consultant servicing a religiously oriented organization, added knowledge from the field of theology would be of great assistance.

This concept of process consultant for the organization, as articulated by Schein, is very much analagous to the "instructor" of the Argyris-Schön model, or the "someone else" in the Kelsey program.

Where does a religiously oriented organization find such a process consultant? Unfortunately, it is most difficult to find individuals who possess all the requirements described here. This is not to say that there is a lack of individuals who possess the capabilities needed. My experience has shown me that there are many individuals who have the natural talent, sensitivity, and awareness needed to be process consultants. A number of these individuals are already part of religiously oriented organizations.

What is needed for such talented individuals, in most cases, is special training. Such training could assist these individuals in gaining the necessary knowledge and/or skills of counseling psychology, organization, administration and theology. An important element of this training would be the process of integration. Integration here is to be understood in a twofold way: 1) an intellectual linkage of the knowledge and skills; and 2) a personal internalization of this knowledge. This last factor is most important. Personal internalization can assist an individual to become more integrated, more congruent. Possessing personal congruency, the trained process consultant can be more helpful in assisting individuals and organizations to become more congruent, and thereby become more effective in the field of religious education.

Perhaps some of our national centers, institutes, or departments of religious education might take up the challenge to create programs for training process consultants for religiously oriented organizations.

Summary
This essay has explored the crucial and vital role that the factor

of congruency plays in the development of more effective religious education programs. There has been a dramatic updating of the content of knowledge in religious education. Now, more than ever before, is there an urgent need to update the *context* which religious education employs. Context can be defined as individual behaviors and attitudes, structures and processes of implementation. It must be noted that only when the content and the context are congruent will religious education programs become more effective.

The factor of congruency centers mainly in the contextual aspect of religious education programs. In discussing incongruence it was shown that this phenomenon emanates from the basic dichotomy of the rational and nonrational aspects of the individuals. Such a dichotomy has been fostered by certain prevalent philosophical systems and by the lack of awareness in society.

Religious educators, concerned with promoting greater congruency in their programs—thereby promoting greater effectiveness—were encouraged to enter into their own personal process for congruency. Two models for this process were offered.

Individuals *are* organization; as individuals lack congruency, so do organizations. Religious educators were encouraged to learn more about organizational theory since there are many points of obvious correlation. To assist religiously oreinted organizations to achieve greater congruency, the model of process consultant was suggested.

Notes

1. H.C. Kelman, "Compliance, Identification, and Internalization: Three Processes of Attitude Change." *Journal of Conflict Resolution*, 1958, Number 2, pp. 51-60.

2. For a more detailed explanation of the impact of Descartes and Kant in terms of the dichotomy factor, see; Charles A. Curran, *Counseling-Learning, A Whole Person Model for Education* (New York: Grune & Stratton, 1972), pp. 32-56; Morton Kelsey, *Encounter with God* (Minneapolis, Minnesota: Bethany Fellowship, Inc., 1972), pp. 62-91.

3. Curran, *Counseling-Learning, A Whole Person Model for Education*, p. 46.

4. Ibid., p. 48.

5. Chris Argyris and Donald A. Schön, *Theory in Practice: Increasing Professional Effectiveness* (San Francisco, California: Jossey-Bass Publishers, 1974).

6. Ibid., pp. 63-84.

7. Ibid., pp. 85-95.

8. Ibid., pp. 96-109.

9. Ibid., p. 134.

10. Morton Kelsey, *Encounter with God* (Minneapolis, Minnesota: Bethany Fellowship, Inc. 1972), pp. 174-209.

11. James Hillman, *Insearch: Psychology and Religion* (New York: Charles Schribner's Sons, 1967), p. 45.

12. John A. Sanford, *The Kingdom Within* (Philadelphia: J.B. Lippincott Co., 1970).

13. A recent publication that might introduce the reader to Jungian psychology is Laurens van der Post's *Jung and the Story of Our Time* (New York: Pantheon Publishers, 1975).

14. Amitai Etzioni, *Modern Organizations* (Englewood Cliffs, New Jersey: Prentice-Hall, Inc., 1964), p. 7.

15. H.R. Niebuhr, *The Purpose of the Church and Its Ministry* (New York: Harper, 1956), p. 27.

16. Avery Dulles, S.J., *Models of the Church* (Garden City, New York: Doubleday & Co., 1974), p. 15.

17. Ibid., pp. 15-16.

18. Etzioni, *Modern Organizations*, p. 9.

19. Victor A. Thompson, *Modern Organization* (New York: Alfred A. Knopf, 1961), p. 11.

20. Dulles, *Models of the Church*, pp. 31-42.

21. Ibid., p. 35.

22. Peter F. Rudge, *Ministry and Management: The Study of Ecclesiastical Administration* (London, England: Tavistock Publications, 1968), p. 38.

23. A very fine summary of some basic aspects of organization and administration can be found in Edgar Schein, *Process Consultation: Its Role in Organization Development* (Reading, Massachusetts: Addison-Wesley Publishing Co., 1969) pp. 13-75.

24. One of the best summaries of the vast body of knowledge treating what I have labeled organizational incongruence is contained in Wendel L. French and Cecil H. Bell, Jr., *Organization Development: Behavioral Science Interventions for Organization Improvement* (Englewood Cliffs, New Jersey: 1973).

25. Schein, *Process Consultation: Its Role in Organization Development*, p. 135.

26. Ibid., p. 13.

27. Ibid., p. 116.

16.
Faith Development Theory and the Aims of Religious Socialization

James W. Fowler

James Fowler locates the problem of religious socialization as the need for standards by which the members of a tradition can evaluate their goals or norms. From his research he distills six emerging structures of faith development and suggests that they are both descriptive and normative. While these norms are presented as universally valid he also suggests that they may be the source of reform and renewal within the individual traditions.

The following paper is premature. It represents an effort on my part to put on "seven-league boots," to leap ahead of my research and theory building on faith development, and to assay the usefulness of our work for the guidance of religious socialization.

Since I first read John Westerhoff's *Values for Tomorrow's Children,* and heard him lecture on "Religion for the Maypole Dancers" and on "What is Religious Socialization?", I have recognized the importance of what he is driving at. By refocusing the concerns of religious educators on religious socialization he has simultaneously widened and deepened our understanding of the ways selves form and are formed religiously. And he has put the role of education—education of the schooling sort—in its proper perspective. Given my limited knowledge of the history of education and religious education in this country I may be forgiven if I am wrong in seeing continuities between Westerhoff's approach and those of Bushnell, Dewey, and George Albert Coe—each of whom, in different ways, understood "growth," "learning" or "development" as a process of interaction between an active inquiring self and a culturing social environment. By drawing on contemporary anthropological perspectives, and by marshalling his own experiences and original insights, Westerhoff is advancing our theory and practice as regards "intentional religious socialization" (Westerhoff and Neville, 1974, p. 42) in quite significant and exciting ways.

Concern with intentional religious socialization can be quite clarifying when what is *intended* is more or less obvious and well established. That is to say, when a given religious communion has relatively clear consensus about the attitudes, beliefs, behaviors, and skills or competencies it values, it can utilize the religious socialization perspective to good advantage in evaluating and reconstructing its nurturing environment and methods. A focus on religious socialization will help the group become more critically aware of why its socialization efforts are succeeding or failing. It will help them become clear about the congruent or incongruent impacts of the "hidden curriculum" as expressed through the community's internal politics, its use of money, sex role discrimination within it, its architecture, community relations and the like. It will help them be more intentional in the provision of experiences and resources which foster persons' growth in the directions that are valued by the group. Even when a religious community is *not* clear or in agreement about the desired outcomes of socialization, the approach of intentional religious socialization can be helpful. It can be the stimulus and model by which the community can work at clarifying and becoming intentional about the generation of beliefs, attitudes, behaviors and competences it values and wants to foster.

What becomes obvious, on reflection, is that in intentional religious socialization the "intentional" or normative element—as regards the *content* of desirable beliefs, attitudes, behaviors and skills—is necessarily specific to the valuing perspectives of the socializing groups. This means that as regards indices of effectiveness in religious socialization the standards, on the whole, are *internal* standards of the particular religious communities in question. Intentional religious socialization assumes the value-relativity of the respective internal standards. It offers no other criteria against which either the content and desired outcomes or the actual attitudinal and behavioral results of a given religious communion's socialization process can be evaluated. With respect to the content and goals of religious and personal development, intentional religious socialization, as a theoretical perspective, can only empathetically enter into the ethos and goals of the particular religious communities to which it may be applied. It neither possesses nor claims to offer evaluative or normative standards for the content of religious socialization exogenous to particular religious traditions or communities.

As regards the *process* of effective religious socialization of course, the picture is different. As remarked earlier, if a given group can articulate its socialization goals, intentional religious socialization as a growing body of theory can provide sound guidance and great practical assistance. Presumably the comprehensive socialization process found to be effective in any given religious community would have much in common with similarly effective patterns in other groups, despite wide variations as regards what each group values as the ideal outcome of religious socialization.[1] Intentional religious socialization will increasingly be able to provide normative guidelines of a valuable practical sort which will facilitate the kind of growth or development hoped for by a consulting group. But as regards the substance or the content of religious socialization, to be self-consistent as a theory, it seems that it must take a value-neutral posture.[2]

This brings us to the question that lies at the heart of this paper. If the foregoing analysis of the role religious socialization can play is accurate, if its only explicit normative contributions apply to matters of process and technique, and if it implies and requires an approach of value-neutrality and relativity as regards the contents and goals of religious socialization, then can we, should we, must we, accept those limits of the theory and resolve to work with and within them?

To many readers these questions may sound either surprising or alarming. What conscionable alternative(s) do we have to a value-neutral perspective on the normative contents of different approaches to religious socialization? Religious tolerance has emerged as a precious gain in the last 400 years in Europe and North America. The institutionalization of religious liberty in constitutional democracies cannot but be considered as a significant advance in civilization. Is there any possible perspective or standpoint, beyond the internal norms of specific religious traditions, which could provide valid criteria for intentional religious socialization while avoiding blatant or subtle religious imperialism? And if such a perspective were found or created, would its application be acceptable and desirable?

Let's examine for a moment the possible consequences of a failure to seek such a valid, normative trans-religious perspective on religious socialization. It is important to reflect upon the reasons for the contemporary emergence of intentional religious socialization as a perspective and as a body of theory, and for its enthusiastic acceptance by a wide cross section of religious educators. Plainly its emergence and acceptance have something to do with the fact that it provides a welcome and much needed theoretical basis for a discipline which has fallen on rocky times for the last decade or so. With the decline of neoorthodoxy in Protestanism, and of dogmatic catechetics in Catholicism, a broad consensus on the objectives, methods, and curriculum of religious education broke open into great ferment. As dogmatic foundations for defining religious education eroded, the theological ecumenicity of the 1960s and early 1970s[3] was converging toward a focus on social-existential and phenomenological analyses and descriptions of faith as *relation* and as *process* in *religious* community. Paralleling (and anticipating) these theological developments, capable religious educators of a new breed, such as John Westerhoff and Gabriel Moran, began to formulate approaches to religious education which put relations, process and community dynamically at the center of things.

What has begun to emerge as a result is a kind of *consultant's* theory of religious education built around what Westerhoff has called intentional religious socialization. By a "consultant's theory" I mean nothing pejorative. Rather, I want to suggest that against the current backdrop of phenomenological and social-existential approaches to theology, and informed by anthropological and psychological approaches which are also dominated by phenomenological methods, religious educators have in a real sense followed suit. The task of the religious education theorist has become that of bringing to bear a rich assortment of sensitivities, experience, and knowledge of the socialization process, which he or she can put in the service of the intentionality of a given religious community or group.

Good consultants, informed by rich, flexible theory and broad experience, can be of immense help to their clients. What concerns me, however, is the clear danger that in falling into the consultant's role religious educators may let the nettle of norms and goals for intentional religious socialization slip entirely out of their hands. To me there is the danger that the religious socialization emphasis may have results in religious education similar to those of values-clarification approaches in the field of moral education. The values-clarification theories and techniques made important contributions in leading educators to recognize the impoverishment of continuing certain didactic approaches to moral education after corporate social moral consensus and socialization procedures had broken down. It offered exciting and useful pedagogical techniques. But in its theoretical and practical concerns (and in its entrepreneurial excesses) the values-clarification approach remained steadfastly consultative and supposedly value-neutral and value-relative. Moreover it fostered a kind of futility at best, and contempt at worst, as regards the effort to develop approaches to moral education which are based on non-relativist, principled approaches to moral decision making.

Put in plain terms, I want to see intentional religious socialization address itself explicitly to the effort to find and found norms which will guide its own theory and provide exogenous standards against which users of the theory may evaluate their own tradition's internal goals and norms of religious socialization. In this respect I am asking religious socialization theorists to be theologians, in addition to being anthropologists, educators or psychologists. I am challenging them (us) to harness the productive approach of religious socialization to a theory of development which aims to be both empirically descriptive and theologically normative. This would mean relinquishing the consultant's neutrality and embracing a new kind of broad theological normativeness—one geared, I believe, to the radical pluralisms of our time, both the *horizontal* and the *vertical* pluralisms with which we must work.[4]

The challenge I am placing before my colleagues who are working on intentional religious socialization parallels almost precisely Lawrence Kohlberg's challenge to the proponents of the values-clarification and of the cultural transmission approaches to values education. Kohlberg has backed up his challenge by providing a theory of moral development which represents a potent advance toward a new basis for normativity in moral socialization. In face of the value relativism underlying the values-clarification and cultural transmission approaches to moral education Kohlberg has offered the following:

(1) A formal, structurally definable account of a sequence of stages in the development of capacities for moral decision making. This sequence of stages appears to be invariant, hierarchical and universal. Culminating in the forms of reasoning required for a universalizing perspective on justice, Kohlberg's theory claims both empirical validity as a description of moral development, and pholosophical-ethical validity as a normative developmental sequence. (See especially Kohlberg, 1971; but also Kohlberg, 1969 and 1973.)

(2) In its focus on the *forms* or *structures* of moral judgments, Kohlberg's work provides a model for dealing with the pluralisms mentioned above. In one sense his most revolutionary contribution to moral education may be the clarification of a set of necessary *underlying competences* which make a moral point of view possible. In this respect Kohlberg is not describing attitudinal or behavioral *contents* which are to be taught and learned; rather he is pointing to *operations* or *patterns of thinking, feeling,* and *valuing* which *underlie* moral attitudes and behavior. These develop largely unconsiously in a person in the process of his or her interaction with an environment that provides moral dilemmas and challenges, an available language of moral discourse, and human models and behavioral precedents.

I have issued a collegial challenge to the theorists of intentional religious socialization asking them to concern themselves explicitly with a normative framework for their enterprise. As my friend and colleague Lawrence Kohlberg has done for moral education, I want now to try to offer a theoretical perspective which may represent a useful step toward building such a normative framework for religious socialization.

Over the past three years I have devoted much of my time to an effort to see if we can empirically establish and refine a structural-developmental theory of what I have called "faith development" (Fowler, 1974 A,B, 1975). In the next two sections I will give a telegraphic overview of the emerging theory and of the assumptions underlying it. Then in the last two sections of this paper I will offer some preliminary reflections on this stage theory of faith development as a descriptive and normative perspective potentially useful in clarifying exogenous norms for intentional religious socialization.

FAITH: THE STRUCTURAL DEVELOPMENTAL APPROACH

By "faith" I mean a dynamic set of operations, more or less integrated, by which a person construes his/her ultimate environment. This construal (or construction) includes and serves the person's centering loyalties and values (conscious and unconscious), and maintains a framework of meaning and value in reference to which the person interprets, reacts and takes initiatives in life. Conceptually, in asking you to think of faith as an integrated set of operations, I am focusing upon it as a patterned process or *structure* underlying and giving form to the *contents* of believing, valuing, knowing and committing. This distinction between the *structure* and *content* of faith is important to grasp and maintain. In a sense the focus of our stages is on the "how" of faith as a dynamic but structured process, as opposed to the "what" of faith, i.e. that which is believed, known, trusted or loved in faith.[5] (A moment's reflection will make it clear, however, that our research must focus on both, for you really have no access to the structure of a person's faith except as you "precipitate" it out of his or her expression of its content.)[6]

Faith, understood in this way, is not synonymous with religion or with belief. In ways that we will try to make clearer in this paper, faith, as a structured process at the center of the self's system regulating orientation and action, has a reciprocal or dialectical relationship with religion and belief as well as with language and ideology more generally. Religion and belief, symbol and ritual, ideology and ethical norms, serve as *models* in a double sense in relation to faith. On the one hand they are models for guiding the construction of a framework of meaning and value, providing vicarious experience and insight. On the other hand they provide media by which faith can express, communicate and apprehend itself. (See Geertz, Smith, and Fowler, 1974 B, Lecture I.)

Our structural-developmental approach derives in important ways from the cognitive developmental theories of Piaget and Kohlberg. In a moment we will consider how, as regards the concept "stage," and as regards the interactional epistemology underlying our theory, we are deeply under their influence. It will also become obvious that in our description of faith stages we have incorporated many insights of both these men and their followers. There is, however, one important respect in which our structural focus differs from theirs. Piaget conceptually distinguishes between *cognition* (the "structures" of knowing) and *affection* (the "energetics" or motive-force of knowing).[7] (See Piaget, 1967, pp. 3-73; 1964; Piaget and Inhelder; and Flavell, pp. 80-82.) Kohlberg tends theoretically to follow Piaget in maintaining this distinction, but making it clear that in reality the two interpenetrate in inseparable ways. (See Beck, Crittendon and Sullivan, pp. 392 ff.) Both claim that cognitive structures tend to dominate over the affective dynamics and that only the cognitive structures can serve as the basis for describing the sequence of developmental transformations which they call *stages*. Cartesian rationalism and Kantian formalism stand behind this approach.

Our work, on the other hand, has significant indebtedness to the psychoanalytic tradition (notably through Erik Erikson's writings), which insists upon recognizing the sharp qualification of rationality by unconscious defenses, needs and strivings, and which emphasizes the role of symbolic functioning in the processes of ego development. Similarly, I am indebted to theological and philosophical traditions in which knowing and valuing are held to be inseparable, and in which *will* and *reason* are seen as serving the dominant affections or loves of persons.[8] Faith, as we are studying it, is a structured set of operations in which cognition and affection are inextricably bound up together. As my associate Bob Kegan puts it, in faith the "rational" and the "passional" are fused.

The structural-developmental approach, represented by Piaget and Kohlberg and including our work, may best be described as *constructivist* and *interactionist* in its understanding of development. In this respect, as in many others, the structural-developmentalist epistemology fits hand-in-glove with the underlying assumptions of the religious socialization perspective. It is a fundamental Piagetian insight that the child's earliest knowing, before language and the symbolic functions have developed, derives from the child's manipulation of objects. Knowing begins with a *doing*, an *acting upon*, and *interaction with* objects and persons. Schemas, structures, or operations are, for Piaget, internalized patterns of action constructed in the child's interaction with objects and persons in order to enable him or her to organize and reliably predict their future behavior. Schemas and structures are generalizable; they become part of a set or repertoire of mental operations which the child brings to any new experience, perception or relationship. When a novelty is encountered the child tries to *assimilate* it to his or her existing schemas and structures. If it proves unassimilable the child experiments with new manipulations on it. As this is occurring new schemas are being assembled and tried. When the child finds an adaptive way of dealing with the novelty, the new schemas become part of his or her structural repertoire and, in Piagetian terms, we can say that a structural *accommodation* has occurred. Out of the interaction with a new object or person the child has developed new, generalizable structures. Development, then, in the structural-developmental approach, is understood as the *accommodatory* construction of new *schemas* or *operations* of knowing (which process is largely unconscious, formal or non-content-specific, and generalizable). In this perspective emphasis is placed on the constructive role of the knower and on the fact that knowledge is not merely an internal mental copy of something that is simply "there" in external reality, but that knowledge is the product, the "construction of reality" a person makes, using his or her available structures of knowing and interpretation. As new structures are developed the construction of reality undergoes changes.[9]

A decisive contribution of structural-developmental theory and research is its demonstration that there are uniformities in the structural patterns persons develop in order to organize and deal with the physical, social, and ultimate environments. The uniformities are described developmentally as a sequence of *stages*. A stage, in this perspective, represents a typical set of integrated operations, a structural whole, available to and employed by a person to construct, maintain and orient him/herself in the world. Stages succeed each other by way of accommodatory structural transformations. Earlier stages are characterized by more simple, global and undifferentiated structures. Successive stages increase in complexity, inner-differentiation, flexibility and comprehensiveness. Later or more developed stages carry forward the operations of earlier stages, but integrate them into more complex and inclusive structural wholes. Each stage, therefore, builds upon previous ones, meaning that the stage sequence is *hierarchical*. Because each stage builds on the previous ones, the sequence of stages is *invariant*. A stage cannot be skipped. Similarly, unless there is organic or emotional-mental deterioration the stage sequence will be *irreversible*. Persons will employ the most adaptive and adequate structures available to them for meeting the problems or dilemmas posed by their physical, social or ultimate environments. Finally, it is the claim of structural developmentalists that stages of the kind we are describing are *universal*. Persons may move through these stages at different rates (structural stages are not strictly determined by biological maturation or chronological age) and not all persons will complete the sequence of stages. But at their rate and to their point of development, it is held, the structural stages will be descriptive of their developmental processes.[10]

The Stages: A Brief Overview

In our effort to give a structural-developmental account of faith we have identified *six stages*—moving from simpler and undifferentiated structures to those which are more complex and differentiated. Faith manifests growing self-awareness as you move through the stages. The ages given with each of these stages represent an average *minimal* age. Many persons attain them, if at all, at later chronological ages than those indicated. Stage attainment varies from person to person and equilibrium of a stable sort may occur for different persons or groups at or in different stages.

Stage 1—Intuitive-Projective Faith
The imitative, fantasy-filled phase in which the child can be powerfully and permanently influenced by the examples, moods, actions and language of the visible faith of primal adults. (age 4)

Stage 2—Mythic-Literal Faith
The stage in which the person begins to take on for himself/herself the stories and beliefs and observances which symbolize belonging to his/her community. Attitudes are observed and adopted; beliefs are appropriated with literal interpretations, as are moral rules and attitudes. Symbols are one-dimensional and literal. Authority (parental) and example still count for more than those of peers. (6½ - 8)

Stage 3—Synthetic-Conventional Faith
The person's experience of the world is now extended beyond the family and primary social groups. There are a number of spheres or

theaters of life: family, school or work, peers, leisure, friendship, and possibly a religious sphere. Faith must help provide a coherent and meaningful synthesis of that now more complex and diverse range of involvements. Coherence and meaning are certified, at this stage, by either the authority of properly designated persons in each sphere, or by the authority of consensus among "those who count." The person does not yet have to take on the burden of world-synthesis for himself/herself. (12-13)

Stage 4—Individuating-Reflexive Faith

The movement or break from Stage 3 to Stage 4 is particularly important for it is in this transition that the late adolescent or adult must begin to take seriously the burden of responsibility for his/her own commitments, life-style, beliefs and attitudes. Where there is genuinely a transition to Stage 4 the person must face certain universal polar tensions which Synthetic-Conventional faith allows one to evade:

individuality	v. belonging to community
subjectivity	v. objectivity
self-fulfillment	v. service to others
the relative	v. the absolute

Often Stage 4 develops under the tutelage of ideologically powerful religions, charismatic leadership, or ideologies of other kinds. It often finds it necessary to collapse these polar tensions in one direction or the other. Stage 4 both brings and requires a qualitatively new and different kind of self-awareness and responsibility for one's choices and rejections. (18-19)

Stage 5—Paradoxical-Consolidative Faith

In Stage 4 the person is self-aware in making commitments and knows something of what is being *excluded* by the choices he/she makes. But for Stage 4, the ability to decide is grounded, in part at least, on the fact that one set of commitments is over-valued at the expense of necessarily viewing alternatives to it in a partial and limiting light.

Stage 5 represents an advance in the sense that it recognizes the integrity and truth in positions other than its own, and it affirms and lives out its own commitments and beliefs in such a way as to honor that which is true in the lives of others without denying the truth of its own. Stage 5 is ready for community of identification beyond tribal, racial, class or ideological boundaries. *To be genuine, it must know the cost of such community and be prepared to pay the cost.* A true Stage 5 requires time and testing and regard for those who are different and who oppose you which Stage 4 does not have. In a true Stage 5 *espoused values and beliefs are congruent with risk, and action taken.* (30-32)

Stage 6—Universalizing Faith

Stage 5's commitment to inclusive community remains paradoxical. To affirm others means to deny oneself. Defensiveness and egocentrism make the affirmation of other's truth difficult and threatening. One's own interests and investments in tribe, class, religion, nation, region, etc. still constitute biasing and distorting loyalties, which have to be struggled with and overcome continually.

Stage 6 Universalizing Faith *is rare.* At this stage what Christians and Jews call the Kingdom of God is a live, felt reality for the person of faith. Here one dwells *in* the world as a transforming presence, but is not *of* the world. The sense of the oneness of all persons is not a glib ideological belief but has become a permeative basis for decision and action. The paradox has gone out of being-for-others; at Stage 6, one is being more truly oneself. Stage 6's participation in the Ultimate is direct and immediate. Their community is universal in inclusiveness. Such persons are ready for fellowship with persons at any of the other stages and from any other faith tradition. They seem instinctively to know how to relate to us affirmingly, never condescendingly, yet with pricks to our pretense and with genuine bread of life. (38-40)[11]

NORMATIVE DIRECTIONS IN THE STAGE THEORY

The overview I have just given of our stages was intended merely to give you a sense of the flow and direction they manifest. That brief account is in no way adequate to describe the structural character of each stage or to suggest the structural transformations and augmentations involved in stage transitions. I want now to give some indication of "what is in a faith stage," structurally speaking, and to give a fuller account of the structural characteristics of each of the stages.

For the sake of convenience and economy of presentation I have produced a chart (Appendix) which summarizes the stage articulation to be offered here. In the reading of this section you will need to refer frequently to the chart. The text of this section is merely a brief exposition of and comment upon the chart.

Across the top of the chart you find six categories descriptive of structural competences involved in faith. In a moment we will examine each category, briefly explaining its focus. Taken as a set (read horizontally) these categories of structural competences suggest what we mean when we speak of a faith stage as an *integrated system of operations, a structural whole.* For in the construction of a worldview, and in the creation of a coherence that reflects a person's most centering loyalties and hopes, this full set of competences and more are employed. The structural wholes, represented by the horizontal set of competences at each stage, are descriptive of what we have found in our analyses of some 227 in-depth interviews conducted with persons from 4 to 84 in the past three years.[12] That is to say, the horizontal "wholes" do hang together and are descriptive of the variety of actual patterns of thinking, believing and valuing we find in the responses of our interviewees.

Now let's look at each of these competence categories: *Category A, The Form of Logic,* builds on Piaget's theory of cognitive development. Its focus is on the patterns of reasoning available to the developing person at each stage. The cognitive competences of each Piagetian stage are *necessary* for the correlative competences described by categories B-F, but are not *sufficient* for them. That is why cognitive development in this theory is treated as one strand of competence intertwined with many others. Readers familiar with Piaget's work will note that we have offered substages in adulthood for Piaget's stage of formal operations. We find that these are descriptive of different patterns in the employment of formal operations in the construction of a worldview, and we believe that they constitute important areas for further research.

Category B, The Form of World Coherence, so far as I can tell, is a focus that has specifically derived from our own work. It represents an effort to describe a sequence of stage-typical *genres* employed by persons to conceive or represent patterns of coherence in their ultimate environment. In the strand of development it describes one finds some important clues for informing communication with persons of each stage.

Category C, Role-Taking, owes most to the important research and theory of Robert Selman of the Harvard Graduate School of Education. (See Selman, 1974, Parts I and II.) Up through Stage 3 we are relying explicitly on Selman's account of development in the ability to take the perspective of others. Beyond Stage 3 we have found it possible and necessary to extend Selman's work, applying it to the person's abilities to take the perspectives of his or her group, and then of groups, classes or traditions other than one's own. As will become clearer later in this paper, the level of role-taking, particularly at the later stages, becomes an important normative element in our stage theory. The later stages require the development of competences in intergroup role-taking which require a relativization of, and distancing from, the values, beliefs, norms and perspectives of one's own group or class.

Category D, *Bounds of Social Awareness*, undoubtedly emerged as a focus for us through general familiarity with reference-group theory. However, our identification of a developmental sequence, so far as I am aware, derives more from theological-ethical than from social-psychological sources. This category focuses on the extent of inclusiveness of a person's primary identification and concern. Here again the dual character of the sequence as both descriptive and normative shows up.

Category E, *Form of Moral Judgment*, is, of course, an inclusion, with slight modifications, of Kohlberg's stages of moral development. The descriptions of his stages here, and the placement of their sequence in the larger stage sets, indicate the correlations we find between Kohlberg's stages and ours. As included here the stages of moral development are an important normative strand in the total theoretical perspective on faith development.[13]

Category F, *The Role of Symbols*, is a focus we have developed in our own way, but in shaping it, as in many of the other categories, I have been influenced from a wide variety of sources too numerous to mention. This category focuses upon a developmental sequence of levels in symbolic competence. Faith, as a construal of one's ultimate environment, involves persons in the effort to relate to realities which can only be symbolically represented or mediated. A person's competence with symbols—whether they are imaginal, linguistic, or ritualistic—is therefore of core importance.

I have neither the space nor the time here to unpack the developmental sequence in each of these categories or to elaborate the character of each stage as a horizontal, structural whole. The reader, for the present, will have to work at those horizontal and vertical readings for him or herself. As an aid in that work, however, and as a way of sharpening a focus on the issue of the normativity of a theory like this one, I want to say a few things in summary fashion.

First, as one examines this chart reflectively, it may seem that the dynamic which lies at the heart of faith—namely, a centering affection, an organizing love, a central object of loyalty and trust—is missing. And this is true. To note this is to be reminded again of the formal and structural focus of this stage theory. It is this formal character which gives the theory the possibility of being applied to a variety of different religious traditions with a variety of *contents* as regards prescribed beliefs, values, attitudes and behaviors. Yet, it should be noted that in its formality the stage theory progression presumes a self that is involved in a simultaneous process of *centering* and *de-centering*. On the one hand it presumes and describes an increasingly *individuating* self—a self which, as it develops, differentiates itself from a nurturing ethos and gradually, stage by stage, assumes the burden of construing and maintaining for the self a vision of reality, and of taking autonomous moral responsibility within it. This process describes an increasingly centered self—a self with boundaries established by increasingly self-chosen, self-aware investments of trust and loyalty. On the other hand, the theory presumes and describes a progressive path of gradual de-centration in the sense that at each stage a more inclusive account is taken of persons, groups, experiences and worldviews other than one's own. Increasing with each stage there is an effort to find and maintain a mutuality or complementarity with a widened cosmos of being and value. Symbolically this centering and de-centering might be represented by a pair of interlocking cones, one upright, the other inverted:[14]

Second, in order for the centering and de-centering just described to occur, the development from stage to stage requires qualitative transformations in the person's structures or patterns of thinking, valuing, committing and believing. Both the centering and the de-centering, as developmental processes, require that the structures underlying faith become progressively more complex, more internally differentiated, more comprehensive, and more flexible. This is another way of saying that each stage represents qualitative gains in structural competences over the preceding ones. A reading of the stage chart both horizontally and vertically should serve to illustrate how movement from one stage to another involves the kinds of structural transformations just described.

But third, we must remind ourselves that the kind of competences under discussion are not skills that can be directly taught. Nor are they operations or acquisitions about which one is usually self-consciously aware. Rather, these competences accrue derivatively in the interaction of a person with the world, as he/she employs (and is employed by) the available relational, symbolic, linguistic, cultic, and ideological resources. The development of faith competences and the movement from one stage to another cannot be the *direct* result of education or schooling.[15] Rather, in precisely the fashion described by the religious socialization theorists, faith development occurs as a person wrestles with the givenness and crises of his/her life, and draws adaptively upon the models of meaning provided by a nurturing community (or communities) in construing a world which is given coherence by his/her centering trusts and loyalties.

Fourth, though it is too complex a matter for the space we have here, I want briefly to indicate that this developmental process and the eventual equilibrated stage at which a person "rests" are both relative to the complexity of her/his environment, and to what Kenneth Keniston (1974) has usefully called "the modal developmental level" of his/her dominant nurturing community. Of course individual givens of genetic inheritance and temperament are also relativizing variables. Then, to a degree that psychologists generally have not taken seriously enough, a person's or group's "place"—in the sense of social class, educational experiences, economic opportunity, and the societal meaning of their racial or ethnic identity—has important implications for the stage of faith development that will support their survival or efforts at change. (See Fowler, 1974 B, Lecture III.) All this is to underscore what I have often said before: that this stage theory is not to be taken in any simplistic sense as saying "higher is better" and/or that persons described best by the later stages are somehow of more worth as persons than those best described by the earlier. "Each stage may be *the* most appropriate stage for a particular person or group. Each stage describes a pattern of valuing, thinking, feeling and committing which is potentially worthy, serene and graceful." (Fowler, 1976, p. 18)

NORMATIVITY AND VALIDITY: SOME CONCLUSIONS

As we come to the conclusion of this paper it may be useful to review what it has tried to do. First there was an appreciative recognition of the contributions of religious socialization theory. There was the assertion, however, that the socialization approach, as so far developed, treats the question of norms and goals of religious socialization primarily as a matter governed by the *internal* norms of particular socializing groups or communities. A challenge was offered to the religious socialization theorists to move through the implicit values-relativism of their approach, and to wrestle with the clarifying of norms for religious socialization that would be both exogenous to particular religious communities, and be capable of empirical and theological validation.

Second, the emerging structural theory of faith development was presented. The reader was asked to think of its stages as a sequence of formally describable sets of structures or competences underlying persons' believing, valuing, committing and acting. These stages and their sequence have found provisional empirical validation. This provisional empirical validation has made it possible to suggest that beyond the theory's usefulness as a *descriptive* account of faith development in structural terms, we should consider whether the implicit and explicit normativeness of the theory commends it as a formal and universalizable description of goals for intentional religious socialization.

In the course of briefly presenting the faith stage theory we tried to indicate some of the ways in which the stages are both descriptive and normative. If the structural competences described by and required for Stages 5 and 6 are to develop, they must come by a person's development through a gradual construction of the entire stage sequence. If intentional religious socialization, through its work in and with the contents of a particular religious tradition, hopes to help develop persons whose faith manifests the qualities described by Stage 5 or Stage 6, then the intentionally selected patterns of socialization for persons at each prior stage must include an openness toward and sponsorship for continuing development.

I am conscious as I write this that my seven-league boots (and the license that went with them) may seem to have given way to 7,000-league pretensions in this projection of the possible usefulness of the faith development theory. It was this anticipated gap between possibility and the sure ground of oughtness which made me say at the outset that this paper is premature. Yet, having come so far, let us not shrink from pushing a little farther, in order to see how this gap might be closed and whether its closure would be desirable.

It seems to me that the adequate validation of a normative theory such as this one has to proceed on three levels simultaneously. The first level, as has already been mentioned, is the level of empirical research. Are the stages, as characterized, truly descriptive of a developmental sequence that is invariant, hierarchical and universal for human beings? In order for us to have more than a provisional confidence about this, our present cross-sectional data will have to be supplemented by longitudinal follow-ups with our present sample, and by extensive, carefully executed cross-cultural studies. Clearly, in the pursuit of empirical validations of these kinds the theory itself will continue to develop, to be refined, and steadily to become less biased in many ways. Across twenty or more years of such work it should become clear whether the theory, as it has evolved, can claim empirical validation. The fact that cognate theories such as those of Piaget and Kohlberg have found impressive longitudinal and cross-cultural validation is a source of encouragement to us in this regard.

At a second level of validation, however, there is a complex set of issues of a different sort which are of crucial importance. These have to do with the religious, political, social and moral implications of a normative theory of this sort. Unfortunately, here I can only hint at the importance of these issues, though we are trying seriously to deal with them. I have already pointed to the growing religious and ideological pluralism of our world. I have suggested that not only the *horizontal*, but also the *vertical* (developmental) pluralism among us must be taken into account. But we should also characterize our world as one which manifests a growing gap economically and socially between the haves and the have-nots. The maldistribution of goods, services and life-chances is *increasing* in our time rather than decreasing. We live in a world with an increasing population and a growing scarcity of life-supporting, life-enhancing resources. And we live in a world of exacerbated tensions between racial, ethnic and religiously defined groups. Yet it is also true that ours is a world of enhanced communication, expanded travel, increasingly inclusive international commerce, and slowly growing success in efforts at international regulation. It is the responsibility of researchers and theory builders in our time to anticipate, insofar as they can, the impacts of their theoretical work—its uses and potential misuses—on the range of persons and groups who have to be counted in the world we have characterized. Every effort must be made to prevent such a theory from developing in ways that will lend support to structures of oppression and provide rationales for exploitative social, economic, political and religious arrangements. This is to suggest that the validation of a theory such as the one under discussion here must proceed on a *social-ethical level* and be subject to an ongoing *moral audit*. It is our considered belief that the competences described by Stages 5 and 6 of the faith development theory include those which are requisite for transcending the biases of religious prejudice and of economic and class self-interestedness. It is our observation and conviction that the persons best described by those stages are persons prepared to seek and pursue justice, sacrificially if necessary, in the kind of world we have described. That these competences or structures which are found to underlie the believing, committing, valuing and acting of those who are most committed to justice among us should be held as developmentally normative, seems to us a necessary constituent of any claim of *truth* for a theory like this.

Finally, the validation of this theory must be undertaken at what we may call the metaphysical or theological level. The alert and reflective reader of this material will have noted an underlying thrust in its normativity at this level. First of all, there is the observation and conviction that we human beings are *ontically disposed* to try to discern and give coherence and meaning to the welter of powers, events, crises, relationships and mysteries that impinge upon us. Second, in the giving of coherence to our collective and individual experience, we are drawn to centers of value and love which represent for us *excellence of being*. We are drawn by these; they kindle our affections. But third, there is that in Reality which awakens our hunger for participation in excellence of being, and which beckons us toward itself in a remarkable variety of ways. And though our apprehending of that by which we are apprehended is inevitably blurred, distorted and partial—and though our responses are similarly blurred and distorted—there is, nonetheless, at the heart of our life a primal transaction, a primal relation, between the deep places of the human soul and a soul of the universe. Theologically then, there is underlying this theory the conviction of an ultimate *Oneness* surrounding, sustaining, and unifying the incredibly complex "manyness" of our experiences and imaginations. This Oneness does not in any way make human moral responsibility or human suffering matters of indifference. Rather, I believe that in the heart of that Oneness is a structure-intending-righteousness and right-relatedness in being. Development in faith fits us for growing intentionality and responsibility in our participation in *that* excellence of being.

Lest it be unclear, let me say in closing that there is likely no way toward Stages 5 or 6 except through the powerful and particular *contents* of specific religious traditions.[16] As Santayana is supposed to have said, we cannot be religious in general. Theological validation of this theory will involve testing whether the characteristics of the culminating stages of the theory capture and describe the structures necessary for fulfilling the highest normative intentionality of the great, particular religious traditions. Given the efforts to validate some such theory as this on the other levels of empirical investigation and social-ethical adequacy, however, is it too much to hope that a theory of formal, structural normativity in faith development might in return contribute to the ongoing renewal, reform and extension of the highest normative intentionality of those traditions, and to the guidance of their efforts in religious socialization?

APPENDIX

FAITH: THE STRUCTURAL-DEVELOPMENTAL APPROACH

A SUMMARY TAXONOMY OF STRUCTURAL COMPETENCES BY STAGE

STAGES:	A *FORM OF LOGIC (MODIFIED PIAGET)*	B *FORM OF WORLD COHERENCE*	C *ROLE TAKING (MOD. SELMAN)*	D *BOUNDS OF SOCIAL AWARENESS*	E *FORM OF MORAL JUDGMENT**	F *ROLE OF SYMBOLS*
1. Intuitive-Projective	Pre-operational	Episodic	Rudimentary empathy	Family, primal others	Punishment-reward	Magical-Numinous
2. Mythic-Literal	Concrete operational	Narrative-Dramatic	Simple perspective-taking	"Those like us" (in familial, ethnic, racial, class & religious terms)	Instrumental Hedonism	One-dimensional, literal
3. Synthetic-Conventional	Early Formal operations	Tacit System, symbolic mediation	Mutual role-taking, (interpersonal)	Conformity to class norms and interests	Interpersonal concord and ↔ Law & Order ↔	Multi-dimensional, conventional

4. Individuative-Reflexive	Formal operations (Dichotomizing)	Explicit system, conceptual mediation	Mutual, with self-selected group or class	Self-aware adherence to chosen class norms & interests	Reflective relativism or class-biased universalism	Critical translation into ideas
5. Paradoxical-Consolidative	Formal operations (Dialectical)	Multi-systemic, symbolic *and* conceptual mediation	Mutual, with groups, classes & traditions other than one's own	Critical awareness of and transcendence of class norms & interests	Principled Higher Law (Universal-critical)	Post-critical rejoining of symbolic nuance and ideational content
6. Universalizing	Formal operations (Synthetic)	Unitive actuality, "One beyond the many"	Mutual, with the commonwealth of being	Trans-class awareness and identification	Loyalty to being (*modified Kohlberg)	Transparency of symbols

Notes

1. As will become clearer later, however, there may also be a "process relativity" involved here. Parallels in the *process* of effective religious socialization between groups may depend upon parallels in the "modal (average-optimal) stage of faith development" sponsored by those groups. Groups whose modal developmental level is best described by Stage 3 will use different socialization procedures than those whose modal level is best described by Stage 4.

2. This is not to overlook the clear statements of personal and communal loyalty to a Christian position made by Jack Westerhoff in such places as p. 117 of *Generation to Generation*. It is merely to point out that the anthropological and educational perspective he is working from provides no inherent criteria for justifying a choice of one version of Christian vision and values over any variety of others sponsored by other religious groups.

3. As contrasted with the largely paralyzed ecumenicity of church union and organizational integration in the same period.

4. By *horizontal pluralism* I mean the obvious variety of values, beliefs, attitudes and behaviors sponsored by different groups and traditions. By *vertical pluralism* I mean to suggest the diversity between and within religious communities that derives from persons and subgroups being at different developmental stages as regards their faith.

5. It is this distinction between structure and content which gives us a way of coping with values and religious pluralism. When, later in the paper, we come to discuss the normativity of the faith stage theory the reader should bear in mind that its normativity has to do with structural patterns *underlying* the contents of beliefs, attitudes, behavior and the like, rather than with those contents themselves.

6. For an account of our research method and interview procedure see Fowler.

7. This distinction between cognition and affection is often mistakenly confused with the distinction made above between structure and content. In Piagetian studies the latter distinction (structure/content) can also fruitfully be discussed in terms of the distinction between operative (structured) and figurative (imaginal or content) knowing. See Furth, 1969, especially Parts III and IV.

8. Some notable representatives of these traditions are St. Augustine, Martin Luther, Jonathan Edwards, Josaiah Royce, Ernst Troeltsch, H. Richard Niebuhr, and Michael Polanyi. See also Fowler, 1974 C.

9. For comparisons and contrasts of this epistemology with those of behaviorist and maturationist theories see Kohlberg and Mayer, "Development as the Aim of Education" in Kohlberg, 1973.

10. See Kohlberg, 1969; 1973. Piaget, Kohlberg and their followers have conducted cross-cultural research establishing empirical bases for their claims of universality. Our theory has yet to be tested and verified either longitudinally or cross-culturally.

11. For more comprehensive expositions of these stages now available see Fowler, 1976 and Fowler, Keen and Berryman. For earlier descriptions see Fowler, 1974 A,B.

12. A description of the 1972-74 sample of 118 and of the research

procedure can be found in Fowler, 1975. A book based on a sample of 340 interviews is now in preparation.

13. It may strike some readers as arrogant and somewhat imperialisitic to incorporate the theories of senior colleagues such as Piaget and Kohlberg as "strands" in this effort at a more comprehensive theoretical perspective. I by no means intend it as such. I merely want to try to show the complexity and richness of the structural competences which faith requires and how the theories of Kohlberg and Piaget have informed and been part of our approach to this task. For a discussion of the relation of moral and faith development, see Fowler, 1976.

14. I am indebted to literary critic, Professor Northrop Frye, for his suggestion of this image to represent what he heard me try to describe.

15. Though, as Greenfield and Bruner point out, schooling is a crucially important ingredient in development of the kind we are describing.

16. For me this would have to include certain humanistic traditions despite the broadly theistic underpinnings of the theory.

Bibliography

Beck, C. M., B. S. Crittendon, and E. V. Sullivan, *Moral Education: Inter-disciplinary Approaches*. New York: Newman Press, 1971.

Erikson, Erik H., *Identity and the Life Cycle*. New York: International Universities Press, Inc., 1959.

Erikson, Erik H., *Childhood and Society*. (2nd Ed.) New York: W. W. Norton Co., 1963.

Erikson, Erik H., *Insight and Responsibility*. New York: W. W. Norton Co., 1964.

Erikson, Erik H., "The Development of Ritualization" in Donald R. Cutler, Ed., *The Religious Situation 1968*. Boston: Beacon Press, 1968.

Flavell, John H., *The Developmental Psychology of Jean Piaget*. New York: D. Van Nostrand Co., 1963.

Fowler, James W., "Toward a Developmental Perspective on Faith" in *Religious Education*, Vol. LXIX, No. 2, pp. 207-219, 1974 (A).

Fowler, James W., *Faith, Liberation and Human Development: Three Lectures*. In *The Foundation*, Atlanta, Georgia: Gammon Theological Seminary, Vol. LXXIX, 1974 (B).

Fowler, James W., *To See the Kingdom: The Theological Vision of H. Richard Niebuhr*. New York, Nashville: Abingdon Press, 1974 (C).

Fowler, James W., "Stages in Faith: The Structural-Developmental Approach" (1975). A chapter for a forthcoming book edited by Thomas Hennessey, S.J., *A Symposium on Moral Development and Moral Education*. In Press.

Fowler, James W., Sam Keen and Jerome Berryman, *Life-Maps: The Human Journey of Faith*. Needham, Massachusetts: Humanitas Press, 1976.

Furth, Hans G., *Piaget and Knowledge*. Englewood Cliffs, New Jersey: Prentice-Hall, Inc., 1969.

Geertz, Clifford, "Religion as a Cultural System" in Donald R. Cutler, Ed., *The Religious Situation 1968*. Boston: Beacon Press, 1968.

Greenfield, Patricia M., and Jerome Bruner, "Culture and Cognitive Growth," pp. 633-657 in David A. Goslin, Ed., *Handbook of Socialization Theory and Research*. Chicago: Rand McNally, 1969.

Keniston, Kenneth, "Psychological Development and Historical Change," pp. 149-164 in R. J. Lifton, Ed., *Explorations in Psychohistory*, New York: Simon and Schuster, 1974.

Kohlberg, Lawrence, "Stage and Sequence: The Cognitive-Developmental Approach to Socialization," pp. 347-480 in David A. Goslin, Ed., *Handbook of Socialization Theory and Research*. Chicago: Rand McNally, 1969.

Kohlberg, Lawrence, "From Is to Ought: How to Commit the Naturalistic Fallacy and Get Away with It in the Study of Moral Development," in *Cognitive Development and Epistemology*. New York: Academic Press, 1971.

Kohlberg, Lawrence, "Continuities in Childhood and Adult Moral Development Revisited," in P. B. Baltes and K. W. Schaie, Eds., *Life-Span Developmental Psychology: Personality and Socialization*. New York: Academic Press, 1973.

Kohlberg, Lawrence, *Collected Papers on Moral Development and Moral Education*. Cambridge, Mass.: Center for Moral Development and Moral Education, Harvard Graduate School of Education, 1973.

Kohlberg, Lawrence and Mayer, Rochelle, "Development as the Aim of Education" in *Harvard Educational Review*, Vol. 42, No. 4, Nov. 1972, pp. 449-496.

Piaget, Jean, "Relations between Affectivity and Intelligence in the Mental Development of the Child." Translation in mimeo from the French text of a course by Piaget in 1953-54 made by Charlotte Ellinwood. University of Chicago, Department of Psychology, 1965.

Piaget, Jean, *Six Psychological Studies*. New York: Vintage Books (Random House) 1967.

Piaget, Jean and Bärbel Inhelder, *The Psychology of the Child*. New York: Basic Books, 1969.

Selman, Robert L., *The Development of Conceptions of Interpersonal Relations: A Structural Analysis and Procedure for the Assessment of Levels of Interpersonal Reasoning Based on Levels of Social Perspective Taking, Parts I and II*. Boston: Harvard-Judge Baker Social Reasoning Project, 1974.

Smith, Wilfred Cantwell, *The Meaning and End of Religion*. New York: Mentor Books, 1965.

Westerhoff, John H. III, *Values for Tomorrow's Children.* Philadelphia: Pilgrim Press (United Church Press), 1970.

Westerhoff, John H. III, Gwen K. Neville, *Generation to Generation.* Philadelphia: Pilgrim Press (United Church Press), 1974.